T0246016

COMEDY BOOK

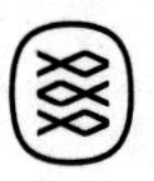

FARRAR, STRAUS AND GIROUX

New York

COMEDY BOOK

*How Comedy Conquered Culture—**and the** Magic That Makes It Work*

Jesse David Fox

Farrar, Straus and Giroux
120 Broadway, New York 10271

Printed in the United States of America
First edition, 2023

Grateful acknowledgment is made for permission to reprint the following material:
Jesse David Fox, "How Jerry Seinfeld Changed Modern Comedy with *Seinfeld*," "How the Internet and a New Generation of Superfans Helped Create the Second Comedy Boom," "What Is the Best Adam Sandler Movie?," "I Watch Saturday Night Live Like It's a Sport, and You Should Too," "'One Giant Nerve That You Were Afraid to Touch,'" "Trump Is One of the Worst Things Ever to Happen to Comedy," "Truth in Comedy After Louis C.K.," "How Bo Burnham Is Deconstructing the Idea of 'Truth in Comedy,'" "The Special Special," "Some Questions About Phoebe Bridgers's Bo Burnham Cover," "How Funny Does Comedy Need to Be?," "What If Improv Were Good?," "Who Should John Mulaney Be Now?," and "Maria Bamford's Masterful Late-Night Eulogy." Articles first appeared, in slightly different form, on the *Vulture* website and are reprinted by permission of *Vulture* and Vox Media, LLC.
Lyrics from Bo Burnham, "Can't Handle This," from *Make Happy* (2016), and "All Eyes on Me," from *Bo Burnham: Inside* (2021), used with permission.

Library of Congress Cataloging-in-Publication Data
Names: Fox, Jesse David, 1985– author.
Title: Comedy book : how comedy conquered culture—and the magic that makes it work / Jesse David Fox.
Description: First edition. | New York : Farrar, Straus and Giroux, 2023. | Includes bibliographical references and index.
Identifiers: LCCN 2023018729 | ISBN 9780374604714 (hardcover)
Subjects: LCSH: Comedy—History and criticism.
Classification: LCC PN1922 .F65 2023 | DDC 809.917—dc23/eng/20230620
LC record available at https://lccn.loc.gov/2023018729

Our books may be purchased in bulk for promotional, educational, or business use. Please contact your local bookseller or the Macmillan Corporate and Premium Sales Department at 1-800-221-7945, extension 5442, or by email at MacmillanSpecialMarkets@macmillan.com.

www.fsgbooks.com
www.twitter.com/fsgbooks • www.facebook.com/fsgbooks

3 5 7 9 10 8 6 4 2

For my parents

Humor is the last stage of existential awareness before faith.

—SØREN KIERKEGAARD, *Concluding Unscientific Postscript to Philosophical Fragments*

Comedy is to make everybody laugh at everything, and deal with things, you idiot.

—JOAN RIVERS, to a heckler in Wisconsin

Contents

COMEDY BOOK

1

COMEDY

This is a love story.

"You nervous?" In my memory, that was the first thing Jerry Seinfeld ever said to me. It was May 2015, and I was about to interview him onstage at Vulture Festival, in front of five hundred people. That afternoon, Seinfeld looked like a cross between a tech CEO and Jerry Seinfeld. Black T-shirt under a well-made gray checked blazer, small glasses surrounded by only a whisper of silver frames, the very close-cropped hair of a man who gets it cut often. It's possible he said something else first—I don't know, like, "Hello" or "How's it going?" But what I remember was, "You nervous?" See, Seinfeld rose to prominence in the comedy clubs of the 1980s, when comedians were forced to see every onstage interaction as a battle to the death—kill* or be killed. I told

* "Kill" is slang for when a comedian or a piece of comedy performs extremely well in front of an audience. "Destroy" and "crush" and words like it are often used similarly.

him, "No," by which I meant, "Yes." How could I not be? I was going to be asking the writer of many of my favorite jokes where they came from.

The audience was younger than I expected, considering how long Seinfeld had been famous. They reminded me of, well, myself. My feeling of *How did I get here?* transformed into *How did* we *get here?* Before that point, I had a narrative of myself as a fan of comedy, starting with me as a kid watching *Seinfeld* reruns every day while doing my homework and building to me talking onstage with the guy with the name. But in that moment I started seeing myself as a part of a much larger cultural shift.

To quote the question asked by many a Jerry Seinfeld impressionist: Who *are* these people? Simply put: comedy nerds. Comedy nerds are nerds, but, if you can believe it, for comedy. People who follow the trends and study the foundational texts, and who, if you asked, would say, "Of course comedy is an art form." A few months before I interviewed Seinfeld, I had been talking to Comedy Central's head of research at the time, Chanon Cook, about a 2012 survey she conducted, which showed that millennials viewed humor as the number-one factor in their self-definition. "Comedy is to this generation what music was to previous generations," she told me.[1] "They use it to define themselves. They use it to connect with people." Comedy Central called them Comedy Natives.[2] If you look at social media behavior—posting funny videos on Facebook, tweeting a joke reaction to the news of the day, lip-syncing a favorite sitcom scene on TikTok—it seems that comedy has enmeshed itself in how millennials and now Gen Z communicate. Cook's analysis pointed to what life started looking like for young people around 2010. Seinfeld had a sense that something had been changing, but he wasn't exactly familiar with us comedy nerds. At one point he referred to us with the close but not exactly right "stand-up geeks." More than he couldn't comprehend who this new generation of comedy fan was, he couldn't appreciate his own role in our emergence. It's hard to say *Seinfeld* is the reason for modern comedy fandom, but it seems fair to suggest the reason it looks the way it does has a lot to do with the show's content and popularity. I'll explain. Let's go back to the beginning.

It was the summer of 1989. Gorbachev was abandoning the Brezhnev Doctrine, Prince had everyone doing the "Batdance," and the team of Jerry Seinfeld and Larry David had a new show about something. Originally called *The Seinfeld Chronicles*, the initial premise was that each episode would show the day-to-day life of a stand-up comedian and how it got turned into material.[3] Though much of that framing dropped when the show went to air, rewatching now, it is amazing how many plots revolved around stand-up. Jerry also periodically tells jokes, but not how a normal sitcom character would. Meaning he knows he's making a joke and, because he's a comedian, he'll comment on how well it worked. My favorite example of this aspect of the show is a scene from the season 8 episode "The Checks," with Jerry and Elaine coming out of a drugstore:

> **JERRY:** Hey, have you seen all these new commercials for indigestion drugs? Pepcid AC, Tagamet HB.
>
> **ELAINE:** Ugh, the whole country's sick to their stomachs.
>
> **JERRY:** Now, you know you're supposed to take these things before you get sick?
>
> **ELAINE:** What is this, a bit?

JERRY: No.

ELAINE: 'Cause I'm not in the mood.

JERRY: We're just talking. Is this not the greatest marketing ploy ever? If you feel good, you're supposed to take one!

ELAINE: Yeah, I know that tone. This is a bit.

JERRY: They've opened up a whole new market. Medication for the well.

The scene continues and Elaine gives Jerry the sort of feedback comedians give each other, telling him to move "medication for the well" to the start and hit "good" harder. When it aired, in 1996, it was the first time I ever heard the term "bit." Many of my peers and I were being indoctrinated to care about comedy. The message of 97 percent of sitcoms is that friends are good or family is good or your office is friends or family and thus also good. Not *Seinfeld*. The idea that it was a show about nothing is misunderstood. It was not that it wasn't about anything, it was about the idea of nothing. It was about nothingness. Famously, Larry David said he wanted "no hugging, no learning." Seinfeld hung a photo of space taken by the Hubble Space Telescope in the writers' room to remind the staff how little what they were doing mattered.[4] Nothing didn't mean the nonsense the *Seinfeld* four tended to focus on; it was an existential nothing. There was one exception: *Seinfeld* was less *Waiting for Godot* and more waiting for good joke. For the makers of the show and the characters in the show, the one thing that mattered was comedy.

And the show was remarkably popular. Truly, it is remarkable for a show *that* specific to be watched by as many people as it was. At the beginning of this chapter, I referenced a well-known line from the second season of the 2019 critical supernova *Fleabag* ("This is a love story"). I imagine there's a good deal of Venn diagram overlap among readers of this book and watchers of the second season of that show, and yet I doubt anyone knew with 100 percent certainty that I was copping the line. The monoculture, the time in which everyone watched and listened to the same stuff, is so far in the rearview that you can't be sure with things like this. Though American streaming numbers for *Fleabag* aren't available, you can sense that it didn't consume mass culture the way *Seinfeld* did. Now, if I said "yada yada," it's unlikely any readers wouldn't know what I was making a reference to. Over 76 million people watched the *Seinfeld* finale in 1998.[5] There were only 276 million people living in the U.S. at the time, and a lot of those people were babies not allowed to stay up that late. Over 58 million watched the freaking clip retrospective that ran before the finale. For comparison, fewer than 20 million people watched the *Game of Thrones* finale, the biggest TV event in recent memory.[6] That is significantly less than *Seinfeld*'s weekly viewership. Also, it's relevant that, given its run from 1989 to 1998, *Seinfeld* was right in the sweet spot for millennials, who were born between 1981 and 1996, making it likely the first big show that many of the largest generation in American history watched. Because of David's no-learning rule, all the show projected to its impressionable fans was that comedy is valuable. Essentially, Jerry Seinfeld and Larry David invented the comedy podcast, or, at least, they deserve credit for generating an interest in the basic premise of funny people sitting around talking about comedy and their lives as comedians.

The story is not that *Seinfeld* premiered and yada yada

comedy is a whole thing now. (I told you you'd get it when I referenced "yada yada.") I don't want to draw a straight line from *Seinfeld* to today, because it was not a linear expansion. It was more of a big bang, with the expansion spreading in 360 directions and accelerating as it moved forward. Starting in the nineties, there were countless entry points for comedy fandom. I was a member of the *Seinfeld* generation, a term I just made up to refer to the sort of millennial who grew up watching *Seinfeld* and, in turn, always knowing and caring about what goes into a stand-up's comedy. But you could also call us the *Simpsons* generation, as I remember at age nine watching an episode and laughing at a joke so hard that something dislodged in my brain and I thought, *Someone wrote this thing. I wonder who? I wonder how?*

We were a generation raised on a new sort of sketch-show-veteran, blockbuster-comedy movie star, from Eddie Murphy, Bill Murray, and Chevy Chase in the eighties, to Jim Carrey, Adam Sandler, Ben Stiller, and Mike Myers in the nineties, to the Wayans brothers, Will Ferrell, and Melissa McCarthy in the 2000s. We were also the *Def Comedy Jam*, *Martin*, *In Living Color*, UPN, WB generation. Or, maybe, the generation who saw prominent women in comedy like Janeane Garofalo, Margaret Cho, and new woman-dominated casts of *Saturday Night Live*. And there was RuPaul's emergence as the biggest drag queen the world had ever seen. Most succinctly, you could say, we were the Comedy Central generation, being the first to grow up with a network that, appropriately enough, centered comedy. I was not aware of any of this at the time, I was just a kid watching what I liked, but the accessibility of this much comedy is part of how you get a generation of comedy nerds.

Comedy has steadily grown in cultural relevance, from

vaudeville around the turn of the twentieth century to *Seinfeld* toward the end of it, but since then it feels like its growth in both scale and value has sped up. This book focuses on comedy made from 1990 through the early 2020s. This is the period in which millennials, and then Gen Z, emerged as cultural consumers. Also, as will be discussed in chapter 2, this represents the period after the comedy boom of the eighties (when hundreds of comedy clubs opened) went bust (when hundreds closed), and comedy puts itself on a path as an art form and a business that would lead it to where it is today, where there are more comedians of a greater variety performing for larger audiences across more platforms than ever. Maybe the most drastic stat to convey how much things have changed is this: When *Seinfeld* premiered, in July 1989, no comedy act had headlined a show at the Madison Square Garden arena; since the show ended in 1998, eighteen acts have, at time of writing.* It's not just that the biggest names are bigger; comedy has built a robust middle class of performers who might not have their own TV show but have millions of followers on social media or a loyal fifty thousand listeners of their podcast.

Moreover, in 2004, a survey revealed that one in five eighteen-to-twenty-nine-year-olds got their presidential campaign news from comedy shows.[7] Ever since, comedians' status in the sociopolitical conversation has only been on the rise, led by Jon Stewart's work on *The Daily Show* and followed by *Saturday Night Live*'s impact on how young people (especially self-identified Independents and Repub-

* Dane Cook, Jamie Foxx, Chris Rock, Eddie Izzard, Kevin Hart, Aziz Ansari, Russell Peters, Gabriel Iglesias, Louis C.K., Bill Burr, Jim Gaffigan, Amy Schumer, Impractical Jokers, Sebastian Maniscalco, Joe Rogan, Trevor Noah, John Mulaney, Jo Koy.

licans) exposed to Tina Fey's impression perceived Sarah Palin.[8] By 2014, comedy was seen as so important politically that when the Obama administration was desperate to boost Affordable Care Act enrollment, their bright idea was to have the president appear on Zach Galifianakis's talk show parody, *Between Two Ferns*, which featured jokes like "What is it like to be the last Black president?" And it worked, with the Healthcare.gov site experiencing a 40 percent boost in traffic, almost entirely made up of people who had never visited the site before. The American socialist magazine *Jacobin* would later call it "The Day Zach Galifianakis Saved Obamacare."[9]

Comedy—broadly, historically—is the art of taking serious things not seriously. In the classroom of our culture, for a very long time, comedians have been placed in the back, cracking jokes at everything in front of them. Comedians were our society's ombudsmen, our official bullshit callers. And, as time has gone on, comedians have done such a good job at this that it's become clearer and clearer that a lot of our assumptions about our society are bullshit. As a result, the media has imbued comedians like Dave Chappelle, Amy Schumer, most current late-night hosts, and the entire cast and crew of *Saturday Night Live* with a status previously granted only to those who claim to be telling us the truth—journalists, politicians, and other public intellectuals. But forget politics. Comedy is, dare I say, cool now. In 2021, the French luxury fashion house Balenciaga chose animated characters from *The Simpsons* as models for Paris Fashion Week. A year later, at New York Fashion Week, the boutique fashion accessories brand Susan Alexandra held its show at the Comedy Cellar, with up-and-coming comedians performing and serving as models. That same week, the cool-kid streetwear brand KITH used its fall lookbook to introduce its newest model—Jerry Seinfeld. For people around my age and older, comedy seems like a bigger deal than it ever has. For those younger, they've never lived in a culture where comedy wasn't an ever-present, important, valued societal force. This is what culture looks like during the second comedy boom. And there are no signs it's slowing down.

Something Seinfeld said that day inspired this book. Our conversation was chugging along nicely but hit a snag when I tried to have him discuss the nitty-gritty of his joke-writing process. "This is my favorite thing to talk about," he said, "but I really think they're going to be so bored to hear it." The interview went on for another thirty minutes, but this sentence played over and over again in my head, as if a DJ had made it the hook of the panel's dance remix. "This," meaning the craft of comedy, is the favorite subject of one of the twenty or so most famous people of the last quarter century, and yet he thinks it would bore the five hundred people who were so interested in everything he had to say that they were able to buy forty-dollar tickets in the minutes between when they went on sale and when they sold out. I could tell some people in the first few rows were disappointed, but I wasn't going to push. I was still quite scared of him. But, upon reflection, I realized this moment of disconnection between Seinfeld and me captured a dichotomy that has persisted, where no matter how much comedy grows in popularity and societal value, there still exists a strong apprehension about appreciating it on its own terms as an art form. This needs to change. So, that's what this book is: an exploration of the ways of seeing the art of comedy. Throughout our time together, I will embrace the extreme subjectivity around what people find funny, but considering comedy as an art is nonnegotiable.

And I believe I'm not alone in this desire to understand comedy better. There are fans, regardless of what Seinfeld says, who are open, curious, and excited to understand how comedy functions as an art form and as part of our culture. Seinfeld's comment was tapping into a long-held view that analyzing comedy is a fool's errand, one that I intend to debunk in this book. See, when Seinfeld was growing up and coming up, jokes were not meant to be explained. If you have to explain a joke, that means it wasn't funny. If you explain comedy, you'll kill it. Which brings us to *the* frog. As E. B. and Katharine S. White wrote in 1941: "Humor can be dissected, as a frog can, but the thing dies in the process and the innards are discouraging to any but the purely scientific mind."[10] Strong premise. Too wordy. It would be punchier if it ended with the frog death. Uh-oh! There I go! E. B. Damned, I dissected their joke. And it is a joke, literally, ironically enough. And like a good joke, it gave people the vocabulary to shape and express their own opinion. The opinion being that by analyzing a joke, you suck the joy out of it.

Before we go forward, we need to establish what a joke is, because the word is used to describe two different, albeit related funny phenomena. There are jokes. Like, joke-jokes. Sometimes called street jokes. They're the things that start with "Knock knock" or "A priest, a minister, and a rabbi walk into a bar" or "What do you get when you cross a _____ with a _____?" Joke-jokes are jokes you find in joke books. They're freestanding, authorless, utilitarian tools to produce laughter. They have been around for millennia. They are a bottom-up, folk-cultural product. Modern comedy's early history—from minstrel shows to vaudeville to burlesque to the borscht belt and chitlin circuit*—started with jokes like these, but now when comedians say they tell jokes, they are talking about something different.

Norm Macdonald made the distinction between joke-jokes and comedians' jokes clear in 2015.[11] An interviewer wanted to know how he wrote the often long, sometimes meandering jokes he would tell on late-night shows and *Howard Stern*, like the legendary "moth joke" he told on *Late Night with Conan O'Brien*, about a moth going through an existential crisis who visits a podiatrist's office ("'Moth, man, you're troubled. But you should be seeing a psychiatrist. Why on earth did you come here?' And the moth says, ''Cause the light was on.'"). Macdonald said he did not write them. No, comics don't write "actual" jokes. "They're just out there," he explained. "No comic in the world can make up an actual joke like 'A guy walks into a bar and this happens.'"

He continued, "They call a comedian's act 'jokes,' but they haven't been jokes for years." Macdonald had a hard time explaining what he had previously thought was ob-

* Minstrel shows were nineteenth-century variety shows in which the performers wore blackface. Vaudeville shows were large, family-friendly variety shows that were popular at the start of the twentieth century. Burlesque was vaudeville's much more adult sibling. The borscht belt is the name for the mid-twentieth-century summer resorts in the Catskill Mountains where Jewish Americans vacationed, at which a style of comedy developed. Chitlin circuit is the name for the mid-twentieth-century venues where Black artists were able to tour to perform in front of Black audiences.

vious. He threw out the word "observations" to describe them, but "jokes" can be anything to a comedian. A joke can be Sarah Silverman telling her audience not to forget God can see you masturbating, but "don't stop. He's almost there." Then she adds, "I'm just kidding. There's no God." A joke can be Wanda Sykes's examination of how it is harder being gay than Black, in which she plays out her parents' responses to if she had to come out as Black ("You weren't born Black. The Bible says, 'Adam and Eve,' not 'Adam and Mary J. Blige.'"). A joke can be Leslie Jones acting out the time she danced so hard to impress Prince, her ponytail flew off her head. To a comedian, a "joke" is a complete comedic idea. And this is how the word will be used in this book. This distinction is necessary because comedy's jokes are carrying the baggage of joke-jokes, including the belief that they should not be analyzed, at least in polite society.

The thing is, the Whites weren't talking about analyzing comedy, as in the art form that is currently thriving, because the genre was still in its nascency. I believe that because of the sentence that directly preceded the dead-frog line: "Analysts have had their go at humor and I have read some of this interpretative literature, but without being greatly instructed." I have also read some of this interpretative literature and similarly found it lacking. Often, it's because it is oriented around joke-jokes.

Instead of summarizing the "Theories of Humor" Wikipedia page, let me tell you a little story about Noel Meyerhof, a beloved office cut-up, who one day is discovered entering jokes into the Multivac supercomputer by a colleague. This is the plot of "Jokester," a 1956 short story from Isaac Asimov, who in his free time was a famed joke-joke freak, releasing three collections over the course of his lifetime. When confronted, Meyerhof explains his intentions are to figure out where jokes come from, as they seem to have no origin and he has not been satisfied with the existing literature. "The people who write the books are just guessing," he argues. "Some of them say we laugh because we feel superior to the people in the joke. Some say it is because of a suddenly realized incongruity, or a sudden relief from tension, or a sudden reinterpretation of events. Is there any simple reason? Different people laugh at different jokes. No joke is universal. Some people don't laugh at any joke. Yet what may be most important is that man is the only animal with a true sense of humor; the only animal that laughs." Fortunately for Meyerhof, the Multivac spits out an answer: Aliens made them up!

Extraterrestrials aside, this is a decent summary of the history of comedy philosophy that would have been available to the Whites. You get references to the three most common theories: 1. Superiority theory dates back to the likes of Plato and Aristotle (though the name wouldn't come until the twentieth century), and argues that we laugh at others' misfortune because it makes us feel better about our own lot in life.[12] 2. Relief theory is most associated with Sigmund Freud, who believed people laugh to release psychic energy associated with a repressed topic.[13] 3. Incongruity theory is the most contemporary of the bunch, with many great thinkers offering their spin on the fundamental idea that we laugh at the juxtaposition of a common/rational concept and an uncommon/absurd one.[14] Besides it being easy to think of disproving examples, they all fail for one reason: They're too focused on joke-jokes. This results in these theories' being too binary, as they are trying to explain the relationship between setup and punch line. All of them, in one way or another, have a before and an after. Like an on-off switch, one goes from 0 percent laughing to 100 percent laughing and then back to 0. I'm dubious that this is what it feels like to experience a joke-joke, but it's *definitely* not what it feels like to experience comedy.

For my money, what it *feels* like to experience comedy is best captured by play theory, the theory of comedy this book subscribes to. Let me show you, reader, how this interpretation of comedy is not simply about jokes, but is part of the broader human condition born out of the evolutionary need for play. Try to think of comedy as less of a discrete moment and more of a state of being. In scripted movies or TV shows, it's the story and its characters (or a premise, if it's a sketch) that put you in the position to laugh when funny things happen. In stand-up, it is the energy created between the comic and the audience. The feeling of mirth one experiences watching comedy is similar at the most basic neurological level to the feeling one has joking around with one's friends and family. Similarly, as we mature, we search for ever more sophisticated versions of laughing at a funny face a relative makes when we're a child. Comedians are able to artificially create that state of play by generating the same feelings of trust and safety that free you up to laugh most easily. *But what does this mean for jokes?* Jokes are the means by which comedians play. Joke theories will highlight the importance of surprise in and of itself, but under play theory, surprise is important only insomuch as surprise is fun. But it's not essential. A pun is not funny because the language passes through some inherently funny linguistic calculation, but because you are literally playing with words. For those with mathematically wired, puzzle-solving brains, it might feel like a funny calculation, but that's just because that's how they play. Free from the need to telegraph what they're saying, as comedians get more experienced, they understand they can get laughs without their sentences sounding so jokey.

To best understand play theory, it helps to think where it evolved from. Man is not the only animal that laughs. Isn't that cute? Though humans are the only animal with the biology to make the noise we think of as laughter, other animals make similar repetitive noises. Our sisters the chimpanzees do it.[15] As do gorillas, orangutans, and other primates. Elephants laugh. Rats make little giggles. It's possible dogs and cats laugh. Again, very cute. "Chimps," writes neuroscientist Robert R. Provine, "laugh most when tickled, during rough-and-tumble play, and during chasing games." He adds, "Physical contact or threat of such contact is a common denominator of chimp laughter."[16] In contrast, though adult humans' laughter often involves verbal communication, over the last twenty years, researchers have argued that we are doing our version of rough-and-tumbling. We use comedy as a way to mess around with each other, in the same way chimps tickle each other. It's why Darwin, who saw comedy in a way similar to how future play theorists would, once called humor a "tickling of the mind."[17]

In the 150 or so years since Darwin, new research has advanced the case for play theory.[18] "There is a growing consensus among researchers that the purpose of play behavior is to sharpen the mind's physical, cognitive, and emotional skills," write the cognitive scientists Matthew M. Hurley, Daniel C. Dennett, and Reginald B. Adams in *Inside Jokes: Using Humor to Reverse-Engineer the Mind*.[19] They add that "laughter is a tool to facilitate nonaggressive play." Other researchers describe how humor, as a social phenomenon, evolved from this use of laughter.[20] To apply this to comedy means to consider the comedian-audience relationship. Comedy exists only when both the comedian and audience are working together to create the state of play. "Comedy is a game, a game that imitates life," wrote the French philosopher Henri Bergson in his influential 1900 book on comedy, *Laughter: An Essay on the Meaning of the Comic*.[21] And it is not a game that can be played alone; as he writes, "Our laughter is always the laughter of a group." Again, this state of play is most naturally entered into with the people closest to you, but the art of comedy evolved into existence because people were willing to pay for professionals to create play and needed to practice processing increasingly sophisticated ideas.

By analyzing comedy, by consuming and considering it, the audience, the critic, the frog dissector is further playing with ideas. Diving deeper into a comedian's joke is a way to continue having fun with it, not to take the fun out of it. So, for example, let's play with Jerry Seinfeld. Though Jerry Seinfeld literally released two joke books of his work, his act is not a collection of jokes. If another comedian read them verbatim, the result would be quite different. People tend to think one-liner comedians have less of a persona onstage, but it's often the opposite. You can't tell a Seinfeld joke without doing an impression of him. Though Seinfeld's form might sound more jokey, it doesn't mean his comedy too can't be considered more deeply. Take his joke about Halloween, which became one of his classics:

> So, the first couple years I made my own costumes,
> which of course sucked:
> The ghost, the hobo, no good.

> Then, finally, the third year, begging the parents, got the Superman Halloween costume (not surprisingly).
>
> Cardboard box, cellophane top, mask included.
>
> Remember the rubber band on the back of that mask? That was a quality item there, wasn't it?
>
> That was good about ten seconds before it snapped out of that cheap little staple they put it in there with.
>
> You go to your first house: "Trick or . . ." Snap!
>
> "It broke. I don't believe it!"

Intentionally or not, Seinfeld is using comedy (play) to give people a space to reckon with the loss of innocence, the Lynchian dark side of postwar suburbia, and capitalism's broken promise. I am not saying this is what makes the joke funny or that it was Seinfeld's explicit intention, but it can be argued these ideas allowed for its resonance with audiences at the time he first wrote it in the eighties. Not unlike a poem, you could also look more closely at the meter and word choice. How he introduces the word "snapped," so the audience is primed to instantly make the connection when he uses "snap!" in the next line. And don't get me started about the aural impact of ending sentences with a hard *p*.

Joke-jokes are an anthropological phenomenon and have largely been researched as such, but the movement in comedy over the last thirty-plus years, the time period we'll be focusing on, has been to treat comedy jokes as an art. Even if there is pushback. When we spoke, Seinfeld captured what makes the proposition of taking comedy seriously so difficult. "There's absolutely no difference between the greatest painting ever made and a joke," he said confidently. "But when there's a two-drink minimum and people are getting drunk to make the guy seem funnier, it's not looked at that way." This is a book, first and foremost, about considering comedy as an art form. It's about appreciating comedy without the need to get drunk. There is no two-drink minimum.

After the panel, back in the greenroom, Seinfeld was much softer toward me than before, and he said one thing that I'll never forget, even though I can't for the life of me remember the exact wording. I have a bad memory. Moreover, I don't really believe in memory as an accurate document of what happened, as much as how your brain has decided to store information based on your present psychology. I consider the memoir portions of this book to be speculative nonfiction. This is all to say, I can't remember if Seinfeld earnestly said to me, "You're really interested in jokes" or "You really care about jokes." Again, it doesn't matter which, but what is notable to me is the relationship between how much I care about comedy emotionally and how much I'm interested in it intellectually—how much I love it and how much I'm fascinated by it.

From a very young age, I don't know if I'd say I took comedy seriously, but it was important to me. For me, comedy has been an outlet for frustration, an escape from personal tragedy, and a salve for the cruelties of existence. My mother passed away in 1993. I was seven. It was like I was Sandra Bullock in *Gravity*, doing routine repairs on the outside of my spaceship, when metal shards from a blown-up satellite came flying through, cutting up the craft, detaching my tether, leaving me flipping and flipping through space, floating away from my ship and Earth. I exhibited obsessive-compulsive tendencies from a young age, but the trauma of losing my mother influenced how deep into my head I could sometimes retreat. My family provided stability, brought me back to Earth, but I was lucky to have an art form like comedy that was able to pull me back when I started floating away again. Jokes offered a state I could stay in that made life seem more manageable, with enough pops of dopamine to keep my attention. Laughing is instinctual—it's without intention—and it's uncontrollable. No matter how bad or how nothing I felt, 1993 was also the year *The Simpsons* entered heavy syndication, and I wasn't not going to laugh when Sideshow Bob stepped on yet another rake. Jokes were how I affirmed I was alive.

And as I do with the things meaningful to me, I've thought about it and thought about it, and I only find myself loving comedy more. I've seen it live up to my level of inquiry. Later in the Whites' piece they make another analogy that I like better than the dead frog. They are describing the state of humor, and after backhand-praising radio comedians and the manufacturers of whoopee cushions, they describe a comedy short they saw at a movie theater. In it, a man blows a giant soap bubble and jumps in and out of it. "It was, if anything, a rather repulsive sight," the Whites write. "Humor is a little like that: it won't stand much blowing up and it won't stand much poking. It has a certain fragility, an evasiveness, which one had best respect. Essentially, it is a complete mystery."[22] I get this. When you see a magician do a trick, it would be great to just accept you're in the presence of a wizard. Now, I am not suggesting it's better to cynically look around for wires or hidden cards. I try to instead see the magic in a well-done trick. Taking comedy seriously does not make it less mysterious to me, it makes it more so. I know how they do it, and yet, how do they do it?

Because of the frogs and the aversion to seriousness, comedy has gone under-considered throughout its history, even as it has ascended as a major cultural force. Comedians have wielded a great deal of influence and have acquired power as a result, but there has been little focus on how they actually do that. This is vital at a time of booming innovation, both in terms of the ways in which comedians are exploring the bounds of the art form and the platforms on which they are exploring it. Though there have been some notable comedy histories, comedy scholars I've spoken to feel they're fighting an uphill battle for legitimacy in academia. Similarly, compared to other art forms, there have been very, very few prominent comedy journalists and critics. One goal of this book is to make it more likely that there are more books about comedy in the future.

Creating a space in our culture for analyzing comedy will improve the viewing experience. Despite dedicating my life to thinking about comedy and cutting frogs into smaller and smaller pieces, I've never stopped laughing. It's not that it is harder to make me laugh now, but I am more demanding. I laugh more deeply, with more of me. I want that for everybody. I want that for comedy. Because comedy is an audience-dependent form, an audience that understands more, that cares more, will continue to push the art forward. The hope is to empower comedians to be more ambitious, be it to write jokes even more sharply, pursue more unusual comedy, or play to larger audiences made up of people who are actually supporting them as a specific artist and not someone just providing a service. Better ingredients, better pizza. Better audience, better comedy.

Still, the number-one rule of this book is "Have fun." To analyze comedy is to play. When people learn I write about comedy for a living, they'll ask if I still am able to enjoy it. I enjoy it maybe more than anyone on this planet, as I now know how to see and hear more. This book will show you comedy through my eyes and ears in hopes that you'll be able to do the same. And I guarantee you will laugh more and feel better for it or your money back! [*This is not legally binding.*]

Comedy has proven, especially over the last thirty years, to have a tremendous power to build empathy, to foster social change, to bring people together, and to relieve societal tension, and yet regularly, people, including comedians, push back on attempts to take it seriously. Enough. It is serious. Suggesting otherwise inhibits its potential growth and expanse as an art form—the potential I hope for comedy. They're "just jokes"? Get bent, man. Personally, I have found jokes a salve and means of processing an at-times too tragic world. It is through comedy that I have come to terms with the "cosmic joke," as the famous mystic Yogi Sadhguru puts it—death: "If you get the joke, falling on the other side will be wonderful."

2

AUDIENCE

"Have you ever tried stand-up?" is the question I get most often from comedians. Some are being nice and are just curious to meet a "civilian" who cares so much about comedy. However, I'd be lying (and I'd never lie to you, baby), if I didn't acknowledge that usually the question is meant to challenge my credentials. Comedy is hardly the only field in which the rebuttal to criticism is a rejection of the idea of the critic. I'm sure the first caveperson who ever offered a grunted opinion about a cave painting was hit over the head with a rock by its artist. Still, the skeptical artist's impulse is misguided here. It is more important that the critic relates to the audience, since that is who their work is for, especially with comedy as an audience-dependent art form. That said, yes, I have.

After years of bothering my friend Halle, a stand-up in her own right, with jokes and tweet drafts, she said in 2015 that I should "just try" stand-up. Not only that, but she had the show for me—"a leather-jacket-themed open mic." A leather-jacket-themed open mic means comedians were supposed to wear a leather jacket and do the type of material Andrew Dice Clay would do if he were making fun of

Andrew Dice Clay. Let's say I was ninth on a list of seventeen acts. Really, I have no idea. I do remember that most people just did regular sets wearing a leather jacket. One guy didn't have a leather jacket, borrowed one, and then proceeded to just talk about how dating was weird or whatever. There is a famous photo of the comedy writer Katie Dippold at a normal, just-drink-wine-and-watch-a-scary-movie Halloween get-together, dressed like the Babadook from the 2014 Australian horror film *The Babadook*. My leather jacket was a Babadook costume. *I only have leather jacket jokes*, I thought. *They're going to know I'm a fraud.* But as I saw more and more comedians do a medium job, it dawned on me, *They have nothing to compare me to.* As far as they knew I didn't incorrectly come dressed like the Babadook, I am always dressed like the Babadook. I *am* the Babadook.

Next thing I knew, my name was called. As I approached the stage, I repeated to myself, *Take the mic off the stand and put the stand behind you. Take the mic off the stand and put the stand behind you. Take the mic off the stand and put the stand behind you.* From years listening to comedy podcasts, I knew this one action is what separated amateurs from professionals. In retrospect, its significance was overrated. The audience wasn't hostile. They were giving me nothing. I was starting at a true 0. I asked if they were ready for "some leather jacket comedy" and they said "woo," less as a cheer and more of a "yes."

And then I did stand-up. That's how I talk about it. "Did." I wouldn't say I *performed* stand-up, but it was, undoubtedly, technically stand-up. I said a joke out loud and the audience made a noise that I thought was laughter. But it wasn't laughter. It was an acknowledgment of a joke, which is better than nothing. I realized that because with my second-to-last joke I said the punch line and I heard a sharp, loud noise, as if the audience was a popped balloon, but instead of helium, it was filled with laughs. (I'm sure you might be curious what the joke is, but I don't want to tell you. First, the expectations for it right now are too great. Second, it's not *not* dirty and it would be distracting. I will tell you eventually.) Then my set was done. I sat back down with the comedians and some said, "Good job." I felt nothing. I was not hooked, thankfully. That night I retired from stand-up.

By that point in my life, I had read or listened to hundreds of comedians talk about their first time, so I knew what was supposed to happen in this moment: Your first big laugh is like a secret door opening and behind it is the path to your new life. There is this idea in the general population that all comedians are sad clowns with traumatic childhoods. Based on my experience, that's not exactly correct. What is, for the most part, true is that all comedians have a compulsion to perform comedy. This is notable because, especially starting out, performing comedy—be it improv, sketch, or especially stand-up—is stupid hard. Multiple times a night, every night of the week, you have to do it poorly in front of people. And you have to do this for years before you bomb* only some of the time. If you want to go through this long, exhausting, disenchanting journey, then comedy must fill a deep need for you. For every comedian the source of that need is different, be it nature or nurture, but there is a reason almost everyone who eventually makes it describes that first laugh as feeling like a high they were chasing.

* "Bomb" is slang for when a comedian or a piece of comedy performs extremely poorly in front of an audience.

This is at the core of the sort of codependency of the comedian-fan relationship—you are only happy with what makes the other person happy. And it is what makes comedy such a unique art form. Most comedy is not only created to be performed in front of people but is also created *by* being performed in front of people. All live performers—musicians, theater actors, dancers—will say that they feed off the energy of the crowd or even that the crowd's energy influences their performance, but they are all working off material already written and/or rehearsed in private. Stand-ups will vary in how much they put pen to paper beforehand, but generally they write by going up onstage with an idea for an area in which a joke might be, and then they use the audience to figure out which parts are funny, or interesting, or both.

I'm focusing on stand-up because it is the most extreme example of comedy's natural selection, but the closeness of the comedian-audience relationship is one that defines all of comedy. Improvisers are creating whole shows based on the suggestions of the audience and what they do or do not laugh at. Sitcoms, for almost the entirety of their existence, were shot in front of live studio audiences for the same effect. The process of having an audience to work off is so important to *Saturday Night Live* that during the coronavirus pandemic they got around crowd restrictions by paying people to sit in the audience and calling them extras. Comedy directors like Paul Feig and Judd Apatow re-create the comedian-and-live-audience dynamic by using a ton of test screenings when editing their films. There are obvious exceptions—like animated or single-camera sitcoms—but still a vast majority of those are worked on by people who come from a live comedy background. That's because audiences more than shape how material grows and changes: They shape how comedians do what they do. And in doing so, over time, it is the audience that has pushed comedy forward as an art form.

The history of stand-up is the history of where comedians performed stand-up. As the stand-up–audience relationship evolved, so evolved the art form and the societal perception of it. And it stands to reason: If the job is to create a state of play, you are going to play by the rules of the place you are performing. To capture just how important this relationship has been, and to provide context for the past forty years of evolution, it's important to understand what came before. By looking back at comedy's history, you see how comedy thrived or regressed as a result of who comedians were playing to and the locations where their audiences had gathered. So, who's ready to run through the entire history of modern live comedy!? [*cheers*] And by modern, I mean starting in early-nineteenth-century America!!! [*standing ovation*]

There are a variety of comedic traditions featuring some form of monologue, dating back millennia. In the U.S., scholars argue the seeds of modern comedy were planted with the creation of minstrel shows in the early 1830s. Variety shows where white people performed in blackface, minstrel shows started as a way for white performers to appropriate the comedy Black people developed to process slavery and to mock their enslavers, and grew more cruel over time in response to the rise of abolitionism.[1] Minstrelsy was designed to appeal to the twisted morality of its racist audience members, resulting in comedy that was degrading and dehumanizing. By the 1870s, minstrel shows, now with

Black performers in blackface, were still popular, but the public lecture circuit, known as the lyceum movement, had also emerged with a proto-version of stand-up comedy that was dominated by something that more closely resembles the contemporary TED Talk. Mixed in with these speeches were the likes of Artemus Ward and Mark Twain—men who'd adhere to the moralist roots of those events, but with the added of bonus of being humorous when they spoke.[2]

Come the twentieth century, everything went wild. Industrialization, population explosion, and economic prosperity led to an eruption of literacy and leisure time. People flocked to variety shows, namely burlesque and vaudeville. Though there were performers who did both, the style of comedy differed based on venue and audience. Vaudeville attracted large audiences of people looking for a family-friendly show. This meant the comedy was big, physical, and often included a mix of music and dance. Burlesque comedians were dirtier, edgier, and all-around more adult, as they were sandwiched between acts featuring women wearing pasties with the little tassels that went awoo-awoo-awoo-awoo when the performer danced.

None of this historical comedic performance was "stand-up." According to the comedy historian Kliph Nesteroff's book *The Comedians: Drunks, Thieves, Scoundrels and the History of American Comedy*, that term, as the legend goes (legend count #1), comes from the mob, which ran most of the venues comedians performed at in the 1940s.[3] In between wearing fedoras and ending sentences with "see," these mobsters managed boxers, see. A dependable, tough boxer was referred to as a "stand-up fighter." A nightclub jokester who could deliver the goods was likewise called a "stand-up" comedian. The ability to provide a consistent service defined this era of live comedy, from the 1930s to the 1950s. It was joke-jokes' last stand, meaning the last time when using stock material was valued. Whether at nightclubs, on the chitlin circuit, or in the borscht belt, comics had a pressure to uphold people's expectation of what comedy was, which was joke-jokes. Also, during this time, comedy moved from theater seating to tables and booths, thus perforating the fourth wall. Comedy then grew a bit more interactive and enabled a rise in insult comedians, like Don Rickles.

The late 1950s and early 1960s—real Mrs. Maisel times—saw perhaps the most radical change in American comedy, and (you're never going to believe this) it was influenced by the audience. It's the story of suburban migration and who was left in the cities when all the squares got their two-car garages in Nowheresville. What happens when the only audience to perform to is downtown hipster jazz freak Communists? Lenny Bruce, Mort Sahl, and Nichols and May. Playing to like-minded crowds, in coffee shops and folk venues, allowed comedians to be more personal, conversational, and politically radical. And since these audience members were spending the rest of their week seeing improvisational jazz, it would make sense they'd want that spontaneity from their comedy as well. The proximity of hippie Greenwich Village, where much of this activity was happening in New York, to the gay West Village is also notable, as both Phyllis Diller and Joan Rivers, despite starting stand-up ten years apart, tell similar stories in Yael Kohen's oral history of women in comedy, *We Killed: The Rise of Women in American Comedy*, about being embraced for who they truly were when they found themselves performing for a room of gay men.[4] "You could work more chicly," Diller said about the time.[5] "You could do some very esoteric stuff." Esoteric is, of course, relative. Audiences with "esoteric" taste demanded it, and the comedians adjusted their acts accordingly.

The comedy club started in the 1960s and expanded in the '70s. This gave comedians more time in front of audiences than any comedian previously, and more time with a brick wall than anyone since the loser in "The Cask of Amontillado." As a result, comedians were able to refine their acts. And since most of these clubs were showcase rooms, meaning lineups of comics doing ten-to-fifteen-minute sets, stand-ups learned how to kill, and kill quickly. Thanks to the massive breakouts of comedians like Richard Pryor, George Carlin, and Steve Martin, and the clubs' proven economic viability, in the 1980s comedy clubs spread like a virus. Worse yet, many of the hundreds of clubs that opened were run by cynical restaurateurs attempting to capitalize on the hot new trend. In these spaces, stand-up was not an art form but dinner theater. "Franchise comedy clubs created franchise comics," Marc Maron said about that time.[6] As material needed to appeal to whoever, wherever, joke-writing reverted, becoming less personal and more generic. Easily digestible, observational comedy ruled the day. As did sexism, homophobia, and racism. Though plenty of comedians, like Ellen DeGeneres, were able to break out without relying on hack* bigotry, it became the de rigueur mode for opportunists who saw stand-up as a way to make a quick buck. It was a time when Andrew Dice Clay was the comedian playing the largest venues with shows George Carlin compared to "fascist rallies."[7] This, everyone, was the original comedy boom. It lasted about ten years. Mercifully, the product got

* "Hack," which derives from the word "hackneyed," is used to refer to an unoriginal comedian or clichéd material.

watered down and bad enough that audiences stopped going. In 1992, Francis Fukuyama marked the early nineties as "The End of History," and many people felt that it was also the end of comedy. It wasn't.

Then, with stand-up left for dead, two disparate movements rewired the comedian-audience relationship for good: the opening of Black-owned comedy clubs and the birth of alternative comedy. Comedy fosters in-groups, but also in-groups foster comedy. If play needs those involved to be comfortable, it makes sense that it would be simpler to achieve the necessary security and ease when surrounded by people who come from the same place as you, who come out of the same situation. It is on the comedian to then understand and harness the sensibility of these like-minded individuals, who have joined together to become an audience. In the 1990s, this resulted in some of the most revolutionary stand-up in decades. Queue up the *Entourage* theme song, reader, because I want to take you to Los Angeles. *Oh. . . . yeAH.*

The legend goes (legend count #2): In the mid-1980s, frustrated by work one day, the fledgling concert promoter Michael Williams went to the Comedy Store to let off some steam.[8] Looking around, Williams realized he was the only Black person in the room and that he hadn't laughed once. Soon after that experience, he was introduced to Robin Harris, a brilliant comedian who had grown disenchanted with trying to make it at the Comedy Store, after the club's legendary owner and gatekeeper Mitzi Shore told him that his act was too Black.[9] Necessity gave birth to invention, and in 1985, Williams opened the Comedy Act Theater on Crenshaw Boulevard, in the heart of South Central L.A., with Harris the permanent master of ceremonies.

The Comedy Act was the country's first true Black comedy

club. There were Black stand-up comedians before 1985. Three of the biggest comedians at the time—Bill Cosby, Richard Pryor, and Eddie Murphy—were Black. But only a select few were able to get booked in the "mainstream" comedy clubs of the 1980s. That discrimination created a need for what would be called Black rooms, filled with Black audiences. In L.A., Harris—who spent years drawing crowds at neighborhood bus stops—set the tone.[10] "He changed everything," Dave Chappelle would later say.[11] Harris would walk through the audience and roast the shit out of everyone. No one was safe. Harris particularly liked giving it to the droves of Black celebrities who'd come to see him, telling Magic Johnson, "Come on down here to the colored section, Magic." But, in a way, everyone was safe. Where Don Rickles would insult his audience as an outsider, Harris would do the same as an insider. A roast might sound mean, but it's another way of saying "I see you," notable in a country, and an entertainment industry, largely committed to ignoring inner-city life. Harris refused to leave the neighborhood, even as movie offers started coming, including a beloved turn as Sweet Dick Willie in Spike Lee's *Do the Right Thing*, in which he improvised all his lines.[12] He knew his act was as much for the community as it was of the community.

In 1990, Harris died, at the age of thirty-six, before ever getting the big break that seemed to be coming his way, but his legacy was in place. By that time the Comedy Act had a branch in Atlanta, and it would soon open a third club in Chicago. In Chicago, it had already influenced the opening of the South Side club All Jokes Aside, which, along with the Comedy Act and New York's Uptown Comedy Club, codified the style that became associated with *Def Comedy Jam*. Running on HBO from 1992 to 1997, when the comedy boom was supposedly over, *Def Comedy Jam* took the tired stand-up showcase format and created a sensation, thanks to acts who had finally been able to get the stage time necessary to hone their voices.

These voices spoke to an audience previously ignored by the mainstream entertainment industry. And yet, at the time, all the mainstream media could talk about was the words they said. Years later, I spoke about this with Tony Woods, a comedian who, in his first-season set, told a joke that ended with him farting on a cat that was licking his balls while he was having sex with its owner. "Most people couldn't get past the profanity," he told me, speaking about the show generally.[13] "There's no other way to say, 'Oh, yeah, we got kicked the fuck out of our apartment today . . .' That's a profane lifestyle. You can't say, 'We've been evicted.' That's bullshit. You can't just serve chicken with no spice on it, baby." The *Def Comedy Jam* audience demanded comedians talk to them about the issues they faced, as they would discuss them with each other.

It's notable that maybe the two best-remembered moments from the series involve the audience. The first came in the first season, in a set from Adele Givens, an infinitely confident comedian who tagged* her dirty jokes by saying "I'm such a lady." She was talking about her big lips ("All my lips are big," one joke ends), and a member of the audience said something to her. She went in:

> See, see, here's the kinda motherfucker, hollering about "blow job" and he's wearing about a size 4.

* In stand-up, a "tag" is a line a comedian throws in after the punch line to get another laugh.

Little ol' feet, so you know his dick's small.

I couldn't give him no blow job. My big-ass lips, his little ol' dick: It wouldn't work.

It would be like trying to give a whale a Tic Tac, motherfucker.

The audience shook and jumped like a chessboard in an earthquake, with multiple members getting up, running around, and giving each other high fives.

The second moment came on a night when everyone was bombing. It was a demanding audience that wanted to be impressed, and the lineup was not fulfilling its end of the arrangement. Out walked Bernie Mac, wearing a multicolored shirt and pants with his own damn face spray-painted on them. You heard murmurs and heckles when he touched the mic. He stared right back at them: "I ain't scared of you motherfuckers." You can hear the audience transform from cold to hot, shouting in laughter. Mac steams ahead, talking about how good the women look in New York and how much he loves sex, before waving his hand over his crotch and informing the crowd, "I'm blessed. I'm big boneded. I'm heavy structured. I'm hung low. If I pull my shit out, this whole room get dark." He tags the joke by screaming "Kick it!" and the DJ proceeds to play a beat for him to dance to. Chess earthquake. And why would he be scared of, you know, those motherfuckers? Mac and Givens were both from Chicago and were able to flourish as a result of having a regular place to perform. Some comedians say stand-up is like a conversation, but only the comedian is talking. That was not Givens and Mac's experience. They heard from their audience, creating a closeness you could feel in the comedy.

In contrast, Janeane Garofalo was given opportunities to

perform at mainstream comedy clubs when she was coming up in Boston in the 1980s, but often begrudgingly. Club audiences and bookers didn't like her. If it weren't for the insistence of other comics, she might've quit. "It was all very, very male dominated," David Cross explained in *We Killed*. "If you didn't fit into that working-class, blue-collar, male-centric comedy mold, then whatever you did was kind of alternative, in a sense. And for a woman to be intellectual was even more off-putting and difficult."[14] Eventually she moved to L.A. to work on *The Ben Stiller Show* and couldn't get consistent work at any of the clubs there, either.

Garofalo, ever a Gen X contrarian, when I interviewed her years ago at a live event, dismissed taking credit for *anything* (including the fact that she even is Gen X). And she barely acknowledges that alternative comedy was a thing, offering some version of "It just means performing in a place that's an alternative to a comedy club."[15] Garofalo hosted a show at the Big & Tall Bookstore, and cohosted a show with Kathy Griffin at a little rented theater. There were shows at coffee shops and laundromats. It was all very nineties. Many of these "venues" didn't even have PA systems, so to someone walking by, it looked like a person talking to a group of friends. This casual vibe continued even when these comics were in front of cameras. In Garofalo's iconic 1995 HBO *Comedy Half Hour*, she looks at her notes and asks the audience if she has talked about things yet. She speaks in a stream of consciousness, with punch lines sneaking their way into what comes off as a caffeinated hang. Garofalo expects the audience to understand exactly what she means when she describes people by their pop culture taste, like "Do you know who Claudia Schiffer's favorite band is? Foreigner." Or take this screed:

> Dave Matthews Band and Hootie and the Blowfish, I gotta bring it up. Seem like nice guys. Seemingly very nice guys. But never has a CD purchase spoken more volumes about a person in their life. Hootie and Dave Matthews Band, I know who you are. I know who you are. You're not an evil person. You're not a lawbreaker. You don't rock, as a rule. But when you do it's in a very VH1 kinda way. You're into Hootie. And, umm, you like the show *Friends*, a lot. A lot. You wish Tom Hanks and Meg Ryan could star in every movie. Every movie!

I know I say in the first chapter that all comedians are trying to re-create the feeling of mirth you have hanging out with your friends, but throughout the special Garofalo *really* speaks to her audience the way you would talk with your friends. It's all rapid-fire shared references that you don't have to explain. Her best material feels like inside jokes.

The origin of the definitive alternative comedy room is not unlike that of the Comedy Act. The performance artist turned comedian Beth Lapides was waiting to go onstage at the Comedy Store. Watching Andrew Dice Clay's version of nonironic-ironic sexism, she realized there had to be another option. Soon after, she did a show at the nonprofit feminist art and education center the Women's Building, and the audience loved her act. "They seemed starved for laughter," Lapides often recalls.[16] She asked them when the last time they laughed was. "We don't laugh," Lapides said they responded. "We're women, we're artists, and we're lesbians. At comedy clubs they make fun of us." Lapides vowed to create a show that would be "unhomophobic, unxenophobic, unmisogynist." She named it UnCabaret.

Sunday nights, in a small, low-ceilinged room multiple people have described as womblike, it was undeniable that the people performing were doing something different. Going up with notes was commonplace. Lapides would be in the back with a microphone asking questions if stories stalled, which led to a more conversational style. And the audience would be filled with friends or people the performers would see around town, at auditions or the local coffee shop. This resulted in material that aspired to radical honesty. Self-loathing was commonplace, as was oversharing. Many of the comedians were dating each other and talking about it onstage. Sometimes at the same show! And because it was L.A., they were open about show business in a way that comedians were otherwise hesitant to share. There was a fourth wall, but the comedian and audience interacted with the mutual respect of fellow artists. The even-footed relationship and a new sort of closeness defined the show.

Alternative comedy and Black comedy were reactions to the cynical heterodoxy of the eighties comedy boom. And chief among the facets of comedy they were responding to was that relationship to the audience. Although comedians have needed audiences for as long as there has been comedy, it wasn't until then that comedians started trusting audiences and embracing their role as integral to the show. I wouldn't say the audience and performer were equal, but they were both playing a part.

Black and alternative comedy got more popular and more widespread in their second decade. There was the Kings of Comedy, its sister the Queens of Comedy, and their alternative cousin the Comedians of Comedy. Performers from these worlds—Chris Tucker, Martin Lawrence, Ben Stiller, Zach Galifianakis—went on to become major players in TV and movies. It wasn't intentional, but these scenes taught future generations how to be comedy fans.

In 2022, Chris Rock was introducing the Best Documentary Feature Oscar, looking good as hell in a luscious, midnight-blue velvet tuxedo. After a few good jokes, he told one so bad it barely even sounded like a joke, and, in kind, the audience barely laughed. Rock was unfazed, because Rock is unfazed by jokes not working. What he did not expect was the husband of the joke's target, one of the most famous people who's ever lived, who was about to receive the highest honor in his field, coming onstage to give him a slap so slappy that it instantly became referred to as *the* slap. On one hand, specifically the hand that slapped, it was the weirdest thing that's ever happened. On the other, Rock has been confronted before. This is because Rock has a very unique relationship to his audience. He takes the standard comedian process of working material out in front of a crowd and pushes it to its limit, by embracing what other comedians try to avoid—bombing. Few comedians have ever destroyed like Rock, and this is directly related to the fact that few have ever had as many bad shows. That's because it has been proven over and over as the best way for him to figure out where the audience is at. To examine Rock's process is to see the stand-up–audience dynamic pushed to its most extreme.

I've seen Chris Rock live three times, and every time he's bombed. The first time was in the summer of 2003, when I used a fake ID to go to the Comedy Cellar. There I was, very young. *How young were you!?* So young, I fulfilled my two-drink minimum with a mudslide and a hamburger.

And the host said they had a special guest. I don't remember him saying Chris Rock, but I remember the feeling of seeing my favorite comedian walk to the stage and everyone bugging out. He told us he was set to host the MTV Video Music Awards soon and was going to test out some jokes. For a split second, I dreamed of going on AOL Instant Messenger the next day and telling all my classmates about my inside info and having them all respond, "Jesse, you are very cool. We should go on a date." But I would continue to have no dates, as Chris Rock told a lot of so-so jokes about subjects like Justin Timberlake and Britney Spears. I chalked it up to a bad set. When I saw him bomb again, fourteen years later, I knew better.

It was the winter of 2017, and I knew something was up when Wyatt Cenac told us we had to put our phones away. Cenac was hosting his weekly Brooklyn show, Night Train, and said if they caught anyone filming the next act, the person would be kicked out. We all nodded and out walked Chris Rock, wearing a puffy coat. This was the first step in communicating this wasn't a performance, but a guy just stopping by. Most comedians want the crowd to settle in, but Rock was making sure we wouldn't, as he was suggesting he could leave at any moment. His performance could be described as amateurish, but ingeniously so. Rock was trying to get a sense of whether each joke, premise, or idea worked in a vacuum, meaning they weren't building off the momentum of the previous joke or his own performance. He would do things that new comedians do that turn off audiences. Things that, in retrospect, I did the one time I did stand-up. He spoke in a soft monotone and kept looking down. If something did work, he would cut off the rolling laughter by murmuring, "What else? What else?" Another cliché of a faltering comedian. Unlike me, he was able to do this for an hour. And when he decided he was done, he said thank you, off to go into Manhattan to bomb some more. It's possible that, later that week, he did shows for old Jews in West Palm Beach, as he often did before tours. "I figure I'm in front of these people, they're a little older," he told Alec Baldwin in an interview. "If I can get them to laugh at this, when I get in front of the Black people, they're gonna go berserk!"[17]

Other than maybe Richard Pryor, there's never been a comedian better at using audiences to generate material than Chris Rock. There are comedians, like Dave Chappelle, who might be better at manipulating the audience or feeling out the audience in the moment, but in the process of using a series of crowds as a means of writing a special, it's hard to say anyone has reached the same heights. At the core of this ability is an understanding that you can learn more from bombing than killing. Most comics know this, but few embrace it like Rock. When I saw Rock, he was famous enough that he could get the audience to laugh just because of his vocal inflection. (Right now, try picturing his voice. You don't need words; you can imagine the cadence.) We are dogs and he is our Dr. Pavlov. The result, however, is that he can't get an accurate read on the substance of his material. Formally, what Rock is doing is what I learned from that one time I did stand-up: If you lock into the right joke, it can open people up to be in the necessary playful state regardless of how they felt before. Rock didn't want to try to get on a roll and stay in that state, however, as most comics would, because he wanted to know which ideas were comedically undeniable. When you multiply that by hundreds of sets, with thousands of different people, you can get close to your material being, as comedians call it, "bulletproof." So, he bombs.

Bombing seemingly doesn't affect Rock like other people. Later in life, Rock was diagnosed with a nonverbal learning disorder (NVLD), after a friend asked him if he'd ever gotten tested for Asperger's. With 70 to 80 percent of communication being nonverbal, Michael Che captured what having an NVLD can look like on *Saturday Night Live*'s first "Weekend Update" right after the slap: "Like how when he saw an angry Will Smith charging towards him and instead of moving out of the way, he put both his hands behind his back, smiled, and said, 'Uh-oh!'" An NVLD can result in black-and-white, all-or-nothing thinking. It's made close relationships difficult, Rock explained in 2020, but "all of those things are really great for writing jokes."[18] Considering he didn't know early on, Rock's process at that time was not him explicitly trying to counter his NVLD. No, after years in front of audiences, he figured out something that worked for him, as it resulted in one of the three or four most acclaimed/talked-about/controversial specials of all time. Here is the story of *Bring the Pain*.

I take you to Chicago's Park West Theater. It is 1993 and Rock is headlining, at both a career high and low. After being discovered by Eddie Murphy while working at the Comic Strip in the eighties, Rock was on *SNL* by 1990 and being heralded as Murphy's heir apparent. However, after three disappointing seasons and the release of his gangster rap parody movie, *CB4*, which he felt was not a success, Rock found himself off the show (a mutual decision, as Rock wanted to instead join the cast of *In Living Color*), with some name recognition but no clear next step forward. Having come up in mainstream clubs and being too big to appear on *Def Comedy Jam*, it didn't occur to Rock to watch his opener—the show's lionized host, Martin Lawrence. "I was in my dressing room and I heard a roar," he would later tell Judd Apatow.[19] "I thought it was a fight or something. So, I got up and went to the side of the stage. When I got there I realized it wasn't a fight, it was people laughing so hard that the building was shaking. People were crying, standing, stomping their feet—screaming laughter. I was terrified. It was like watching somebody fucking your wife with a bigger dick." And then it was Rock's turn, and . . . "crickets." "It was one of those sets where you panic," he later explained in a documentary made by the comedian W. Kamau Bell about *Bring the Pain* for the series *Cultureshock*.[20] "Okay, I'm going to do my closer right now. That'll get 'em back. And then the closer doesn't work. And now you got forty more minutes with lesser material. Horrible." Unlike the times I've seen him, the bombing was not on purpose, but he did learn a lot from the experience. "He just annihilated me," Rock remembered in 1998.[21] "He was incredible. He was animated, he was actin' out shit, stalkin'—all this shit. Blew my ass away. That was a pivotal moment, because I wasn't really prepared. I'd been working with too many white guys. It just made me realize I had to change my whole game." Rock needed to perform more. A lot more. And, for a comedian who came up through only mainstream clubs, he would now have to play everywhere.

For the next three years, Rock performed three shows a night almost every night. Sets of all-new material, for crowds of barely ten, and he'd bomb and bomb and bomb until he bombed less. He was trying to figure out how to perform his jokes in a way that would read as organic to the audience, while navigating a complex internal dynamic. "I had this great combination of big ego and low self-esteem," he explained.[22] "And the ego gets you out onstage, but the low self-esteem is the thing that makes you practice so much because you don't believe in yourself at all." He didn't trust himself to know what was funny; he needed the audience. Maybe it came from being famous fairly young, or maybe it was his NVLD making him feel like an outsider, but this need of the audience's response transformed into an almost anthropological interest in how they thought and felt. This fascination extended offstage, with Rock acting like a pollster, surveying public opinion. Besides reading multiple newspapers a day, he'd go to the local barbershop. "He'll go around the way and throw out a topic," Tony Rock, a stand-up comedian and Chris's brother, explained about that time, in Bell's documentary.[23] "'Hey, you see this thing about . . . ?' And just let everybody else go, just to see what the pulse is. 'Okay, that's the bit.'" The goal was to build himself as a comedian in the image of his prospective audience.

Bring the Pain was the result. Even when you rewatch it decades later, Rock's mastery of the form is apparent. Rock is a tremendous joke writer and a tremendous performer, but what stands out is his precision. Many comedians who try to push boundaries and explore uncomfortable areas tend to be sloppy, if not callous. In *Bring the Pain*, you see a comedian who put in the time to be in touch with exactly where his audience was at. This is best exemplified by the special's most audacious bit, "Black People and N****s," a joke in the pantheon of comedy history. The joke is about a "civil war [going] on with Black people," in which a segment of the community resents being represented by the behavior of another segment. If it weren't for time in front of countless audiences, the joke could've ended Rock's career instead of defining it. "I think about all the times I didn't have it precise and it was like people were ready to kill me," Rock remembered.[24] There was one memorable night in Oakland, in front of an all-Black audience. "That shit damn near started a fight," Tony Rock added.[25] As harrowing as those experiences were, the jokes got better. If you watch the joke back, you can see how it likely grew or shrank based on audience response.

When the joke rebuts the idea that the distinction is the media's fault, you can almost hear him responding to a specific complaint he was heckled with along the way. Parodying the complaint, Rock suggests, "It ain't us, it's the media. The media has distorted our image to make us look bad." To which he replies:

"When I go to the money machine at night, right? I ain't looking over my back for the media, I'm looking for n****s!

"Shit, Ted Koppel ain't never took shit from me! N****s have!"

Watching back, what is undeniable is how on board the audience that night was. "N****s always want some credit for some shit they're supposed to do," starts one section. Rock repeats the premise, as is his signature. "For some shit that they're supposed to do! A n***a will brag about some shit a normal man just does." When he says his first example, "A n***a will say some shit like, 'I take care of my kids.' You're supposed to, you dumb motherfucker!" you hear an explosion of laughter and applause. Tony Rock: "That's because all the Black men in there that take care of their kids are like, *Yo, that's so fucking true.*"[26] "The joke was perfect for Washington, D.C., because these are the people who are being judged by the standard of *are you a n****r*," the journalist Farai Chideya said years later.[27] "It's upperly mobile Black people," added Tony Rock.[28] "It's Black people who got their shit together." Mel Watkins, the journalist–comedy scholar–author of *On the Real Side: A History of African American Comedy*, puts it in even clearer focus: "He knew they'd be aware of two things—current affairs and the underside of African American culture."[29] Still, Rock wasn't just reflecting his audience's opinion back at them, as if they were one monolith. He had spent the years he was working on his act collecting information, processing it, and making sure he was able to communicate himself in a way that people would best comprehend. Through understanding comes trust, and through trust comes laughter.

"I wanted to do the Blackest special ever," is how Rock put it, before clarifying, "*My version* of the Blackest special ever. I did all this stuff that no Black people saw. And, you know, I wasn't a *Def Jam* guy. I missed all this Black stuff. Meanwhile rap is through the roof. Black is just happening. And I wasn't a part of it."[30] In 1998, Rock's friend the music executive Bill Stepney argued, "If Nixon's supporters were the silent majority, then Chris's black audience sort of mirrors that."[31] Leaving aside whether this is an accurate description of Rock's politics, it is a fair description of any comedian. They are the spokespeople for the unspoken perspective of their fan base. Stand-ups do not hold up a mirror to society, as is commonly said. No, at their best, they create a picture of a society that is rendered more and more accurate with each performance, so when they film the special it looks like a perfect reflection. The comedian is trying to bring aspects of the collective unconscious into the collective consciousness.

This is not to say everyone was happy with the bit. There were some who felt it was just a new spin on respectability politics. There were also members of the hip-hop community who felt targeted. One night, for example, Tupac

Shakur confronted Rock about the routine. It was meant to be provocative, and it provoked; however, the controversy never overwhelmed the acclaim because Rock understood his audience's thinking in that moment. "It just came out like any other routine," Rock said in 1998.[32] "There's nothing controversial about it if people are laughing." It's the comedy version of "the customer is always right": The people who are laughing matter more than the people who aren't. Rock acknowledges there are boos in all of his specials.[33] He knows they're there and he knows they are coming. From doing all the shows in preparation, he understands these are not the boos of bombing, but boos of discomfort that come from getting too close to saying the unsaid.

And yet, there is one critique that did seem to stick with Rock a little, which is, what does it mean for white people to see and laugh at that particular joke? "The 'N****s vs. Black People' thing causes worry in some Black people because they think that white people are picking up on our inside information," Mario Joyner, a comedian and friend of Rock's, said in 1998, adding, "or that it will make white people feel entitled to say 'n***a.'"[34] This is maybe best captured in the "Diversity Day" episode of the American version of *The Office*, where Michael Scott (Steve Carell) launches into a retelling of the routine without a second thought. The scene captures a culture's tendency to consume Black comedy without consideration of Black pain. On *60 Minutes* in 2005, Rock said he never will do the joke again: "Some people that were racist thought they had license to say 'n***a.' So, I'm done with that routine."[35]

Rock worked as hard on *Bring the Pain* as any comedian has ever worked on a special, making sure he and his prospective audience would be on the same page, but he never could've predicted how huge it would become, reaching people he had not expected to reach. So what did he do? Started bombing again. He put himself in front of more people, new people, different people, accounting for how big his platform had become. The result, in 1999, was *Bigger & Blacker*. I'm not sure any comedian has ever killed as hard as Rock killed at that moment in time. One of the many standout jokes targeted privilege. Though he does make this connection explicitly, he is speaking about the same white privilege that led people to believe they could impersonate him. Talking about the belief some people have that they are losing the country, Rock asks, "If y'all losing, who's winning?" He continues, "Shit, there ain't a white man in this room that would change places with me. None of you would change places with me. And I'm rich!" Same as before: Rock figured out where his audience was, so when he made his point, it would be undeniable.

Oh! The last time I saw Chris Rock bomb. I almost forgot. I'll tell you later.

Talk is cheap. And stand-up is talking. So, by the transitive property, stand-up is cheap. Person, stool, mic stand, mic. Because of the low overhead and the unending search for audience, comedy has always been quick to adapt to new technologies. Like Marshall McLuhan's idea that the medium is the message taken to the extreme, comedy fits itself in whatever time and space is available, like water in a vessel. For example, physical comedy thrived during the silent film era, and then, with the introduction of talkies, comedy got talky. The best example is how long-playing records influenced two stand-up trends in the 1950s and '60s. First, the extended running time meant you didn't need to constantly get up to change the record, making LPs ideal for parties. Party records, like those made by Redd Foxx and Moms Mabley, were designed for gatherings of adults.[36] This meant they were dirty as hell. Concurrently, there was also a value to comedy that could be played at home, for one person, alone. This plus the longer run time resulted in a new appreciation for the cohesion and flow of an act.[37] Jokes and stories grew longer. Compared to the turn-of-the-century comedy singles, comedy records prioritized the comedian's point of view. When they had titles like *Inside Shelley Berman*, audiences were expecting to get to know the person. If you were wondering just how big these comedy records were, let me tell you about *The Button-Down Mind of Bob Newhart*. After spending fourteen weeks at the top of the *Billboard* charts, the album won Album of the Year at the 1961 Grammys. Not Comedy Album, but Album, period. It didn't win Comedy Album, because its follow-up, *The Button-Down Mind Strikes Back!*, won that category.[38] This time is sometimes referred to as the comedy record boom, or even the first comedy boom. Which would make this current moment the third.

I say that, but—I hope you're sitting down—I don't think comedy booms exist. I'm aware that I used "comedy boom" five times already in this chapter. I'm aware that in chapter 1, I referred to this current moment as the second comedy boom. (Also, I said I'd never lie to you. Umm, sorry to tell you this, but my fingers were crossed behind my back!) When you zoom out, comedy booms are not defined by unique time periods when America loved laughing. There was popular comedy before and after. Booms are simply periods where the industry and trade publications could define comedy by a new, discrete way in which it was making money. What is considered the first comedy boom should be called the comedy club boom.

The so-called second comedy boom is similarly the product of emerging venues. If comedy's history is a series of paradigm shifts related to who the audience is and how they are receiving the comedy, the internet has allowed for an eruption of places comedy can infiltrate—YouTube, Twitter, Instagram, podcasts, streaming channels, TikTok, and whatever new app just came out whenever you're reading this. Think about it. What even *is* an audience now? For centuries, it meant whoever was within hearing distance. Right now, a comedian can perform a joke in front of three hundred people, film it, and have it watched as part of a special by 5 million people on Netflix, record it and have it listened to by 300,000 people on Spotify, clip it and have it watched by 1.2 million people on YouTube, 640,000 on Instagram, and 1.1 million on TikTok. This is what adapting to the audience looks like today, and the audience responds accordingly. Where for decades, the only way for a comedian to find an audience was through a five-minute set on Johnny Carson's *Tonight Show*, at this moment, with podcasts, social media, video sharing, and streaming services, comedians are building audiences faster and with more loyalty than any time before. Concurrently, the value of comedy in our culture has continued to increase. I'm not sure if you can call this a boom, as if it is a limited time period. We're approaching fifteen years of this and it doesn't appear to be stopping soon. This isn't a boom—it's just the way it is.

Okay, so here is the joke. Please, don't tell anyone:

The other day, a skeleton was giving me a blow job, and when I came it sounded like someone spit on a xylophone.

3

FUNNY

"Funny is funny" is a phrase you'll often hear when people are asked to justify their opinions on comedy. And it makes sense. Those words are the same word. A = A. Reflexive property. It's a phrase I most associate with two very different but very similar boomers—Jerry Seinfeld, the guy from before, and RuPaul. For Seinfeld, it is often a way to push aside any sort of identity politics, mixing postracialism with a naive belief in the legitimacy of meritocracy. With RuPaul it often materializes in his use of the phrases "you gotta make it funny" and "you better make me laugh" interchangeably when talking to competing queens on *RuPaul's Drag Race.* When both RuPaul and Seinfeld espouse some version of "funny is funny," they are essentially saying "If you're funny to me, you're funny to everyone." In both their defenses, they have been extremely successful and have had their senses of humor validated to such an extreme degree that I'm sure it feels universal. And, again, though they are extraordinary cases, the feeling is not special.

Often people say things like "punching down is just not funny" or "it's not funny when you're preaching to the choir." These statements will often ignore that there are people, in fact, laughing at these things. What this tells us is that the sense of what is funny is so subjective—so completely built into your persona—that it feels objective. That is how you get an idea like "funny is funny" in the first place. It's a throwing up of the hands, when you know comedy is subjective but are unable to articulate beyond your own taste. Most people know intellectually that there are other people out there who laugh at different things than they do, but when confronted with those things, the reaction is visceral and often dismissive.

Like, in 2007, Christopher Hitchens wrote a piece for *Vanity Fair* entitled "Why Women Aren't Funny." It brought intellectual heft to an opinion long voiced by the stupid. Some women wrote rebuttals, but in doing so, they played into Hitch's hands, as he later published a sequel where the main point was *See, see, see how serious these women are?* Well, he's dead now. I have no interest in arguing with a dead guy. It's no fun. Either way, he has already lost.

Also, women don't need me to argue their case, as the evidence has always spoken for itself. Like, it's good Hitchens was already dead by 2013, because I'm sure watching Tina Fey and Amy Poehler host the Golden Globes three years in a row would've killed him. (I assume he'd rather be dead than admit he was wrong.) Their performances set the bar for modern award show hosting and included, to me, two of the most undeniable jokes ever told. First, in 2013, Amy Poehler said about Kathryn Bigelow: "I haven't been really following the controversy over *Zero Dark Thirty*, but when it comes to torture, I trust the lady who spent three years married to James Cameron." And then, in 2014, Tina Fey joked about the film *Gravity*: "It's the story of how George Clooney would rather float away into space and die than spend one more minute with a woman his own age." To spend time on the question if women are funny would be like Neil deGrasse Tyson having to spend time explaining that the Earth is round. But it's not like Hitchens's argument was based in any sort of reality. No, whenever men say women aren't funny or that women aren't funny around them, it says less about women than about what it's like to hang out with these dudes. When I read what Hitchens wrote, I see a person with an aesthetic preference, who knows more about being a misogynist than about comedy. It's not just him. Because there isn't a history of taking comedy seriously, people are left to create value systems around their own senses of humor and ideas of taste.

The fix for this misguided way of thinking is to consider funniness as an artistic metric and not as an intuitive fact. This is vital, because comedy has really taken to the content boom, providing people with algorithmically created niches of their specific senses of humor, to the point that Hollywood has essentially abandoned the idea of the big-comedy-movie-star movie that was present for my entire life. Funniness subjectivity has strengthened, often laying bare our inability to value comedy beyond the service it provides. While it is obvious to take seriousness seriously, how do you take funniness seriously, when so much of the art of comedy is to not take things seriously? Add to that the fact that ideals of good taste fail in judging comedy, as that standard was created in opposition to funniness.

So often, from ancient Greek philosophers to the people who vote on the Oscars today, those in charge of interpreting our culture have dismissed comedy as being juvenile, as dumb, as merely funny. *Merely funny!?* Umm, funniness rules. It's one of my top-three favorite things about comedy.

It is difficult to achieve. It is rare. It is an exception. As Will Rogers once said, "An onion can make people cry, but there's never been a vegetable invented to make them laugh." So we must understand why funniness was depreciated, dismantle that value system, and in its place offer a new way of considering it.

This chapter is going to be about Adam Sandler and *The Simpsons*, but first it's about William Shakespeare, who, despite being British and dead, had his work become *The Simpsons* of 1800s USA. As was captured in *Highbrow/Lowbrow: The Emergence of Cultural Hierarchy in America*, Lawrence Levine's 1988 book about the invention of the norms of taste, Shakespeare's work was really gosh-dang popular.[1] And with everybody, not just the fancy. Accordingly, how Shakespeare was performed shifted to become broader, with bigger acting, more melodrama, and frequent mugging.

As the century wore on, the rich grew tired of being in the same room as poor people. Separate sections weren't enough; they needed separate theaters. Soon, separate theaters weren't enough. Like a fifth-grade bully who holds a third grader's ball up in the air, out of reach, turn-of-the-twentieth-century rich dicks sought to elevate certain cultural products out of the grasp of the common man. This was achieved by charging higher ticket prices, by convincing people that to understand the work of someone like Shakespeare they would need to have studied it in college, and by policing audience behavior. "The relative taming of the audience at the turn of the century," Levine writes, "was part of a larger development that witnessed a growing bifurcation between the private and the public spheres of life. Through the cult of etiquette, which was popular in this period, individuals were taught to keep all private matters strictly to themselves and to remain publicly as inconspicuous as possible."[2] Levine is alluding to activities like "eating, coughing, spitting, nose blowing, scratching, farting, urinating," or, as suggested in etiquette books from the time, laughing loudly.

Around the same time emerged the proliferation of the ideals of "high comedy." The British author and seven-time loser of the Nobel Prize in Literature George Meredith, in *An Essay on Comedy and the Uses of the Comic Spirit*, defined its terms.[3] Meredith thought comedy was good but argued that "true Comedy . . . shall awaken thoughtful laughter." I am aware that "thoughtful laughter" sounds like some junk I would say, but to Meredith "thoughtful" means rational, balanced, and restrained. You know how rich men, dressed in tails, top hats, and monocles, laugh in cartoons, like "Ha, yes, very good"? In kind, the comedy for polite society was to be about polite society. Whatever you picture Oscar Wilde to be like, whether you've read any of his work or not, it's that, but straight. "Thoughtful laughter" is laughter that never overwhelms good taste.

These standards proliferated during the twentieth century with the explosion of popular culture, despite the fact that to the real elites, *all* pop culture was lowbrow trash. I blame film critics, as the early decades of film criticism were a fight to get the form to be seen not just as a popular art but a fine art. This push created a value system that comedy often found itself on the wrong side of.

Looking at the original reviews of movies that are considered comedy classics, I was overwhelmed by the condescension. Even in good reviews, the critics needed to make sure they hedged. Like when reviewing Billy Wilder's *Some Like It Hot* in 1959, *The New York Times* called it "overlong, occasionally labored," writing, "two hours is too long a time to harp on one joke."[4] *Variety* praised the film's director and performances, but wrote, "Even so, the film has its faults. It's too long, for one, being a small joke milked like a dairy; one or two scenes skirt the limits of good taste."[5] Again, these were positive reviews, of a film that would top the American Film Institute's list of the "100 Funniest American Movies of All Time" in 2000, but still critics wanted to make clear that they knew it was still a comedy. This is just the start. The *Times* critic said of the ending of *Dr. Strangelove or: How I Learned to Stop Worrying and Love the Bomb* (AFI's eventual third-funniest movie ever), at the time of its 1964 release, "It isn't funny. It is malefic and sick."[6] This is a movie critics like, and yet he still feels the need to make his skepticism clear. When reviews were less mixed and more wholly negative, the language was more harsh. Like for the Marx Brothers' 1933 *Duck Soup* (AFI's number five), the *Times* declared it was "for the most part, extremely noisy."[7] I was most insulted reading the *Times* review of 1974's *Blazing Saddles* (AFI's number six), which the critic compared to Chinese food, in how it left him unfulfilled. "One remembers exhaustion, perhaps because you kept wanting it to be funnier than it was."[8]

If these movies received mixed responses at the time, how did they find themselves decades later considered all-time classics? Looking at the other films that top this AFI list—*Tootsie*, *Annie Hall*, *M*A*S*H*, *The Graduate*—I have a theory. All those movies are great, well-made comedic films, but they aren't laugh riots. They aren't films those in the business refer to as "hard comedies." There are humor and solid laughs in each, but these movies are also all understated and mix in a good deal of drama. It would make sense, then, that *Blazing Saddles*, *Duck Soup*, and *Dr. Strangelove* appear in the AFI top ten not because they've gotten funnier as time passed, but because they've gotten *less* so. As the huge laughs mellow with the passing of relevance, these films seem less jokey and, as a result, more "respectable." A film like Buster Keaton's *The General* (nineteenth on the AFI list) can go from being called "elementary" and a "flop" by *Variety* upon its 1926 release[9] to "genius" and a "masterpiece" by the same publication decades later.[10] No longer does the trivial laughter distract from the important technical innovation. Film created its own version of good and bad taste, partly by generating a value system that looked down upon funniness. And this perspective became more prevalent as pop culture grew in prominence in our society. Routinely comedies, be it the Halle Berry and Natalie Desselle fish-out-of-water comedy *B.A.P.S.* (15 percent on Rotten Tomatoes),[11] Will Ferrell and John C. Reilly's delayed adolescence farce *Step Brothers* (55 percent on Rotten Tomatoes),[12] or Will Forte's tremendously silly action movie parody *MacGruber* (47 percent on Rotten Tomatoes),[13] have come out over the last thirty years that critics didn't love, only to become beloved fixtures of the American comedy canon. More recently, in the last fifteen or so years of the Golden Age of Television, the single defining feature of so-called prestige comedies is that they are less outwardly funny than the sitcoms that came before them (more on this phenomenon in chapter 7).

In 2021, I had the opportunity to interview the former writer and current professional opinion-haver Fran Lebowitz, and I asked if she'd noticed the increased prominence of comedy in our culture since 1990. Of course she had. When I asked her what she credits that to, she said, "The general lowering of standards."[14] Starting in the nineties, she began noticing an accelerated shift in what educated New Yorkers were taking seriously. Well-executed TV shows were being held up to the level of books and theater. "[If] everything is great and everything is important," she said, talking about the flattening of brows, "then comedians are great artists." Lebowitz is an old-school snob and a willful Luddite, so what she sees as the end of elitism is more a democratization of elitism. It's oxymoronic, but this shift reflects an evolution of taste combined with the maintenance of standards. Now, over a century since these standards were codified, the terms "highbrow" and "lowbrow" have lost their specific meaning in our culture. Still, in an era of algorithmic consumption habits, you can see the remnants of their ideals in how people talk about what is good or bad art.

Between 1995, when he came out with *Billy Madison*, and 2015, when he started making movies exclusively for Netflix, Adam Sandler starred in seventeen live-action movies that each grossed more than one hundred million dollars worldwide. During that twenty-year period, that's more hits than Ben Stiller made, more than Jim Carrey, more than Will Ferrell, more than Julia Roberts, more than Will Smith, more than Tom Cruise. It's tied with Tom Hanks, but if anything, that proves the point, given that the Sandman's and Hanks's careers are rarely rated on the same scale. Unlike Hanks, only two movies that the Sandman starred in and produced in that period have received higher than a 50 percent, aka "Fresh," score on Rotten Tomatoes—*Happy Gilmore* and *The Wedding Singer* (though both are inflated by positive DVD reviews, so it's possible that none of his movies topped 50 percent). The Sandman has twelve Razzie nominations (with three wins) for Worst Actor and thirteen acting nominations from the People's Choice Awards (with nine wins). The biggest comedy star of a generation, yes, but these are some things critics have written about him and his movies: "he's smug, vain, mean-spirited . . . and not funny";[15] "savagely unfun and relentlessly generic";[16] and "It's all painfully unfunny."[17] Specifically, this was all said about *one* of his movies—his 2011 drag comedy *Jack and Jill.* Adam Sandler (my editor said I was only allowed three "Sandman"s, and I got too excited and used them right away) is not the only popular comedian to be loathed by critics and the critically minded, but no one has ever sustained such a stark divide. Examining Sandler's career allows you to see how serious people value funniness.

Consider what it looks like when Sandler gets the occasional positive review. Besides always being for a more "serious" movie, the critic must note that it is an exception, often proclaiming that the film—and his role—is his best since *Punch-Drunk Love.* Is Sandler better as Danny Meyerowitz in *The Meyerowitz Stories* than he is in *Jack and Jill* playing Jack *and* Jill? If you have an answer, that means you have a personal opinion about the relative value of being funny. To argue, however, that the personal opinion that Sandler is better as Danny is universally correct is implying that the relatively few who find Sandler compelling being largely dramatic and only slightly funny have superior taste than the many, *many* more who enjoy him being essentially entirely funny. This is not a behavior exclusive to professional critics, as social media has given a platform to anyone who wants an opportunity to argue their taste. Everyone's a critic.

Nothing against the critic. Some of my favorite coworkers are critics. I use them as the stand-in for people who assert a highbrow perspective while residing in the world of middlebrow. They are watching Sandler's career through the prism of cinema. When critics reviewed *Jack and Jill*, the same week in 2011 they also reviewed Lars von Trier's masterpiece *Melancholia*, which *Vulture* later called the best film of the decade.[18] If you are judging the quality of a Sandler movie based on a definition of "good" represented by movies like *Melancholia*, of course you are going to write things like "Yet the pic's general stupidity, careless direction and reliance on a single-joke premise that was never really funny to begin with are only the most obvious of its problems," as *Variety* did.[19]

But what happens when you are judging Sandler's movies against other Sandler movies? To answer this question, I watched them. Every single one. Again. But this time all in a row. The first thing you notice when you don't assume all his movies are bad is that a lot of them are pretty good. Sandler's films have been able to maintain a certain quality because he's had an unparalleled amount of control over the movies he has made. Executive producing through his Happy Madison production company, he's handpicked his collaborators for all his movies and is able to be very hands-on through the entire process, from scripting through release. That said, I do not want to argue for Sandler through the auteur theory, because, as far as I can tell from watching his movies, he does not subscribe to that perspective on filmmaking. Sandler appreciates that his films have a sort of take-home lesson, that he has fun making them with his family and friends, and, most importantly, that the most people as possible find it funny. "I didn't get into movies to please the critics," he said in 2013.[20] "I got into it to make people laugh and have fun with my friends." Here he is espousing a comedian's value system. Sandler took the idea that comedy is about creating the feeling of laughing with your friends literally. However, again, it is a value system directly in opposition to cinema's.

When thinking about Sandler's approach to moviemaking, I'm often reminded of when Judd Apatow was promoting *Funny People*, the movie many interpreted as revealing Sandler's insecurities over the movies he makes, when, in reality, it was much more about Apatow's. Apatow told Terry Gross on *Fresh Air* that when they were starting out in comedy at the same time, "Adam had so much energy to be funny that he would be very funny with strangers on the street."[21] And that's it. Sandler is driven by the desire to make as many people laugh as he can—he doesn't care about how old they are, where they live, if they are the movie critics for a major newspaper. *Jack and Jill* made nearly $150 million worldwide. It's not about the money; it's about the people, and specifically the people laughing. More people saw and laughed at *Jack and Jill* than *Punch-Drunk Love*. *Jack and Jill* was a success. Again, I'm not arguing it is better (whatever that means), just that it is a better articulation of what Sandler strives to achieve. But the amount of care Sandler invests in making his movies funny to his audience is also at the core of why they are poorly received.

To be fair, it's not just that his movies are comedies, but the sort of comedies they are. This is the crux of the matter: If I'm to make the case for taking comedy seriously, for taking funniness seriously, I must defend the lowest of low comedy—the poop joke. Which brings us back to *Jack and Jill*. If you haven't kept up with Sandler since *Big Daddy*, give or take, it is probably the movie of his that you assume is the worst. (That or *I Now Pronounce You Chuck and Larry.*) It's telling of what "the worst" means for people. But there is one scene in particular in *Jack and Jill* that captures everything we talk about when we talk about Sandler.

While visiting her successful twin brother in L.A. from the working-class hometown they grew up in, Jill returns from a date farting and desperately needing to use the bathroom to "make some chocolate squirties." Having gotten into a fight earlier about her overstaying her welcome, Jack comes after her to talk. Separated by the bathroom door, Jack tries talking with her, but Jill is still mad. She tries to tell him about her date and how nice it felt to be welcomed by someone, but she keeps on interrupting herself by the loudest, wettest farts, maybe, in cinema history. Imagine the loudest, wettest farts and double their volume and fluidity!

Whatever bad taste is, it's this. Farting and pooping and laughing—all the things the turn-of-the-twentieth-century dweebs felt were not appropriate for polite society. These are low laughs, sure, but they are intentional laughs. If you want to get technical, the comedy is in the contrast between Jill finally confronting her brother and the humbling sounds of her chocolate squirting. It's a deeply human joke—as much as we pretend we are high-minded beings with our little jobs and conversations about the debt ceiling, we have a room in our house where we excrete waste like we're cattle. "[Man is] a god who shits," wrote the cultural anthropologist Ernest Becker in the Pulitzer Prize–winning *The Denial of Death.*[22] Speaking of death, there is a tendency to treat the discussion of it as inherently sophisticated. This is best captured by the opening scene of *When Harry Met Sally*, when Billy Crystal's Harry, trying to prove his sophistication, asks Meg Ryan's Sally, "Do you ever think about death?" When she says, "Yes," he snobbishly retorts, "Sure, you do. A fleeting thought that drifts in and out of the transom of your mind. I spend hours. I spend days." This brilliant little scene is meant to communicate that Harry is deep or, more accurately, thinks he's deep. Now imagine if he instead asked her, "How often do you poop?" We would think the screenwriter, Nora Ephron, was trying to tell us he's a juvenile doofus. (Also, can you imagine!?) However, what is going to the bathroom but a little death, a physical reminder of your decomposition. Why is that less serious than a *thought* of nothingness—because it smells bad? What do you think a dead body smells like!? My guess is it is because, unlike dying, going to the bathroom is something you do in your daily life, and there is a shame associated with the juvenile parts of our life. This makes it an even more complex issue than dying, which is scary but just happens once and the individual is not even there for it. Rooted in the highbrow denial of death is a lowbrow denial of life.

But that's not all. This contrast of our higher and lower selves can be applied to the scene on a metatextual level as well: It's funny that a bunch of grown-ups went to work one day and planned shots around coordinated diarrhea noises. While we're in the meta, it's also compelling because the audience is aware that both parts are played by Sandler and that means the movie will create scenarios so that two characters interact but aren't in the same frame. "When I was a kid and a teenager I was obsessed with Adam Sandler and Jim Carrey stuff," Andy Samberg, who played Sandler's son in 2012's *That's My Boy*, told me.[23] "My friends or parents would be like, 'I don't know. It just seems stupid.' I would always say, 'Yeah, but they know it's stupid. That's the difference.' They're choosing to be stupid from a place of intelligence, and therefore that is making me happy. They're saying, 'We know what the world is, and in spite of that we're going to spend our time on this as adults.'" Samberg, who would go on to make his own version of well-made stupidity with his comedy partners in the Lonely Island, understands lowbrow does not mean low quality.

Which is not to say lowbrow always means high quality, and that the only thing a good comedy needs is to show a person going to the bathroom. It's a matter of trying to see and appreciate the quality regardless of the brow. You can do dumb comedy, smartly, by offering something new that twists or subverts expected joke formats. You might still have a poop joke, but there is a distinction to be made in how you get there. I compare it to pop music. Do you know the story of Kelly Clarkson's "Since U Been Gone"?[24] The pop music supercomputers Max Martin and Dr. Luke were listening to the Yeah Yeah Yeahs' "Maps"[25] and were frustrated by the moment when it gets to the chorus, because it doesn't go up in energy, vibe, melody, etc., the way a traditional pop song would. So they ripped it off and put a generationally huge chorus on it to great effect. Both songs are giving you pop, but one gives you the expected in a big way and the other is playing against it.

Playing against it can look a lot of different ways. A recent example comes from an episode of Comedy Central's *Detroiters*, one of the great smart-dumb pieces of comedy in recent memory. In it, Sam and Tim, two local advertising executives played by the show's stars and cocreators, Sam Richardson and Tim Robinson, are invited over to the futuristic smart home of a genius inventor (played by Kevin Dorff). The Elon Musk type wants the boys to help promote his zero-emissions car. Showing it off, he explains it "takes all of its harmful carbon emissions and exhaust and expels it into a nontoxic blob." Cut to the back of a car, where it appears the car is, well, shitting. It's a poop joke, but a very specific, odd way into one. Often, the twist on the form comes down to who is doing the pooping and where and how and why. What made the pooping scene in *Bridesmaids* so comedically explosive was that the ways pooping was depicted felt fresh and new—the buildup from the sketchy lunch scene; the contrast with the women being in wedding dresses; the farce of all of them rushing to find anywhere to go, resulting in Maya Rudolph's shitting in the street; the fact that this sort of scene features women at all. (The scene reminds me of a line from Chris Kraus's *I Love Dick*, "What happens between women now is the most interesting thing in the world because it's least described,"[26] if she were talking about pooping.) In contrast, the *Jack and Jill* scene is literally set in a bathroom. It's in an Adam Sandler movie—you are supposed to know fart and poop jokes are coming. This doesn't make the scene more or less funny, or better or worse, as it really comes down to personal preference. What matters is understanding all of these as intentional formal decisions rooted in specific artistic perspectives.

"We can intellectualize as much as we want to," Richardson told me, "but the idea of this brown thing that comes out of your butt and stinks and you have to deal with it and you're ashamed of it, there's nothing funnier in the world."[27] He added, "And it makes a sound when it comes out and sometimes the sound is just a sound, but it reminds you of a thing and this thing stinks like the poop—like, it's just objectively funny." One last thing from Richardson for the critics: "You will never get smarter than the idea of a fart being funny and poop being funny." Look, I agree, clearly.

But to take it a step further, I don't mind funniness's associations with the scatological or the fact that it might not be smart. Comedy's ability to be juvenile, to tap into the audience's juvenile self, is one of the things that makes it special. While critics are literally paid to seem smart and the rest of us are just doing it because of social pressure, all of us would benefit from having our stupid sides appealed to.

For example, the most emotional experience I ever had watching a movie was during *Blended*, a Sandler–Drew Barrymore rom-com about two single parents that *The New York Times* said "has the look and pacing of a three-camera sitcom filmed by a bunch of eighth graders and conceived by their less bright classmates."[28] I had a profound personal realization about the sacrifices my own parents made blending my family. This was not in spite of some of the dumbest jokes of Sandler's career, but, in my opinion, because of them, as they told the overthinking part of my brain to take ninety minutes off, so I could *feel* something. In *The Denial of Death*, Becker discusses Otto Rank, the colleague of Freud's who was known for working with authors and artists, like Henry Miller and Anaïs Nin. Rank believed the only cure for neurosis was the "need for legitimate foolishness." I understand there are potential negative sociopolitical ramifications of a culture of thoughtlessness, but part of what comedy does is relieve pressure; often the pressure is that of trying to appear like an adult. Comedians like Sandler make movies that appeal to both an actual child and everyone else's inner child.

I saw *Blended* at a press screening, and people were laughing. Yet the *Times* review called it "not funny on so many levels."[29] This is not a one-off phenomenon. Bilge Ebiri, one my favorite coworkers, who happens to be a film critic, tells the story of going to a press screening of *That's*

My Boy and seeing all the critics there laughing, the *whole* movie. He later explained, "They laughed their asses off and they all went home and they all wrote their little, snippy, snide *pans* talking about how it's bad, how it's inappropriate, how it's offensive."[30] What Sandler's career shows is that you cannot effectively judge comedy by a value system that was created specifically in opposition to comedy's primary goal. And, in turn, funniness cannot be expected to adhere to a value system that doesn't value funniness.

Sandler's recent surge in being respected is a warning sign for comedy because it is directly related to him doing less funny work. I am happy for him, but that is not the way forward for the art form. Because comedy is in a position not unlike film was one hundred years ago, in a fight for legitimacy, but, unlike film, the answer cannot be to be less funny.

I was an actual child once. It's true. And my favorite show/comedy/anything was *The Simpsons*. I'm sure I laughed in the years between my birth and my introduction to the show (keys, jingled), but *The Simpsons* was the first time I was like, *this* is for *me*. I cannot tell you when I started watching. When I picture myself as far back as I can picture myself, I was watching. And *The Simpsons* was, I thought, the funniest thing that ever existed. Who would've guessed I was right?

My viewership reflects that *The Simpsons* was very popular in the early nineties, but I didn't watch it *because* it was popular. How would I know? I could barely read, let alone comprehend the Nielsen rating system. Similarly, I thought it was good, but it had nothing to do with the fact that it was supposed to be good. So it's quite comical to read the pretentious writing about the show from the time and imagine the blank face of baby me not knowing what the hell it was talking about.

Going through a lot of the early writing about *The Simpsons*, the Harvard of it all stands out. While none of the show's three creators went to Harvard (Matt Groening went to Evergreen State College, James L. Brooks dropped out of NYU, and Sam Simon went to Stanford, like an idiot), four of the original seven staff writers did (Al Jean, Mike Reiss, Jon Vitti, George Meyer). Season 2 included writing from two more Harvards (Jeff Martin and Nell Scovell). Seasons 4 and 5 brought on another four (Conan O'Brien, Bill Oakley, Greg Daniels, Dan McGrath). In 2021, *Harvard Magazine* reported that over thirty writers from the show were alumni.[31] *The Simpsons* was the shining example of a growing trend, with the *Los Angeles Times* reporting in a 1992 piece entitled "America Laughs with Harvard Accent, But It Doesn't Know It" that an improbable 10 percent of all TV comedy writers went to Harvard.[32] This is partly the result of the prestige and training of *The Harvard Lampoon*, and largely the result of the professional connections they fostered with each other. *The Simpsons* lacked the prestige signifiers of the more dramatic comedies of the modern age, but the show's association with Harvard proved to be a feather in the cap for the show and comedy generally.

Even when critics weren't talking about Harvard, it was the highbrow, intellectual parts of the show that got most consistently celebrated. "Matt Groening's cartoon family is one of the few current works of popular art that possess wit and integrity," read an *Entertainment Weekly* review of *The Simpsons'* second season. "*The Simpsons* as role-model programming, as intelligence-affirming fare? Bart would probably tell me to blow it out my ear. But it's true."[33] Even the jokes journalists chose to showcase—be it the heavy-handedly satirical or fancy-pants reference—conveyed that what made *The Simpsons* good was how elevated it was. Like a 1990 *New York Times* profile of Groening that praised the cartoonist for "sneaking references to Diane Arbus or Susan Sontag into the show."[34] Or the 1992 *Times* review, which was clearly quite tickled by Maggie being placed in the Ayn Rand School for Tots run by an "unctuous director" who reads a book called *The Fountainhead Diet*.[35]

Here is the thing: Structurally, there is no difference between a highbrow reference, like Sontag, and any of the myriad lowbrow ones the show made. The construction is often identical, and the joke functions the same way, with a mix of the spark of recognition and the unexpected contrast between the reference and what you're watching. A highbrow reference might benefit from its specificity, but the show made just as many great, specific mass-culture jokes. Regardless of the brow, a reference has the added effect of bringing in the people who get it. The difference is in who gets it. But is a joke more intelligent just because a smart person gets it? Isn't that like saying a portrait of a college dean is superior to that of a stock boy at the campus bookstore, because more professors would recognize the former than the latter? Unless you have an exclusivity-for-exclusivity's-sake value system of the kind that has long defined the highbrow, jokes for "smart" people aren't necessarily the smartest jokes.

In my opinion, there were smarter jokes made using more broadly recognizable references in each of the episodes the above jokes appeared in. In the same episode in which Arbus's work is used as a comparison to Bart's photo of Homer (season 1, episode 10, "Homer's Night Out"), Homer is trying to check out at the Kwik-E-Mart when Apu, who has the photo taped behind him, says, "You look familiar, sir, are you on the television or something?" To which Homer responds, "Sorry, buddy, you got me confused with Fred Flintstone." A couple weeks later, in the same episode in which Sideshow Bob shows an "amusing caricature" of Sontag from the *Springfield Review of Books* ("Krusty Gets Busted"), he responds to being proven guilty of framing Krusty by yelling at Bart and Lisa, in the style of an uncovered *Scooby-Doo* monster, "And I would have gotten away with it, too, if it weren't for these meddling kids." Maggie doesn't just get placed in the fascistic day care in season 4, episode 2, "A Streetcar Named Marge"; she breaks out of the room she's placed in to get back her pacifier via a full-on *Great Escape* homage, including scenes like her bouncing a rubber ball against the walls of her crib in a perfect mirror of the iconic scene from the 1960s World War II film classic. While all the highbrow jokes are quite good, the alternative, pop-culture-oriented bits are more lived-in, ambitious, structurally sophisticated, and philosophically complex. Where the former relies on a simple juxtaposition (that the juvenile medium of cartooning references the world of intellectual adults), the latter demands the sort of technical precision, critical elasticity, and postmodern self-awareness that is associated with *The Simpsons*.

I'm not saying the higher-brow references make *The Simpsons* worse in any way. What made *The Simpsons The Simpsons* was that it can and did do it all. Take the "A Streetcar Named Desire" musical they put on for that aforementioned season 4 episode: They took Pulitzer Prize–winning source material and wrote the silliest songs over it, with lyrics like "Can't you hear me yell-a? / You're puttin' me through hell-a! / Stella, STELLA!!!!" At the same time, Homer is seen wordlessly watching. It's beautifully directed; you can see him put together the parallels between his oafish treatment of Marge and Stanley's treatment of Blanche. At the end of the episode, Homer tells Marge, "It made me feel bad. The poor thing ends up being hauled to the nuthouse when all she needed was for that big slob to show her some respect," adding, "Hey, you know, I'm a lot like that guy." Marge responds, "Really?" Homer: "Yeah, like when I pick my teeth with the mail and stuff." To me, that's *The Simpsons* at its best—just everything, everywhere, all at once. It's high. It's low. There's an undeniable irony and yet the result is touching. More than a reference, it reflects a true cultural fluency.

At the time of its 1990s peak, it had an unprecedented concentration of comedy and an uncommon range of comedy. Smart wordplay, dumb physical gags, obscure references, trenchant commentary on contemporary conventions, funny voices. The perspective was undeniably white, male, Harvardy, so a ton of people never got *The Simpsons*, but, just in terms of numbers, it reached more people than any other piece of comedy. Despite Fox not being available in all markets when the show premiered, the show brought in between 20 million and 34 million viewers per episode for its fourth season, then stayed just south of 20 million from seasons 5 to 9, and remained at over 8 million through its NINETEENTH season. (Reminder: 19.3 million viewers tuned in for the *Game of Thrones* series finale.)[36] There have also been decades of syndication. Moreover, *The Simpsons*, after the Fox-Disney merger, became an unexpected hit for Disney+. Also, because animated comedy traditionally translates better than live action, because it's easier to swap in different languages with less concern for matching mouth movements,[37] *The Simpsons* has long been a massive international hit, airing in over two hundred countries (as of 2007),[38] including, just for a numbers perspective, the world's most populous countries, India and China. By my calculations, over 750 episodes and a smash movie with more jokes and more types of jokes reaching the most amount of people translates to the funniest piece of culture our society has produced.

I say that, but the thing is, bear with me, funny is funny. Despite years of rejecting the phrase, I came back to it during an interview with Brian Regan, a stand-up comedian who is as respected as anyone among other stand-ups for his understanding of the audience.[39] "Over my career, you always hear people say, 'This is funny,' 'This isn't funny,'" he told me, "and I've always been intrigued with who gets to decide. Is there a committee?" Since there isn't, instead "everybody has their own version." So, he deduced, "If I think something is funny and then there's one person in the Amazon rain forest who also thinks it's funny—we're the only two—well, it is funny. Eight billion people might disagree, but they're missing out, because two people think it's funny." This is not to say that if you're funny to me, you're funny to everyone. This is saying that if it's funny to *anyone*, it's funny. It doesn't mean comedy is beyond criticism or thoughtful consideration, obviously, but that you have to focus on how it tries to achieve its funny and what it is trying to communicate, instead of debating if something is funny at all. If you find something funny, there is fun and insight to be had in trying to explain why, but if someone else finds something funny that you don't, there is nothing you can say that can make the person revoke their laugh. Later, jokes might not be funny to someone anymore, but when it was funny, it was funny. It's really a matter of . . .

4

TIMING

In 2017, *I'm Dying Up Here* premiered on Showtime, telling a fictionalized version of the birth of the L.A. comedy club scene in the late 1970s. The show takes place at a club called Goldie's run by the titular Goldie, subbing in for the real-life Comedy Store and Mitzi Shore. The show wasn't great, but there is one scene from one episode that captures what this chapter is going to be about. For context, the comedian Judy Gold plays a legendary borscht belt comedian named Judy Elder, who uses her friendship with Goldie to get booked at Goldie's, in hopes of trying her hand at performing for a hipper crowd. But, after seeing her act, Goldie tells Judy she can no longer perform at her club, as her style is just too dated. At the same time, Cassie Feder (Ari Graynor) is a young comedian struggling to connect with the club's audience because of the darkness of her material and their expectations of female comics. Toward the end of the episode, Judy and Cassie find themselves together literally outside and metaphorically at a crossroads in time. Judy's time has passed; Cassie's is in the future. Cassie is too soon; Judy is too late. Still, having experienced the full arc of a comedian's career, Judy sees the situation clearly and tries to offer Cassie some perspective. "A hundred years from now, people are still gonna be listening to Beethoven and oohing over Michelangelo, reading Shakespeare. But us?" she asks. "Jokes and shoulders, that's what we are. Yeah. Jokes for people to laugh at and shoulders for comics down the road to stand on." Judy continues, "Trust me, I am not whining. We get something better. We get the moment. You know, we get the right fucking now." What this scene captures is the idea that while all art should respond to its given time, none are as tied to it as comedy is.

Chapter 3 noted how the fading funniness of classic comedies helped in their being taken seriously, and that is true in those cases; but, as a whole, it has hurt comedy's esteem as an art form. It's hard to understand the artistic merits of comedy when its fundamental appeal—that it's funny—is removed. This is more than just saying comedy is very context dependent, which it is and will be explored further in chapter 9, but that rather to appreciate comedy is to appreciate its timeliness.

And never is its timeliness more valuable, impressive, and special than in times of difficulty. Because in contrast to books, movies, and television shows that are worked on in private, and even, potentially, live entertainment like theater, dance, and music, which is performed in public but conceived over time in private, comedians are writing material onstage in response to a tragedy, in front of people, the day, week, month after it took place. Insomuch as we process our lives through art, comedy is doing this in the moment, with the audience. This is hard. Because unlike musicians or performance artists, comedians are expecting a specific response—laughter—that is especially difficult in periods of trauma. And yet sometimes they are able to create a space for comedy, at the least comedic of times.

In 2021, the professor Philip Scepanski released a thorough examination of how comedy has responded to national trauma in recent American history, offering insight into the particularities that make comedy valuable in tough times and the evolution of comedy's role in our culture.[1] In *Tragedy Plus Time: National Trauma and Television Comedy*, he argues there is a great power in the fact that "comic speech often takes the form of play, [as it then] stands outside the regular rules of discourse" that can be constraining in the moments following tragedy. The original *Tonight Show* host Steve Allen's formula of comedy being tragedy plus time is inexact, but it does capture that there is a relationship among all three elements. What the comedy is and when it is happening in relation to a tragedy impacts how it is perceived and received. Stemming from this relationship is the popular idea and visceral feeling of a joke being "too soon," as in it might be funny and useful in coming to terms with a traumatic event but the audience isn't ready for it. To understand this imperfect equation, we must consider comedy's relationship to tragedy and comedy's relationship to time, with the hope of better understanding how these elements intersect. While not all comedy is about trauma, how comedy is created out of tragedy illustrates comedians' most significant role in our culture—helping people process their lives.

On September 29, 2001, in New York City, of all places, Gilbert Gottfried was bombing. He was at the Friars Club, his home away from home, on one of the ugliest stages you could ever stand on. Gottfried fit right in by dressing terribly, swimming in a hopefully rented tinfoil-silver tuxedo. It was the roast of Hugh Hefner, and Gottfried looked like a baking potato. He was just taking old dick jokes and throwing the guest of honor's name in them. "Hugh Hefner's so old, his first condom was made out of bark." You get the idea. In between the titters where laughter usually was, you have to imagine the audience members started thinking, *Should we be doing this?* Or even, *Did we inhale ash from the Trade Center on the way in?* Things were going as planned for Gottfried.

If I tell you not to picture a pink elephant, you will. That's what it felt like to be Gilbert Gottfried when disaster strikes. "Maybe I'm self-destructive, maybe I'm just plain stupid," Gottfried told me about the evening years later.[2] "But if someone tells me don't do something, then I want to do it." Other comedians, usually unafraid to go *there*, were hesitant to take on 9/11. (Bob Saget explained to me, "There will never be anything funny about 9/11."[3] DeRay Davis admitted, "I couldn't find a joke in it because I imagined if I had a family member in it.") But Gottfried could not help himself, even if there was a hole in the ground four miles away that was still smoking. "I have to leave early tonight. I have to catch a flight to California. I can't get a direct flight," he told the room toward the end of his set. "They said they have to stop at the Empire State Building." According to Gottfried, he lost the audience more than anyone has ever lost an audience. "People were booing and hissing. One guy yelled out, 'Too soon.'" Gottfried was confused. "I thought it meant I didn't take a long enough pause between the setup and the punch line." Gottfried had never heard the expression "too soon" before, so, being in a room of comedians, he assumed it was a comment on his comedic timing, when it was really on his *comedy*'s timing.

Comedic timing you are probably familiar with—the pace and rhythm in which a comedian speaks—whereas comedy timing is about when the audience is ready to receive a joke. Gilbert Gottfried, that September night, was jeered like a heretic because *that* audience was not ready to receive *that* joke. The man in the crowd yelled, "Too soon," but what he meant was, "It is not the time we tacitly agreed for this joke we had not heard before to happen." The equation goes: Comedy is tragedy plus time. This just means time is a factor, not that the more time that passes, the better. That's because jokes can also be too late. In 2014, Peter McGraw, Lawrence E. Williams, and Caleb Warren published a study in which they measured how responses to three Hurricane Sandy jokes progressed from a day before the hurricane made landfall, in fall 2012, to ninety-nine days after.[4] The appeal of the three jokes they shared dipped for the first week, before slowly surging, reaching their peak about five weeks out, only for the perceived humor scores to start going down again, ending up with its lowest score at the end of the hundred days. Gottfried's joke told the exact same way a hundred days later might not have made sense at all, as it demanded people have September 11 on their minds. Gottfried should've been near McGraw and co.'s sweet spot, but 9/11 was different. Still, regardless of the reaction to this one joke, looking back, comedy thrived following 9/11, in a variety of ways that illustrate how comedy can be made out of tragedy.

"Too soon" does not mean too soon to tell a joke, but too soon to get the audience to be on board with it. Comedians know this, but will try anyway. As a result, after 9/11, comedians were figuring out what the audience needed, regardless of what the audience thought they wanted. This ethos is best captured by Marc Maron, who was onstage in New York City days after the attack and saw it as his mission to start the process of unpacking this shit. "I'm not frequently asked to lighten things up," he told me decades later.[5] This was especially the case after 9/11, as his upstairs neighbor had died in one of the towers. And there was a man downstairs who had signed up to work with the recovery effort downtown. Maron remembered, "He came back one day and this macho guy just broke down crying." It was at that moment Maron realized, "There was no 'too soon.' We were living in it." Scepanski writes, "Because national traumas are so important to America's politics and larger sense of identity, comedy's role as both an active agent of boundary-stretching and a passive test of changing discursive rules makes it a critical site in defining the way we speak of significant historical events."[6] For Maron the only way out was through, and that meant going past the fearful reverence of a nation in mourning.

It didn't always, or often, go well. One response to a joke has stuck with him ever since. Maron can't remember what joke it was for sure, but maybe it was the one the *Los Angeles Times* quoted him telling the weekend after the attack: "My manager called me yesterday to see if I was OK. He said, 'So, are you going to move to L.A. now?' And I said, 'Well, you know, you got earthquakes out there. Our city may be the target of terrorism, but yours is the target of God.'"[7] The routine continued—again, this is four or five days after September 11—by wondering if "God might be the greatest terrorist of all time." One night, this joke or a joke like it caused a marine to stand up and tell Maron to stop. He did not, replying, "Look, I appreciate you defending my right to say these things." Decades later, he would reflect upon the confrontation to me, saying, "For me, comedy was a way of processing whatever my sense of truth was and my sense of righteous indignation. I saw comedy as a platform that you worked through things on. For me, the challenge was: *How do we make this funny? How do we make this relevant through comedy?* It's sort of our duty to try to disarm this a bit and process it so people can move through their fear and anger to a degree. I didn't feel like I was entertaining the troops; I felt like, *We've got to process this collectively and it's going to go through me, the way I do it.*"

Comedy can play with hard feelings and complex situations, but for it to feel like comedy, it demands that an audience be in a playful state. Which demands that they feel safe and that they can trust the comedian and the people around them. It's easy to imagine why this might've been difficult that evening. But even if it didn't succeed in generating laughs, Maron and the marine were still working through things. If loving is suffering, and surviving is finding some meaning in the suffering, to paraphrase Nietzsche, it's not hard to see where comedy fits in. As McGraw, Williams, and Warren wrote in their original paper: "The human capacity for taking a source of pain and transforming it into a source of pleasure is a critical feature of the psychological immune system."[8] In Maron's telling, trauma is a toxin that comedy, as society's liver, is helping to process.

What is notable about the Maron story is that the marine was even there at all. What was he looking for that night? Based on some of the comedy that was getting made around Maron at the time, my guess is something closer to how *South Park* handled 9/11, something closer to jingoism.

No matter how antiestablishment comedy is thought to be right now, there is a history of comedy made to support the American war machine. During World War II, Disney won an Oscar for *Der Fuehrer's Face*, a satirical short in which Donald Duck is a bad and overworked Nazi, saluting every single image of Hitler he sees and poorly screwing in artillery shells, scored by a Bavarian "oompah" track. After 9/11, *South Park* offered their version of this with "Osama bin Laden Has Farty Pants." The *South Park* creators, Matt Stone and Trey Parker, are not stand-ups, but, in contrast to animation's usual time-consuming process, each episode of the show is produced in just six days so it can best respond to the moment. "Farty Pants" aired in November 2001. In it, the boys fly to Afghanistan to meet their Afghani counterparts. The irreverence jumps out compared to a lot of comedy made that year. The episode makes fun of Stan's mom, who is traumatized by the news; the uselessness of celebrity attempts at being helpful; the American military's senseless bombing of civilian areas; and the naivete of American patriotism, blind to why the world might hate us. And while the episode is sympathetic to Afghani people, it is shocking how it treats bin Laden (well, it would be if it weren't *South Park*). An homage to those World War II–era *Looney Tunes* propaganda cartoons, this episode casts Eric Cartman essentially as Bugs Bunny to bin Laden's Elmer Fudd, viciously putting the terrorist leader in cartoonishly insulting scenarios. At one point, bin Laden puts a gun in Cartman's face. Cartman says, "Hey, look, an infidel." When bin Laden turns, Cartman pulls down bin Laden's pants to reveal nothing between his legs. Then, as if coming up from behind the camera, a magnifying glass is revealed—nothing—then another—nothing—then a whole bunch of magnifying glasses, finally revealing a very small penis. Then, again coming from off-screen, as if held up by the creators, a sign is revealed that reads TINY AIN'T IT!?

Putting aside who the target is for one sentence, it is just so grotesquely, arrestingly dehumanizing. It feels a bit Abu Ghraib-y. This is not to accuse *South Park* of anything, necessarily, or to defend the honor of Osama bin Laden, but to reckon with the text of the joke. This was an attempt to speak truth to power and the truth was "We really hate you." People were angry, and it was cathartic to see our enemy treated brutally. And *South Park* did, as *South Park* does, try to get its audience to take things less seriously. It is degrading, literally. And it speaks to the potential of animation to push the boundaries the furthest, because it feels less real and mature. To paraphrase Mr. Rogers, another child entertainer, if it's mentionable, it's manageable. Well, if it's mockable, it's manageable.

What is clear from this *South Park* episode and much of the comedy from that time is the fear. Fear that leads to anger. Anger leads to hate. Hate leads to—wait, I'm quoting Yoda. Truthfully, jingoism gave way to bigotry. A good example: The ventriloquist megastar Jeff Dunham's idea of addressing the attack was to make a Dead Osama bin Laden puppet for him and his audience to get their anger out on. After some time, he switched it to the more general Achmed the Dead Terrorist, who he strongly insists is not Muslim, though I'm not sure I or his audience believes him.

Still, Dunham was not the worst of it in those early days after 9/11. Maron told me there was a point, sitting with the other comics he thought he knew at the Comedy Cellar, when he thought, *Wow, you're a lot more conservative than I am* and *Wow, you might be a little bit racist*. One comedian who was performing there at the time was Nick Di Paolo. I want to mention his 2002 *Comedy Central Presents* half-hour special to give you a sense of what things were being not just said but televised. Complaining about the new airline safety precautions, he tells a joke about seeing a TSA agent hassling an elderly woman, and saying to the guy next to him, "She's got the diaper around her ass, not her head." Or there's this joke: "The FBI is having trouble penetrating this terrorist cell. Bullshit! Move to my neighborhood. I've been buying fruit from the Taliban for four years." You don't need me to tell you that people were bigots after 9/11, but it's still striking that this passed for comedy.

While many, if not most, comedians would identify as progressive, in practice stand-up comedy is reactionary. Many stand-ups prowl the stage, guarded, in an attack position. Try to say something, and the comedian will strike down upon thee with great vengeance and furious anger. The viral video titles are in the vein of "Comedian Destroys Heckler," not "Comedian Takes a Moment to Understand Where a Chatty Audience Member Is Coming From." And they must be fast. Often when a comedian has good comedic timing, it means they are quick-witted. I've seen enough crowd work* to know that the audience is often more amazed with how quickly the comic responds than with the content of their reply. This results in interactions like:

> "What do you do for a living?"
>
> "I am a phys—"
>
> "That's dumb!"

* Crowd work is when a stand-up interacts directly with a member or members of the audience.

Are they a physician, physical therapist, phys ed teacher, fizzy-drink manufacturer? No time to find out! After 9/11, the lack of consideration given to the member of this hypothetical crowd-worked audience member was being applied to millions of Americans. When you extend this lack of processing time to sensitive issues, like national tragedies, the resulting comedy is id-driven and regressive. It is here where the superiority theory of comedy applies, as it speaks to, as Scepanski writes, referencing Sigmund Freud and Henri Bergson, "the tendency of jokes to be at the expense of some, separating humor's targets from the more unified community."[9] He continues, "Separating out some people forms a social bond among those laughing at them." Talking to Maron, he believes a seed was planted among certain comedians and a certain sort of comedy fan that would mature into the transgressive comedy discussed in chapters 8 and 10.

This climate is what made it especially difficult for Middle Eastern comedians at the time. One comedian, Dean Obeidallah, who is half Palestinian, confronted a comedian who told a joke with the "punch line" of "punch your cab driver in the back of the head and feel more American." The Palestinian American comedian Aron Kader told me about confronting Carlos Mencia for something similar. But more than pushing back against what they saw, the Middle Eastern comedians wanted to offer something in its place. At a time when media was trying to villainize them, these comedians wanted to make it clear that Middle Eastern Americans are Americans, and they are funny.

"On September 10, I went to sleep a white guy," Dean Obeidallah told me. "On September 11, I woke up an Arab." Following a recommendation from a club manager, Obeidallah went by "Dean Joseph" for a week after the attack before changing back. Aron Kader was told to pretend to be Italian. But both realized there was a newfound curiosity about their perspectives, both for good and bad. There was a sort of "fascination, almost," Kader would say.[10] "People need this," he was told by audience members. "People need to put a face or a voice to the enemy, for a lack of a better word."

Mitzi Shore made the Egyptian American comedian Ahmed Ahmed a regular at the club a year before the attack. "There's going to be a war between America and the Middle East, so get ready," she told him. When Ahmed called Shore on 9/11, she replied, "I told you so." The club reopened the Friday after the attack and Shore had Ahmed open the first show back. "Hi everyone. My name's Ahmed Ahmed . . . and I had nothing to do with it. Please don't follow me out to my car after the show." The audience laughed.

This is not to say it was all happy memories. Ahmed and Maz Jobrani, an Iranian American, told me a story about receiving death threats at a show they did in San Diego a month afterward.[11] "Well, if we're gonna die, might as well die laughing," they said. There was not a bomb, thankfully, and afterward, white couples approached the all-Middle-Eastern-American lineup, saying things like "Thank you for making us laugh" and "We had no idea your people had a sense of humor." It's gross to read that response now, more than twenty years later, but Ahmed and Jobrani saw an opportunity, if not a call to action. In the years that followed, along with Obeidallah and Kader, they traveled the world as the Axis of Evil Comedy Tour, confronting negative feelings as well as offering some relief to their fellow Middle Eastern Americans and Middle Easterners not in America, eventually resulting in the first stand-up special featuring Middle Eastern American comedians. The goal was to loosen people up, as comedy does, in terms of both that night and people's understanding of society. Jobrani, for example, has a joke about talking to his friends who assume he's Arab: "We're similar. We're all getting shot at, you know. That's one thing." It continues, "But Iranians are actually ethnically . . . Aryan. We're white. We're white, so, stop shooting." Jobrani and the entire Axis of Evil tour were able to expand the idea of who an American is, while certain forces were trying constrict the definition.

But mostly comedians just made people laugh. Of the dozens of comedians I spoke to about comedy in those first few weeks, almost all remarked on how weird the laughter was. It was loud. Inappropriately loud. Jokes that used to get a 5 were getting a 10. Though relief theory still fails as conceived, it is undeniable that comedy can relieve and release tension. The tremendous release of comedic energy is why Gilbert Gottfried's 9/11 joke wasn't lost to time, despite it being cut from the eventual broadcast. It didn't explode into the ether like most bombed jokes do because of what happened after the joke took the air out of the room, as the legend goes (legend count #3). "Up there [after the Empire State Building joke], it was like, *Well, I'm at the bottom level of hell and this show seems pretty much over*," he told me. "I figured, *Why not go to an even lower level of hell?*"[12] That lower level of hell housed a talent agent's office. Gottfried told a joke known as "The Aristocrats," which up until that point was told only among comedians. The joke starts with a family—that night, it was a father, mother, son, daughter, and little dog—entering the agent's office in hopes of getting representation. The agent asks them to perform their act. Gottfried then describes a variety of combinations of everyone having sex with one another. It all builds to a disgusting crescendo:

> The daughter starts licking out the father's asshole. Then the father shits on the floor. The mother shits on the floor. The dog pisses and shits on the floor. They all jump down into the shit and piss and come and they start fucking and sucking each other. And then they take a bow.

Frank DiGiacomo, there for the *New York Observer*, would write, "Tears ran throughout the Hilton ballroom, as if Mr. Gottfried had performed a collective tracheotomy on the audience, delivering oxygen and laughter past the grief and ash that had blocked their passageways."[13] When the family is done shitting come or what have you, the agent asks, "So, what do you call yourselves?" Gottfried milks this even longer, asking if he should start over. Finally, with the room out of breath with laughter, he says, "The Aristocrats." Writing about it later, Frank Rich described the aftermath for *The New York Times*: "As the mass exodus began, some people were laughing, others were appalled and perhaps a majority of us were in the middle. We knew we had seen something remarkable, not because the joke was so funny but because it had served as shock therapy, harmless shock therapy for an adult audience, that at least temporarily relieved us of our burdens and jolted us back into the land of the living again . . . At a terrible time, it was an incongruous but welcome gift. He was inviting us to once again let loose."[14] "Tragedy and comedy are roommates," Gottfried would tell me. "Wherever tragedy's around, comedy's a few feet behind them sticking his tongue out and making obscene gestures."[15]

A number of studies have tried to prove whether laughter is actually the best medicine, and always the answer seems to be that it's not. But it depends on what ails you. If you have hay fever, medicine is the best medicine; if you haven't laughed in weeks and are afraid you'll never laugh again, seeing a funny comedian will do the trick. It's in situations like this that comedians prove their value. People weren't able to find comedy in their everyday life, with their family and friends similarly frozen in a state of numbed shock. They needed to go to the professionals. "Humor, more than anything else in the human make-up, can afford an aloofness and an ability to rise above any situation," wrote Viktor Frankl in *Man's Search for Meaning*, "even if only for a few seconds."[16] Comedians specialize in that aloofness, allowing them to be ready to process the moment right when it happens. It's why in those first few weeks, when journalists were questioning if we'd ever laugh again and if irony was dead, comedians were already back at work proving them wrong. Because that's the other thing about livers: Beyond being able to process toxins, they have a unique ability to regenerate after being damaged. Give tragedy enough time and you'll get comedy.

Nothing captures comedy's relationship to time like *Saturday Night Live*. Each word in *Saturday Night Live* communicates something about time: "Saturday" is a day of the week; "night" is a time of day; "live" says when it is being filmed and watched. It's like when actors say in press junkets,

"New York is a character in the movie." Time is a cast member on *SNL*. Maybe it's the most important one. It's why the show exists and happens on Saturday nights. Before *SNL* premiered, NBC used to air reruns of Johnny Carson's *Tonight Show* in that time slot. In the mid-seventies, Carson asked the network to stop. He wanted to save the reruns for during the week, so he wouldn't have to tape as many shows. Carson had so much cachet at that point that the network would create the most significant comedy institution in the history of the world to honor his free time.

Live, however, was the real difference maker. Doing a live show every week, such that every sketch must be written, every set and costume designed, and the whole thing produced in five days, is comically challenging. It makes watching *SNL* a mix of a local theater just "putting on a show" and some sort of social experiment reality competition. Why did they decide to do it this way? Besides cocaine, you mean? When Lorne Michaels pitched the original cast members on the show, he said it was going to be like "a cross between Monty Python and *60 Minutes*."[17] It is notable that Michaels didn't say the nightly news, but *60 Minutes*, a *magazine* show. It reflects that Michaels wasn't just thinking of a variety of styles and entertainment—as variety shows of the past might've been conceived—but a variety of subjects that covered all of contemporary life, at any point in time.

SNL's timeliness also largely benefits from the fact that the whole show, not just the newsy bits, is written the week of, so when things really, really work, it feels like it is tapping into the zeitgeist. I am prone to a more spiritual way of looking at it, but even the more rational take—*SNL* is a popular show that airs so many episodes, with so many different sketches, that things are bound to pop periodically—still affirms that *SNL* reflects the tastes of the public at a given time, as the public is deciding what breaks through. The show's ability to mirror the public is why *SNL* is most itself when responding to a moment of national reckoning. Take the show's definitive moment:

At 11:30 p.m. EST on September 29, an hour after Gilbert Gottfried's bomb and only a few blocks away at 30 Rockefeller Plaza, *Saturday Night Live* opened with the announcer Don Pardo introducing the mayor of New York City, Rudolph Giuliani. There Giuliani, flanked by the city's police and fire commissioner, stood in front of four rows of police and firemen, not so fresh off twenty-hour shifts at Ground Zero. "I can remember patting a fireman on the back," Tracy Morgan would later recall, in a 2021 *Rolling Stone* oral history about the first episode back.[18] "I saw this smoke, this dust, come off his jacket from 9/11 and I broke down crying, right on stage, man." After a few words about heroism and not living in fear, the camera panned to Paul Simon playing "The Boxer," at the behest of the show's creator and longtime boss, Lorne Michaels. The song choice was much debated. *You can't do entertainment*, he remembered thinking at the time. *We can't open upbeat. But we also can't do a dirge.*[19] "The Boxer," he eventually decided, summed up New York, as the song's titular boxer doesn't quit. Throughout the song, the camera kept panning over the faces of the essential workers. When it finished, Michaels joined Giuliani to thank him and the other men onstage. "Having our city's institutions up and running sends a message that New York City is open for business," Giuliani responded, clearly reading a cue card. "*Saturday Night Live* is one of our great New York City institutions, and that's why it's important for you to do your show tonight." "Can we be funny?" Michaels, a trained straight man, asked Giuliani earnestly, getting a few snickers from the audience. Giuliani paused a bit too long and then responded, "Why start now?" Michaels gave a "why, I oughta" smirk and looked away. They smiled and embraced and the audience cheered.

Years later, Mike Schur, who was a writer on *SNL* before going on to write for *The Office* and create *Parks and Recreation* and *The Good Place*, called it "the best moment in the history of the show" and "Lorne's greatest triumph."[20] Again, same night as the Gottfried joke. Same subject. But the audiences couldn't have reacted more differently, and that's because while Gottfried was always trying to be ahead of where people are at, *SNL* has built a reputation of being, for better and for worse, on time. It is our culture's great reflector.

Being live on Saturday night, at the end of the week, means the show can both be current and summarize the overall state of the culture. After 9/11, they waited over three weeks, deciding not to come back when the country was still in the disorienting fog. The show couldn't go on if the only other thing on TV was loops of planes crashing and buildings falling. *SNL* needs the nightly news and morning shows and personal interest stories and popular culture. It needs a culture to curate and reflect, tea leaves to read and brew. Will Ferrell appeared on *Fresh Air* days after the "Why start now?" premiere and was asked if he intended to continue playing Bush as a sort of frat boy doofus. He said he wouldn't, as that wasn't how people perceived the president in that moment. Instead, they were opting for a "take-charge Bush." "So much of our approach," Ferrell explained to Terry Gross, "is taking what the perception is and turning it back around, regurgitating to the audience."[21]

And it's true, if you watch that season back, it reflects how attitudes within the country were shifting. From the somber "We're all in it together" cold open in the first episode to the second episode, where Ferrell plays a character so overwhelmed by his need to display his patriotism that he wears a USA crop top and a very small American flag thong to work. It captures the show's tendency, especially then, to make a statement about politics but not a political statement.

Though *SNL* continued doing political cold opens throughout the season, as is standard, none of it was pointed. There was no mention of the Patriot Act that passed that October, for example, or the Guantánamo Bay detention camp that opened in January 2002. The focus was largely on the Bush administration's folksy demeanor. One sketch that jumps out came from the December 1, 2001, episode. In it, Darrell Hammond plays Attorney General John Ashcroft explaining the administration's stance on terrorism and how they determine who is a terrorist. "If you traffic in weapons of mass destruction, you are a terrorist." "If the return address on your mail reads 'A Cave,' you just might be a terrorist." "If you have just renewed your subscription to a magazine called 'Nerve Gas Weekly,' you just might be a terrorist." Then Ferrell joins as President Bush, noting that Ashcroft is starting to sound a lot like Jeff Foxworthy. When Ashcroft apologizes, Bush responds, "Sorry nothing! That's a good thing!" and joins in, "Hello, America. These are trying times. But defeat is not an option. Make no mistake—we will prevail. And let this be a warning—if you have a really long beard and hang out in the desert and are not ZZ Top, you just might be a terrorist." Somewhere in there is a criticism of the Bush administration's fearmongering, and the racist imprecision about potential terrorists. But the joke, even when it is on them, doesn't seem to be targeting their policies as much as their personalities.

And maybe all of this is bad. People thought so at the time. Speaking in 2021, Hugh Fink, a writer for the show that season, discussed what he felt watching the Giuliani cold open. "Wow, this is not the message I was expecting *Saturday Night Live* to be sending. This is flag-waving. This is very patriotic. But there's absolutely no edge and it's not funny. It's just dead serious."[22] Harper Steele, another staff writer, responded to this line of criticism by saying, "This is where people look back in time and think there's something maybe mawkish or uncritical or not very ballsy about that opening. And so my response to that would be, there's just no way to go back in time and give people a feeling of what the world was like at that moment. It's almost indefensible at this point, but I defend it by saying that it was a different world."[23] This is the *SNL* defense—it is not the show's fault; it's the culture at the time.

When the culture sucks, *SNL* will suck. And wouldn't ya know, the culture has always sucked, if only just a little bit. *Key & Peele* never would've had Elon Musk on, like *SNL* did in 2021. Part of this would be for ethical reasons, but part of it is because that's not their show. *Key & Peele* was about marrying impeccable sketch-writing technique, with generational sketch-performing talent, with a clear-eyed perspective on the supposed postracial America. *Key & Peele* aspired to be a great sketch show in a way *SNL* doesn't. There are great sketches on *SNL*, but it is at its core a variety show. Both in terms of mixing monologue, sketch, and music, but also in how it deliberately casts the performers, hires writers, and builds episodes around the idea that no one should like an entire show. Some cast members and writers relish trying to appeal to the largest group of people possible; others relish showcasing the nichest possible material on such a big show. It's not completely artless. They are sometimes trying to paint a picture of how they see the world; it's just that more often, they are trying to offer a series of snapshots of how thc world just is.

It's why you'll most often see people express excitement for an upcoming *SNL*, if the host feels particularly timely or something ridiculous is happening in the news, and not because they have a general excitement for live sketch comedy. I'm not trying to make an excuse for Musk hosting, or Donald Trump, for that matter. Did having Trump host normalize him or was the show just reflecting the fact that the culture already had? I don't know. What I'm saying is that having Musk and Trump host was not out of the norm for the show. That's *SNL*. They were maybe cynical attempts at relevancy, but that's also the whole *60 Minutes* thing. It is seeing yourself as a capturer of culture, not the maker.

What I'll never say, however, is some version of *SNL* hasn't been good since [*insert the year you graduated high school*] or [*insert the most popular cast member when you were a teen*] left. I don't think you watch *SNL* because it's good; you watch it because it's eleven-thirty and it's a nice coincidence when there are some sketches you think are good.

The one time I interviewed him, Lorne Michaels pushed back on the idea of *SNL* being part of the establishment, but just as Giuliani became America's Mayor in the aftermath of 9/11, *SNL* became America's variety show. Giuliani slowly drowned his goodwill in a puddle of farts and forehead bile, but, as the monoculture crumbles, *SNL* has doubled down on its purpose. It is *the* mainstream comedy institution. To be so demands compromise and the smoothing of edges. It can't lose the audience like Gottfried.

In maybe the most definitive segment of the show since "Why start now?" you can see how *SNL* taps into the median potential viewer when faced with a pivotal moment in time. It was November 12, 2016, the first episode after Donald Trump was elected president, when the show opened with Kate McKinnon, as Hillary Clinton, wearing an all-white pantsuit and sitting at a piano. Once again, the show's producer felt it was best to start with a song, and because Leonard Cohen had died that week, McKinnon as Clinton sang his "Hallelujah." Later, *GQ* would report that the show originally was going to open with all the female cast members sharing how they were feeling in that moment and end with McKinnon singing John Lennon's "Imagine," but Michaels thought that would be too partisan. "In the end, we're a comedy show," he said. "You can't forget that."[24] In the days, weeks, years that followed, the cynically minded would refer to this moment as "a bunch of B.S."[25] and the show's "worst idea,"[26] but McKinnon would later tell me it was one of the two moments she felt closest to the viewers in her entire eleven-season run. "For the people for whom that was a tragic event, I felt very connected and in a very real way," she said.[27] Both responses can be correct. That's *SNL* for ya: neither too soon nor too late, but the line that separates the two.

On June 24, 2022, the Supreme Court published its opinion in the case of *Dobbs v. Jackson Women's Health Organiza-*

tion, in which it decided to overturn *Roe v. Wade*, reversing nearly fifty years of precedent. The news wasn't surprising, as the decision had leaked seven weeks earlier, but for many that didn't make it any less tragic.

That night I had tickets to a comedy show. My partner wasn't sure she had the appetite for comedy if they weren't going to talk about it. I assured her that, though I wasn't positive the comedians would really get into it, I couldn't imagine they wouldn't say *something.* We thought maybe it would be a pleasant enough respite after going to protests. Address it and move on, that's it, like a comedian would if there was anything fraught in the air. A simple act to communicate self-awareness, so the audience doesn't feel like they're the only ones thinking what they're thinking. What was necessary was a more sophisticated version of how baby stand-ups will open their sets by acknowledging their own appearance (for example: a young Nick Kroll used to say, "I know what you're thinking—I look like the love child of Harry Potter and Jeff Goldblum"). There is a legend (legend count #4) of the first Lenny Bruce show after the Kennedy assassination. The audience was in a tense tizzy, not knowing what Bruce might say and how they might react. Bruce came out and, referencing the extremely-famous-at-the-time JFK impersonator, said, "The only thing I'm gonna say is Vaughn Meader is screwed."[28] There was a huge laugh of relief from the audience, because of both the fact that Bruce didn't go too far and the mental weight of the president's death.

But, that night in 2022, three (male) comedians went up and three (male) comedians said nothing whatsoever. It was like trying to look at a painting with a giant hole cut in the center: You were staring at the thing you came to see, but it was hollow. "It's malpractice," my stand-up comedian friend

J. F. Harris responded, when I told him about the show a week later. It was not what I have grown to expect more than twenty years after comedians had proved adept at acknowledging what was hard to acknowledge. The show not only didn't offer relief but also amplified our bad feelings, because it felt like no one cared. Say what you will about Gottfried's and Maron's 9/11 jokes, but they were their way of acknowledging what happened and pushing back against the instinct that led those three men to ignore what happened. Too soon is still better than not at all. They turned their back on the timeliness that makes stand-up so special.

We went to the wrong show. The same night, somewhere else in the city, Alison Leiby was in the middle of her run performing her one-person show, *Oh God, A Show About Abortion*. In contrast to how fraught the topic had become over the three years since she had an abortion, and extremely heightened by the recent news, Leiby treated abortion with a plainspoken mundanity. She just as easily could've done a show about her root canals, as she'd later say, as "those were much more devastating than my abortion."[29] Once again I'm reminded of Frankl's quote: "Humor, more than anything else in the human make-up, can afford an aloofness and an ability to rise above any situation." For example, she got a big laugh with a joke in the middle of the show, in which she describes what it's like to find out you're pregnant when you don't want to be pregnant: "[It] feels a lot like . . . You know when you trap a cockroach under a Tupperware in your apartment? And you're like [*screams*] AAHHHHHH! I know it's there and I have to kill it but I need a MINUTE to deal with this?"

Though the main text of the show stayed the same, the night of the *Dobbs* decision, Leiby started with an unscripted address to the audience. She thanked those who came and discussed the privilege she felt being able to talk about her abortion onstage. It was still going to be a comedy show, she explained, so people should laugh, but she also told the audience to feel free to feel whatever they were feeling. And she started crying. "That was a moment where it felt like I wasn't a performer with an audience, but that we were all in a room together, feeling what we needed to feel, and providing community in a world where there really often isn't any," she'd later tell me, sounding a lot like McKinnon talking about the first show after the 2016 election.[30] That night, Leiby took a breath, regrouped, and put on a comedy show.

Not unlike the comedians I spoke to about the weeks after 9/11, Leiby remembers the shows that weekend as a "deeply emotional blur of lots of laughs." She told me, "Some jokes were really hitting hard with the rolling laughs and applause breaks you only dream of most nights in comedy." It might sound surprising, but to Leiby, "it is human nature to stand in the face of something horrific and find a way to laugh." What she did that evening was, as the hack description of comedians goes, say what people were thinking. Often that saying is used to suggest comedians can reveal some dark hidden truth, but what Leiby did that night, and what the comedians I saw didn't do, was make the audience feel less alone. And Leiby herself felt less alone by doing it, as she'd get messages after the shows from people who had similar experiences.

Before *Dobbs*, Leiby was trying to get people to care about abortion as a conversation topic. This wasn't a problem afterward. Instead she focused on being open and allowing people to "use the show to inform or process their own experiences and feelings." "In the wake of the decision a lot of people were looking for a place to put all of their anger and sadness," she told me. "It's not like there were rallies and marches every day to attend. The show became a place for people to come and engage with their own feelings about the loss of *Roe* while also not being too bogged down in legislative next moves or defeatist lamenting."

Scepanski writes, "For viewers attuned to jokes that comfort, deflate the senses of fear and mourning, or otherwise respond to the emotions surrounding national trauma, comedy acts as a significant method through which we feel our way through history."[31] Comedians' ability to detach, to observe, to rise above any situation, puts them in a unique position to process the world and, because of the nature of the gig, if they allow themselves to be present, do it in real time. There will be art made, books written, movies filmed about abortion in this time in history that will be watched and written about decades from now. But they will never have what Leiby and her audience—or any comedian who talked about it and their audience—had that weekend. They were in the exact same place at the exact same time, processing what happened together. They got the moment. They got the right fucking now. They got something better.

5

POLITICS

Jon Stewart is the entry point for the mainstream media to take comedy seriously, because of his actual influence and because his influence was related to something they themselves took seriously—politics. It is why, as soon as he left *The Daily Show* in 2015, journalists wanted to know who the Jon Stewart of today was. After Trump got elected, the question grew more urgent. It's funny, since Stewart was still alive. But no one wanted to know what the actual Stewart was up to in those years off the air (doing advocacy work and making *Irresistible*, a movie that many did, in fact, resist); they were talking about the idea of Jon Stewart.

To talk about the idea of Jon Stewart is to talk about not just the concept of political comedy, but also the question of what comedy does. And it was being frequently asked because under the Donald Trump administration—though there seemed to be more comedy being made about him than about any one person in history, someone who seemed more sensitive to jokes about him than any president we've had—it felt like comedy wasn't *doing* anything.

My answer, then, is that there are thousands of Jon

Stewarts now and there are also none. By examining who these people are and who Jon Stewart the actual person was when he became Jon Stewart the idea, a picture emerges of how comedy does and does not foster political progress.

I first heard the term "fake news" in the nineties, when Norm Macdonald, as "Weekend Update" anchor, would start his segment by saying, "And now for the fake news." A decade later, Jon Stewart became the "Most Trusted Name in Fake News." During the 2016 election, it was a phrase that was out there because of *The Daily Show* and because of the rise in intentionally faked news stories that dominated Facebook. Then Donald Trump did what the modern Republican Party has shown a real knack for, which is redefining a term to mean nothing in particular but still convey an abstract sense that people are out to get them and their way of life. This shift was further made possible by the fact that satirical late-night shows didn't feel *fake* anymore, especially compared to what was being passed off as real news on other channels. *How did we get here, where comedy is being treated at times more seriously than the news the comedians are satirizing?* was a question I asked myself a lot over the four years of the Trump administration. Looking back, so much of it was the result of what Jon Stewart created and needed to create with his *Daily Show*. Specifically, how he became a person people could trust, by providing his audience both the news and the perspective on how to process it.

This shift, of course, didn't just happen. And it wasn't just the influence of a singular visionary. The ascension of political satire is as much, if not more, about the audience's desire and, arguably, need. In *Irony and Outrage: The Polarized Landscape of Rage, Fear, and Laughter in the United States*, the communication and political science professor Dannagal Goldthwaite Young tells the story of the twin rises of political satire on the left and outrage programming on the right. According to Young, *The Daily Show* and Fox News premiering within three months of each other in 1996 was not a coincidence. "Both [*The Daily Show* and *The O'Reilly Factor*] are logical outgrowths of simultaneous changes in the economic and regulatory underpinnings of the media industry and the development of new cable and digital technologies," she writes.[1]

The story, according to Young, starts in the 1980s, with Ronald Reagan and his desire to deregulate anything that was regulated.[2] In 1987, his FCC repealed the Fairness Doctrine, which had required broadcasters to devote airtime to issues of public interest and provide equal time to opposing views. The Reagan administration also cleared the path for the formation of large media conglomerates driven by a clearer profit motive. As Young argues, the business interests of these media giants overtook their public service goals and, in a tale as old as America, over time the business interests won out. The result was an increase in every bad thing you ever thought about the news—overdramatization, a focus on personal interest stories, celebrity obsessions, horse race politics—and a decrease in original, albeit expensive reporting and boring facts.[3] This was then magnified by the era of media fragmentation that started with the explosion of cable channels (more Reagan deregulation) and eventually the internet. As a consequence of all of this, Young writes, "Profit-orientated changes in the newsroom of the 1980s and 1990s degraded the practice of journalism." In 1976, Gallup reported that 72 percent of the American public had a "great deal" or "fair amount of trust" in news organizations. By 2016, that number was 32 percent.[4]

This is bad. Faith in journalism is essential to a healthy democracy. And yet it is undeniable that Americans were breaking off from news organizations through the first fifteen years of the new millennium in search of someone to trust. For many on the left, including your author, this person became Jon Stewart or any number of his successors.

The reason I knew who Walter Cronkite was as a teen was because Jon Stewart was compared to him. Cronkite retired five years before I was born, which was well before I ever watched television news. That absence reflects how millennials and younger generations have never lived in a time of trusted TV news, or trusted established news, period. I read *The New York Times* a little bit when I got to high school, but by the time I graduated, partly because of Stewart, I associated it with the spread of misinformation in the lead-up to the war in Iraq. But the massive cultural shift to empower political comedians was not just the right place, right time; it was the right person, right show, right art form.

The reason I watched *The Daily Show with Jon Stewart* was because I watched *The Daily Show with Craig Kilborn*, and it was habit-forming enough that a new host didn't stop me from watching. *SportsCenter* was my previous main late-night destination, and I thought its former anchor Kilborn was [*sigh*] very cool and funny. If I could avoid bringing up this fact about me, I would, but it's important, because imagine Kilborn hosting that first *Daily Show* after 9/11. Just footage of planes hitting buildings, with Craig quipping, "Oooh, that's gonna leave a mark." A good indication that Kilborn was not meant for that moment is the fact that he was hosting a late-night show then, returning to air before Stewart did, and yet it was quickly lost to time. The nation was looking to turn to someone, and Stewart, with fifteen years of comedy behind him, had an innate sense of what the audience needed. Or, at least, what his audience needed. At minimum, what I needed. Maybe because it's maudlin, people don't talk much about the aesthetics of heartfelt addresses after tragedy. But Stewart's response was lightly funny (starting by acknowledging the show was late to discuss the tragedy: "I'm sure we're getting in right under the wire before the cast of *Survivor* offers their insight into what to do in these situations"), free of cheap platitudes (focusing on the privilege of being in "a country that allows for open satire," as opposed to rah-rah jingoism), and emotionally honest (the way he felt almost embarrassed by tearing up, saying, "We're going to take a break and I'm going to stop slobbering on myself and on the desk," felt genuine, where him just crying might've come off as a performance). Going through traumatic experiences together bonds people; being there in times of need creates loyalty.

Trust is not only necessary to facilitate play, it is essential to joke writing structurally. To show why, I am going to share two perfect Mitch Hedberg jokes:

(1)
I don't have a girlfriend.
I just know a girl who would get really mad if she heard me say that.

(2)
I used to do drugs.
I still do, but I used to, too.

For these jokes to work, to even register as jokes, the audience needs to trust that the first sentences are true, regardless of the fact that they are ostensibly not. As one-liner jokes these are very distilled examples, but a lot of comedy has a "Trust me . . . you shouldn't have trusted me" structure. Comedy often demands you believe and invest in the world the comedian creates before something funny happens, so when the funny thing happens, you notice. Like you need to understand you are watching a businessman walking normally to work, so when he slips on a banana peel, it reads as unusual, unexpected, and funny. Studies show a significant correlation between humor and trust. Specifically, the more trustworthy people find individuals to be, the funnier they find them.[5] And this all goes back to play, right? To enjoy comedy, you need to enter into a playful state, a nonthreatening environment, as Young puts it.[6] This demands trust, trust nurtured by consistency. After 9/11, every night I trusted Stewart to make light of a complicated situation.

Comedians had talked about current events before. Great stand-up comedians have served as social satirists for decades. Mort Sahl read from a dang newspaper onstage. There were decades of late-night monologues. "Weekend Update." What made *The Daily Show* different is that it did something Stewart would often say it didn't do—provided people the news. People like your friend, me! This is in contrast to the traditional late-night talk-show monologue, which was designed to play after the local news. Or take *The Wilton North Report*, the infamous late-eighties news-satire flop. Ironically, the original intention was for it to open with the actual news of the day with the hosts adding commentary to real footage, but that plan was nixed out of fear of turning off viewers. And maybe it would have in the eighties, at a time when TV news was still trusted. But by the early 2000s, pulling from real news heightened the comedy and proved to be increasingly necessary.

"Without credibility the jokes mean nothing," Adam Chodikoff, *The Daily Show*'s head researcher, explained in Chris Smith's *The Daily Show (The Book): An Oral History*.[7] *The Daily Show* didn't have better joke writers than other late-night shows of the past (*The Wilton North Report* possessed what was once called "the greatest writers room you've never heard of,"[8] including Greg Daniels, the cocreator of *King of the Hill* and the American version of *The Office*; Nell Scovell, the creator of *Sabrina the Teenage Witch*; and, oh, Conan O'Brien); the difference was the credibility.

There were a lot of funny things in a given *Daily Show* episode (including correspondents like Steve Carell, Stephen Colbert, Samantha Bee, Kristen Schaal, John Hodgman, Ed Helms, Jessica Williams, John Oliver, Wyatt Cenac, and Hasan Minhaj, who were often free to do fully silly bits), but the show's major innovations were in how it collected, processed, and conveyed information. "Jon was really adamant about keeping up with the pace of the media that we were making fun of," the *Daily Show* writer Jason Ross explained.[9] "So instead of being satisfied by sticking with some *Not Necessarily the News*–type format," he continued, alluding to the jokier 1980s satirical sketch show, "he wanted to make sure that our graphics were just as good as Fox's graphics." Even more significant was the show's use of footage.

For years, *The Daily Show* depended on Chodikoff's storied memory and half a dozen researchers mainlining cable news, watching a wall of TiVos for clips. However, in late 2009 a technological advancement was made that would change political comedy forever. *The Daily Show* worked with a company called SnapStream to develop a program that automatically transcribed TV shows, allowing the *Daily Show* staff to search keywords across every network they follow. "Say you need to find out who said, 'good guy with a gun,'" Alison Camillo, a *Daily Show* producer who later moved to *Full Frontal with Samantha Bee*, explained in *The Daily Show (The Book)*.[10] "Instead of blindly searching through hours of clips, you can put in quotes, 'good guy with a gun,' and it pulls up the last ten different things on *Good Morning America*, the *Today* show, CNN, and you can just put them all in a little playlist." It's a technique still used today, in essentially every single episode of every single political late-night show. When you imagine a John Oliver bit, it is some version of this followed by a simile-based joke. It's one thing to say TV relies on dangerous clichés, but, to use the language of comedy, it's heightening to present this as a cavalcade of examples.

More than being just as good, comedy has some advantages over traditional news. Where biased political commentators and politicians are incentivized to fudge the truth, if not outright lie, to make for more exciting TV, structurally, *The Daily Show* needed truth to make jokes from. "When you try to put false premises on things, you're just wringing comedy out of a dry cloth," Samantha Bee explained about what worked on *The Daily Show*.[11] "I like a real story that means something to me or means something to other people." Though the relationship of comedy to truth is complicated, as will be discussed in the next chapter, on a basic level factually reporting information presents the baseline reality for the comedy to subvert. If you make a joke on false nonsense, when you twist or heighten it, it can often come off as weightless, arbitrary randomness. (Obviously there is a place for randomness in comedy, but even that is playing off the assumed truth of our baseline everyday reality.) Comedically, a bedrock of truth also means a more informed audience more invested in the comedy, increasing the stakes of the setup and thus the payoff of the punch line. This is why, though Stewart believed he wasn't informing anyone, he was so good at it. In a 2007 study looking at knowledge of national and international affairs based on where you got your information, *Daily Show*/*Colbert Report* viewers landed on top.[12]

Being the sugar that helps the medicine go down is consistently the number-one thing scholars and comedians point to when asked what comedians can do to impact politics. I'm aware that being a "fun way to get people to hear information" is also the description of a cool substitute who teaches poetry through the lyrics of Taylor Swift, but social change demands an educated citizenry. The Trevor Noah–era *Daily Show* correspondent Roy Wood Jr., the son of a prominent civil rights era journalist and activist, put it to me this way: "I don't know what change looks like on the other side of a joke. I just hope that there's some degree of awareness. That you can't say you're not informed."[13]

It's not just being informed—it is what comedians are informing their audience about. Stewart, who is prone to self-deprecation about his own impact, will accept his ability to attract attention and then deflect that attention to people and subjects and issues that matter to him.[14] Actual activism is hard work, and it is slow work. It is, as Stewart puts it, "manual effort [over] time." As another *Daily Show* correspondent, Larry Wilmore, put it, "The satirist's job is to have the flashlight and say, 'Look at this.'"[15] And the biggest wins credited to Stewart and his disciples' shows are examples of that job coming to life. Stewart himself set the precedent through his work advocating for the health care of 9/11 first responders and victims. In 2010, he dedicated an episode of *The Daily Show* to the cause, which was later credited by a number of politicians for pushing a bill forward at a time when federal funding was stalled.[16] Again in 2015, when funding needed to be reauthorized, he returned to *The Daily Show*, after recently having just left, and helped extend the fund. In 2019, with the Victim Compensation Fund running out of money, he went to Washington, met with senators, drew a ton of media attention, and gave a passionate speech in front of Congress. Months later, the Never Forget the Heroes Act, a bill that would permanently fund the Victim Compensation Fund, was signed into law. *Full Frontal with Samantha Bee* showed similar results in 2020 after airing a segment hosted by Sasheer Zamata and Amy Hoggart that explored the gender bias in country music. Soon after, the show received credit when CMT announced it would have complete gender parity in the videos it plays. And there's "The John Oliver Effect," which describes Oliver's hard-to-deny influence in making visible issues like the net-neutrality debate and protecting chicken-farming whistleblowers. A lot of the conversation surrounding political comedy is about whether or not it can change minds, but the bigger impact it can have is on an issue its audience doesn't have an opinion about until the comedian gives it a platform.

Lastly, Jon Stewart's *Daily Show* taught viewers like me how to process the news and look at politics. It goes back to the basics of play. While chimps play-fight to better prepare them in case of a dangerous situation, comedians help people play with the ideas that might threaten them. Stewart's *Daily Show* trained the audience in the art of skepticism and sharpened their eye for hypocrisy. In a 2015 interview, Stewart explained *The Daily Show*'s focus is on "the space between the public face of our leaders vs. the private strategies that produce that face."[17] It was a perspective born out of the decision to have the show go to the Republican and Democratic conventions in 2000, as the real news did, instead of just throwing spitballs from afar. "Everything that happens publicly in politics there's a meeting—so what's that meeting?" he said, talking about his 2000 convention breakthrough.[18] "It always struck me as, 'We're always covering the wrong thing. We're always covering the appearance, but we're never covering that meeting.' When you watch that pack of cameras follow a presidential candidate, you go, 'That's not interesting.' What's interesting is to stand behind them and watch that, because then you learn a little bit about the process . . . The show came to exist in the space between what they're telling you in public and the meeting that they had where they decided to do it that way." It's the space between the bull and its shit.

Speaking of, let's talk about the Bush administration and one word: "truthiness." Unveiled in the first episode of *The Colbert Report* in 2005, it is one of the definitive satirical concepts of the twenty-first century and would become a sort of mission statement for the show, with Colbert, in character as a conservative blowhard idiot, declaring, "Anyone can read the news *to* you. I promise to feel the news *at* you." "Truthiness is what you want the facts to be, as opposed to what the facts are," Colbert would later explain, out of character. "What feels like the right answer as opposed to what reality will support."[19] Colbert, of course, was continuing the fight that defined *The Daily Show*. Take the definitive bit from Stewart's run, 2003's "Bush vs. Bush," a debate, using clips, between President Bush and candidate Bush meant to convey the president's brazen hypocrisy.

> **JON STEWART:** Mr. President, let me just get specific. Why are we in Iraq?
> **PRESIDENT BUSH:** We will be changing the regime of Iraq for the good of the Iraqi people.
> **JON STEWART:** Well, Governor, then I'd like to hear your response on that.
> **GOVERNOR BUSH:** If we're an arrogant nation, they'll resent us. I think one way for us to end up being viewed as the ugly American is for us to go around the world saying, "We do it this way. So should you."

The show's writers considered it "a Rosetta Stone piece" for the show. For Stewart, hypocrisy fit nicely into the comedic framework of juxtaposition, but in the years since it has influenced political comedy and, in turn, political thought, with audiences trained to listen to politicians skeptically and to hyperfocus on contradiction. On *The Daily Show*, intense focus on proving hypocrisy led to increasingly intense critique. Stewart became known for his version of righteous indignation and a willingness to hold interview subjects' feet to the fire. While *The Daily Show* started as a work of Horatian satire, wryly pointing out the absurdity of the whole charade, it grew to be more Juvenalian, rooting its comedy in realism and anger.

What it wasn't, at least to Stewart, was cynical, despite what President Obama and his administration would argue about *The Daily Show*'s unwillingness to universally support a health-care bill that lacked a public option.[20] There is some research to back this accusation. In 2004, the political scientists Jody Baumgartner and Jonathan Morris split a sample of 732 college students into three groups, one watching *The Daily Show*'s coverage of the 2004 election, one watching the *CBS Evening News*, and one watching no election coverage.[21] *The Daily Show* group showed a more negative view of both candidates and a greater sense of cynicism about the electoral system and the news media at large. However, because of a lack of controls, the study doesn't prove *The Daily Show* directly made the people cynical, it just shows a correlation between *Daily Show* watchers and cynicism. It is very possible that the thing that made people more cynical is . . . the truth. "Do I think Jon contributed to the cynicism about politics?" the *Daily Show* producer Judith Miller asked herself, answering, "Oh, I don't think you can get too cynical about politics."[22]

That 2006 study possibly supported the reading that Jon Stewart was not the root source of the cynicism, but a person holding up a mirror to it. As Baumgartner would later explain, "These same students who viewed *The Daily Show* who trusted government less were more likely to report that they had greater confidence in their own ability to understand politics."[23] Though he says that greater and greater cynicism might lead people to disengage, "political science research tells us that people who are more confident in their own ability to understand and engage in politics, they will participate more." In 2018, Baumgartner, along with Brad Lockerbie, studied this exact phenomenon, looking at 2012 data from the American National Election Studies, and found that "advocates of political satire may be correct when they suggest that satire mobilizes viewers to political action."[24] They saw that viewers of *The Daily Show* and *The Colbert Report* were more likely to contribute to political parties, talk about politics, and attend rallies. A number of other studies support these claims and also, for good measure, rebut an argument that you'll sometimes hear from the left that watching *The Daily Show* made people complacent by giving them the feeling that by watching the show, they were already doing something. That argument uses a relief theory reading that *The Daily Show* and its ilk are only offering its audience catharsis, when, with a play theory reading, aka this book's reading, shows like *The Daily Show* create a space for the audience to play with complicated ideas, to engage with them more than if they were just passively presented.

In February 2022, after hundreds of doctors and scientists wrote a letter to Spotify to try to prevent Joe Rogan's spread of Covid-19 misinformation, and many more (including celebrities like Neil Young) agreed in the press and on Twitter, Whitney Cummings came to Rogan's defense by tweeting: "Don't look to why so many people trust Joe Rogan, look to why so few people trust the mainstream media."[25] The question is not why so many people trust Joe Rogan. I know why. You know why, having read this chapter. The question is how to contextualize his appeal. Because unlike when Jon Stewart was Jon Stewart, now Joe Rogan is just one of a thousand Jon Stewarts, across the entire political spectrum. Before Jon Stewart, satire was what closes on Saturday night, as the popular saying went. But after Donald Trump, satire was open 24/7.

Days after he released his original "long-form" birth certificate, in late April 2011, President Obama walked out for his speech at the White House Correspondents' Dinner to Hulk

Hogan's theme song, "Real American." That would not be his only reference to the birther controversy, as Obama had a few minutes of material on Trump, who at the time was best known as the host of *The Apprentice* and for propping up the conspiracy that the president wasn't born in America. One joke went, "Now, I know that he's taken some flak lately, but no one is happier, no one is prouder to put this birth certificate matter to rest than The Donald. And that's because he can finally get back to focusing on the issues that matter—like, did we fake the moon landing? What really happened in Roswell? And where are Biggie and Tupac?" Seth Meyers, the host of the proceedings, followed, and went after Trump even harder.

"Donald Trump said recently he has a great relationship with the Blacks," starts what, for my money, is the best pure joke ever told about the man. It continues: "But unless the Blacks are a family of white people, I bet he is mistaken." The joke that is better remembered from that night, for obvious reasons, is "Donald Trump has been saying he will run for president as a Republican, which is surprising since I just assumed he was running as a joke."

Years later, when Trump was running for president as a Republican, people started looking back to that evening. Adam Gopnik wrote in *The New Yorker*: "On that night, Trump's own sense of public humiliation became so overwhelming that he decided, perhaps at first unconsciously, that he would, somehow, get his own back—perhaps even pursue the Presidency after all, no matter how nihilistically or absurdly, and redeem himself."[26] Jon Rineman, the writer of Meyers's second Trump joke above, ending up leaving late night, blaming himself for what he did.[27] It's a great story, but it ignores the fact that the whole reason

Rineman's joke *exists* is because Trump had been considering running. Not to mention, if Trump was so POed, why didn't he run in 2012? His deep love of Mitt Romney? In 2016, a reporter who sat next to Trump at the dinner debunked the theory. "I had a phenomenal time," Trump told her, though he felt Meyers was "too nasty."[28] The jokes didn't make him run, but they also didn't stop him from running. Though it was years before he became president, that night offered the first glimpse of how undeniable Trump is as a subject for political comedy, and yet how little it has impacted him. It's a trend that would lead many to call into question the value of political comedy in general.

After he was elected, Trump proved to be a uniquely large target, but also a uniquely poor one. It was as if, for four years, every painter had to use the same color, and that color was day-old street vomit. Patton Oswalt faced this problem with his 2017 stand-up special, *Annihilation*, starting the show, which was supposed to be about the unexpected passing of his wife, with jokes about Trump. After ten minutes, he told the audience, "That's it for the Trump material." He continued:

> People tell me, "You comedians must be so happy. Trump is president. All this free material." You know what, yes, there is a lot of material, but there is too fucking much. It's exhausting. Being a comedian while Trump is president is like, *imagine there's like an insane man on the sidewalk, just shitting on the sidewalk and yelling about Hitler.* So, you're looking at him and immediately think of the funniest joke about shitting on the sidewalk and you turn to tell it to a bunch of people and behind you he's taken the

> shit and made a sombrero out of it. So, you turn and you tell your amazing shitting on the sidewalk joke and everyone goes, "Oh . . . Turn around, he made a sombrero out of it. Do a sombrero joke." Ah, fuck! I can make fun of the shit he did the last couple of days, but by the time this thing airs, you guys are going to be like, "Wait, what was that again?"

What this joke gets at is it's not just that Trump was bad at being president; it was the frequency and rate of his being bad at it. Some of which was by design, as the Republican Party had realized the shortness of the American outrage span. Comedians aren't desperate for material. It's like assuming the thing that held Vincent van Gogh back was that he didn't have enough starry night skies to paint. What they need is people to be interested in something long enough for the comedian to be able to keep on trying the material out and making it funnier. The stand-up Sara Schaefer explained in 2017 that comedians "[struggled] to get the distance needed to make something awful hilarious."[29] This pace results in comedy that is reactionary or first thought. Cheeto, weird hair, wants to kiss Putin and/or his own daughter, etc. It's why probably the most famous stand-up joke about him is not about anything he did, but about how hard it is to keep up with something we've never seen before. "This guy being the president, it's like there's a horse loose in a hospital," starts maybe the definitive joke about Trump, from John Mulaney's 2018 stand-up special, *Kid Gorgeous at Radio City*. "I think eventually everything's going to be okay, but I have no idea what's going to happen next. And neither do any of you, and neither do your parents, because there's a HORSE LOOSE IN THE HOSPITAL. It's never happened before.

No one knows what the horse is going to do next, least of all the horse." It continues and is very funny, but comedy that is satirical, that is aspiring to *reveal* something, proved difficult as the years of Trump's administration went by.

Part of the reason it was so difficult is there isn't much second thought to the guy. As the comedy writer Noah Garfinkel put it in a tweet: "Donald Trump is the least complicated president in history. There are like four things about him in total."[30] "Satire is about revealing a truth," Larry Wilmore once explained. "Revealing a truth" is different than just telling the truth. It implies exposing something deeper, but with Trump there wasn't something deeper to expose.

Compare Alec Baldwin's Donald Trump impersonation, which he won an Emmy for despite being largely critically reviled, to the two most iconic political impressions of the last quarter century—Will Ferrell's George W. Bush and Tina Fey's Sarah Palin. Where Ferrell's and Fey's impressions revealed something about their targets that had not yet been expressed—specifically, how each used a sort of aw-shucks folksiness as their sheep's clothing—Baldwin's just reflects back, thoroughly and confidently, what everyone already thinks about Trump. There is no point in the satirist's using their flashlight to say, "Look at this," when Trump already puts a spotlight on himself and says, "Look at me." Not only that, but the dude was always doing the worst possible thing and saying the most outlandish possible stuff to the point that it became difficult for comedy writers to use one of their go-to political comedy devices of exaggeration. Across the board, when watching political comedy during those years, it felt like the normal playbook no longer hit the same way.

In spite of the formal problems Trump created for political comedy, there was so much of it. *The Daily Show with*

Trevor Noah, The Opposition with Jordan Klepper, The Jim Jefferies Show, The President Show, The Fake News with Ted Nelms, Full Frontal with Samantha Bee, Last Week Tonight with John Oliver, Wyatt Cenac's Problem Areas, Patriot Act with Hasan Minhaj, Late Night with Seth Meyers, The Rundown with Robin Thede, Tooning Out the News, Our Cartoon President. Jimmy Kimmel got way more political and it helped him in the ratings against Jimmy Fallon's *Tonight Show,* which only got a little bit more political, with both losing to the wholeheartedly political *The Late Show with Stephen Colbert. Saturday Night Live,* which during a normal period in history might do one political sketch a week max, was doing three to five and seeing a ratings boost for it. *The Break,* the show Michelle Wolf created for Netflix with the explicit goal of being a break from the endless barrage of comedic political commentary, ended up becoming largely politics-focused after her highly publicized turn as host of the White House Correspondents' Dinner. And then there were so, so, so, so, so, so, so, so, so many stand-up routines and so, so many tweets from comedy writers trying to be journalists and journalists trying to be comedy writers. I had an off-the-record coffee with one of the hosts of the above TV shows, and they told me the show wasn't their idea. The network/platform asked them, despite already having shows dedicated to Trump. They weren't invested in the idea but weren't going to turn down a TV show. The networks had realized there was gold in them thar hills, and by "gold" I mean eyeballs and by "hills" I mean liberal Trump-related anxiety.

The sheer volume of the Trump-related comedic content proved to be the most extreme example yet of the sort of algorithmically influenced funniness subjectivity discussed in chapter 3. Everyone got a joke or an impression of Trump geared toward their sensibility. A lot of people loved Baldwin's Trump, but if it wasn't your thing and you preferred a Trump that was less buffoonish and more toxic and nihilistic, you watched Anthony Atamanuik's *The President Show*. Or maybe you thought the *real* way to get at Trump was to use his words against him and thus thought Sarah Cooper's lip-syncing of his most ridiculous audio clips was brilliant. In the last few months of the administration, James Austin Johnson, an L.A. comedian who did a very accurate vocal impression of the president but used it to talk about unrelated topics, emerged. This seemed to appeal to those tired of Trump impressions and antiestablishment comedy leftists who landed on the idea that *actually* Trump was the funny one and liberals were unstoppably uncool. (Johnson would then go on to join the establishment, getting cast on *SNL* in 2021 and doing his Trump there.) And there were those whose favorite Trump jokes were parodying resistance clichés, like calling him "the orange buffoon," but with a cartoonish, over-the-top irony. A joke making fun of Trump jokes is still a Trump joke.

It's not just jokes. It's hard not to see the boom in podcasts in which comedians discuss politics as further proof that people still want the type of political comedy that Stewart once provided. These podcasts live across the political spectrum, from shows like *Chapo Trap House* and the dirtbag left to the libertarian-minded, right-leaning podcasts that are part of the *Joe Rogan Experience* extended universe.

The by-product, however, of so much political comedy and so many subjective political comedy niches is the inevitability of being exposed to hundreds of Trump jokes and pieces of political comedy you find off-putting, which in turn creates a cynical feeling that only the comedy *you* like is an exception. There are two examples of this dynamic that stick with me. One is Malcolm Gladwell arguing on his podcast, *Revisionist History*, that the problem with political comedy is that it is too funny and that if it were meaner it would be more effective.[31] What it would be more effective at exactly and how meanness would achieve that is never clear. It just seems that, like a lot of people, Gladwell would've found it cathartic to watch people be mean. The other take that I always think about came toward the end of Trump's run, when *The Ringer* ran an article that claimed that comedy over the course of the administration "failed to produce laughs."[32] How can this be true? If people didn't want to hear Trump jokes, why did Stephen Colbert overtake Jimmy Fallon in the ratings during those four years?[33] *SNL* is only about 10 percent political sketches, but on the show's YouTube page, the most-watched videos since the fall of 2016 are Trump-related cold opens. Did millions of people watch these late-night shows out of social obligation? Over thirty million people have watched *SNL*'s first 2020 debate sketch on YouTube. I'm guessing a lot of them did so because they . . . wanted to.

Okay, but [*to the tune of "Rude" by Magic!*] why it gotta be so cringe? Though cringe will be discussed further in chapter 9, the cringiness here stemmed from the disconnect between Trump-era political comedy's perceived earnest self-importance and its fecklessness. Over those years, I never saw an American comedian earnestly claim to be on the front lines against fascism, but the mix of outsized media attention and inherent "I am right; everyone else is wrong" righteousness gave off a similar enough smugness.

This too-cringe perspective on Trump comedy is philosophically the flipside to the question of who the new Jon Stewart is. Though the people looking for a new Stewart are more likely to believe comedy can make an impact, both perspectives start with the observation that comedy is not doing so at the moment. For a while, there was the question, "Why isn't all this political comedy doing anything?" But after four years of that question, it was replaced by a cynical statement: "Political comedy doesn't do anything."

Let's take a break and put politics aside for a second. Okay? Cool! In New York every few years, a new class of up-and-coming twenty-eight-year-old comedians leaves for L.A. As a result, to cover comedy in New York turns a man into a McConaughey—I get older, but the comedians stay the same age. What often surprises me about seeing comedians under the age of thirty is how much they talk about dating. Audiences can't get enough of the stuff. Under thirty: Dating is weird. Thirty to thirty-five: Marriage is weird. Over thirty-six: Kids are weird. I thought this would die off as comedy grew less heteronormative. Nope. Different pronouns, same jokes. Jokes is jokes is jokes is jokes. And yet people remain single. They still get into fights with their partner. The dating apps all remain operational. Sex happens! Maybe some things are just too difficult for comedy to meaningfully upend.

[*Knowingly peers over glasses*]

Then why do we do any of this [*gestures wildly*]? Hmm. Well, because it's fun and nice and good to know you're not alone. That's why I believe, in general, the conversations around political comedy are too focused on its impact on the *out*-group, whereas much of its power is in building and supporting the in-group. Comedy brings in people who get the joke, separating out those who don't. But, more than that, comedians' ability to generate the feelings of trust and safety necessary for play is helpful in fostering social bonds. When Stewart left the air, the *New Yorker* TV critic Emily Nussbaum captured how *The Daily Show* did that for its audience: "*The Daily Show* became a gathering place for the disenchanted—a place that let viewers know they weren't crazy."[34] The first presidential election I voted in was in 2004, and it was a rude awakening. *How could THIS country vote for a guy like Bush?* I thought, stupidly, as I stayed up all election night. Stewart would serve as a reminder that not everyone did vote for Bush. The value of feeling not alone and not crazy intensified under Trump, a president with so little regard for honesty that the term "gaslighting" became mainstream.

However, it's hard to feel less alone when you are less unified. In the years since Stewart left *The Daily Show*, it is less that there is no one who can do what he did than that no one can live up to the myth of his legacy. During the Bush administration Stewart felt like the second-most-prominent public figure in the country to many left-leaning young people. My cohort believed he spoke truth to power and made an actual difference. But looking back, he was just the spokesman of a certain liberal bubble disproportionately made up of people living in media centers. His popularity was so total to this group of people, and this group of people was so siloed, that it felt to me as if Jon Stewart spoke to and for everyone. Today, that is impossible because of a fractured media climate. So much so that when Stewart himself returned to TV in 2021, with AppleTV+'s *The Problem with Jon Stewart*, he couldn't feel like the old Jon Stewart. This disconnect between legacy and actuality was further accentuated by the new show's initial focus on fostering difficult conversations instead of taking hardline stances, frustrating audience members who'd grown to expect their political comedian to represent them. It's unsurprising that the first of the show's segments to go viral for positive reasons was when he returned to his old form and stuck it to Leslie Rutledge, the Arkansas attorney general responsible for pushing an anti-trans agenda.

When I watch Stewart now, I can't help but think about what would've happened if he'd never left. Frequently asked, Stewart does not regret not sticking around for Trump's 2016 run.[35] He doesn't think he would've made a difference, considering how many other people were out there, including people who had worked with him, making the jokes and pointing out the hypocrisy as he would have. But maybe Stewart underrated the value of the coalition he had built with *The Daily Show*, a personal mix of commonsense centrism, antiestablishment radicalism, hard-fought patriotism, righteous progressivism. Say what you will about the smug failure that was the Rally to Restore Sanity, but 215,000 people came to see Stewart and Colbert's attempt at parodying the Fox News anchor Glenn Beck's Restoring Honor rally, with high-profile musical performances and partly jokey, partly genuine speeches celebrating reasonableness in the face of mounting political divide. The Democrats didn't need another person making jokes; they needed someone both Sanders and Clinton supporters trusted.

More than helping the medicine go down, humor smooths conflicts and unites disparate groups. As shown by the history of Black comedy, this is especially vital for members of marginalized communities, which the powers that be are often found trying to divide. "We cannot have a meaningful revolution without humor," bell hooks said in an interview in 2015.[36] "Every time we see the left or any group trying to move forward politically in a radical way, when they're humorless, they fail. Humor is essential to the integrative balance that we need to deal with diversity and difference and the building of community." Comedians can do this, by being very catchy talkers who give, even teach, their audiences the vocabulary to advocate for their side. "If someone's going out to try and make a point about something and they can't quite articulate it, they can't quite put it into the structure," Roy Wood told me. "They can go find a clip of mine and then put that on their Facebook wall and go, 'This is what the hell I was talking about.'"[37]

Wood continued, discussing how a comedian can help foster difficult conversations within a community, citing the work of another *Daily Show* alumnus, the Trump-era "Weekend Update" anchor Michael Che. Specifically, Che's joke about Black Lives Matter, from his 2016 Netflix special, *Matters*:

> That's a controversial statement. Black lives matter. Not matters more than you, just matters. Matters. Just matters. That's where we're starting the negoti-

> ations. Matters. We can't agree on that shit? What the fuck is less than matters? Black lives exist? Can we say that?

It's a joke that the professor and comedy scholar Danielle Fuentes Morgan mentioned to me as epitomizing her idea of "laughing to keep from dying," as captured in her 2020 book of the same name.[38] In its intro, she writes:

> Laughing to keep from dying is the survival tactic that operates in two registers—the ability to inspire laughter in those who would cause harm becomes a form of protection in the plausible deniability of *just jokes*; the necessity of inspiring knowing in-group laughter opens up black interior space that wards off psychic, or even, physical, death.

So much of the conversation around political comedy is about the offensive, but Morgan points to a history of Black comedy and the value of the defensive. Instead of *How can comedy change?* it is *How can comedy protect?* This is of dire importance for people who, because of this country's history and power structures, are legitimately in danger.

Maybe it stems from my not growing up in a proselytizing religion, but preaching to the choir seems reasonable if it helps them keep the faith. "Humor breaks fear and builds confidence," wrote Srdja Popovic and Mladen Joksic, two prominent Serbian pro-democracy activists.[39] Stewart and Colbert spoke truth to power, expecting not to bring down their opponents but to inspire confidence among the opposition. Colbert's turn hosting the White House Correspondents' Dinner in 2006 was unbelievably daring, but it's not like the jokes were going to be so damning yet so funny that Bush would resign in shame. When Colbert said, "It is my privilege to celebrate this president, 'cause we're not so different, he and I. We both get it. Guys like us, we're not some brainiacs on the nerd patrol. We're not members of the factinista. We go straight from the gut. Right, sir?" it wasn't that he stood up to the president. It's that he followed Bush's attempt at spinning his own presidency with a rebuttal. He put the power of the people who disagreed up against the president himself. It was a symbol that motivated people or, at least, helped ward off hopelessness. *That* is political comedy doing something.

To understand what America has, look at other places that are fighting for it. "There are many countries I've been to where people don't have free speech, and one of the biggest things an authoritarian leader tries to remove is the ability to make jokes about them," Trevor Noah told Seth Meyers, two years into his gig as the host of *The Daily Show*.[40] At the same time Trump was dressing up in fascist dictator drag—asking advisers if he could get the Department of Justice or FCC to punish *SNL* and the other late-night shows that were mean to him—actual totalitarian governments were arresting comedians. In 2016, two television executives in Algeria were jailed for airing a satirical talk show.[41] Since Narendra Modi took over as India's prime minister in 2014, comedians in the country have lived in fear of arrest. As the biggest English-speaking comedian there, Vir Das, explained to me, persecution has become so common that Indian comics have created a secret network, in which they send each other money to cover legal fees and missed work that comes from political harassment.[42] In 2021, multiple comedians, including Munawar Faruqui, were arrested and jailed for unsubstantiated claims that they insulted Hinduism.[43] Also in 2021, Russia's Interior Ministry tried to ban the prominent stand-up comedian Idrak Mirzalizade, who is of Azerbaijani origin, for life from entering or living in the country, only to reduce the sentence to fourteen years.[44] In 2022, Zeinab Mousavi, an Iranian comedian who was critical of the government's treatment of women, was sentenced to two years in prison.[45] Maybe the least terrifying but most ridiculous example is that in 2021, to mark the ten-year anniversary of his father's passing, Kim Jong-un banned laughter for eleven days.[46] Noah continued, in that conversation with Meyers, "A person is less frightening when you're laughing. It doesn't diminish what they do, but it's how we cope."

There will always be a certain sort of wishful thinking around comedy's impact. This ethos was captured by Volodymyr Zelensky, the former comedian turned wartime president of Ukraine, when he said, talking about Russian president Vladimir Putin, "Laughter is a weapon that is fatal to men of marble."[47] But I favor the perspective of another Ukrainian stand-up comedian, Yehor Shatailo, who gave the Russian invasion three weeks before starting to book live shows again.[48] "There's no need to overestimate the power comedy has," he said. "It's not a weapon; I don't think I can heal any wounds. But it might help us to stay sane."

Regardless of how funny or insightful they are, no comedian will ever lead a one-person revolution of social progress, because that is not a solitary act. Comedians can unite, they can empower, they can restore the psychic energy of those on the front lines of change. If comedy did all that *and* kept people sane, it would be a lot.

6

TRUTH

Kind of like the song "Bad Company" off the album *Bad Company* by the band Bad Company, "The Machine" is the title of the closing story of the 2016 Showtime special *The Machine*, by Bert "The Machine" Kreischer. "When I was twenty-two, I got involved with the Russian Mafia," the story starts, followed by nearly fourteen minutes of Kreischer, a bearded big boy with no shirt on, recalling a series of Russian mob high jinks. In the story, it is the mid-nineties, and Kreischer is a state-school party animal on a school trip to Russia. There, he befriends Igor, the mobster the teacher had paid to "protect" the class. Upon first meeting Igor, Kreischer is nervous, which, when combined with the fact that he never learned any Russian leading up to the trip, results in him not saying what he had planned—"Hello, my name's Bert. It's very nice to meet you. I work pussyyyy"—but instead "I am the Machine!" And so it was written. The majority of the story focuses on when Igor introduces Kreischer to *Big* Igor, the Russian mobster who "protects" the train Kreischer's class is taking to Moscow. Knowing him to be the Machine, Big Igor quickly "invites" Kreischer to assist in robbing the dining car, after which one of the teachers who is chaperoning comes to give Kreischer a talking-to. In response, as Kreischer tells it, Big Igor "takes a big sip of vodka, spits it in her eyes, and goes, 'No one talks to the Machine like that.' Shuts the door in her face and goes, 'Fuck that bitch. This is Russia!'" Then Big Igor tells Kreischer they're going to rob the entire train. And they do. Kreischer even ends up assisting them in robbing his own luggage. At the station, a drunk Kreischer learns that the teacher had informed the police. "Don't worry, I talk to police for both of us," Big Igor tells Kreischer, vodka bottle in hand. After they chat, the officer approaches Kreischer and says, "So, I understand you're the Machine. Tonight, you party with us." A confused Kreischer asks if he's in trouble. The police officer gets close and goes, "No . . . Fuck that bitch, this is Russia."

No, he didn't. The police officer did not say that. For years, the story would end with "So, I understand you're the Machine," because that's what happened. And, for years, what happened was the story would bomb. The problem, all along, was the truth. "I was attached to proving it was true," Kreischer told me years later.[1] He thought the key was the chaperoning teacher being of Puerto Rican descent, but the audience didn't care, even if she was. He explained to me, "I wanted to share things that couldn't be faked. And that was a mistake." Sure, if someone was listening, looking to fact check, they would clock how unlikely it is that the police officer said "Fuck that bitch, this is Russia," considering he wasn't there when Big Igor said it the first time, but if you're just going along for the ride, it works because it gives the story closure.

"I don't think anyone really cared if it was true or not," was Kreischer's diagnosis. I agree, depending on how you define the word "true." Truth, as discussed in chapter 5, is fundamental in comedy, but veracity is not. In the moment, audience members are not clocking if a joke is factually accurate; they are responding to if it feels true—if what happens affirms their brains' understanding of reality. Because a comedian writes a story like any other joke told onstage: They listen to how the audience responds and shifts details to get the desired reaction. If the audience laughs more at the exaggeration than reality, the exaggeration becomes the reality. For Kreischer, the audience needed more than what exactly happened to appreciate the ridiculousness of the story, so he made things up that would result in them better understanding his personal truth. If the audience finds certain made-up details truer than the real turn of events, then those details become the story. Fuck that bitch, this is Russia.

All comedians play with the truth the way Kreischer does in this story, albeit not always consciously. Some might punch up or make up dialogue. Others, like a sculptor, will carve out only the parts that are the heart of the story, excluding the details that might confuse or undermine the cleaner truth. Judd Apatow re-creates this formula when he has comedians develop scripts about their lives, asking them to start with exactly what happened and then alter it more and more with each draft until they get to what feels most genuine as a story, even if it is less autobiographical. Heidegger said—okay, actually, a TikTok philosophy professor once said that Heidegger once said—our present idea of self is based on the future we want to strive for, and as a result, our ideals for our future shape how we interpret our past. A similar idea is shared in psychoanalysis, where there is the belief that our "memories" are more of a reflection of our present interpretation of the past than what actually happened. Of course, this impacts all people when they tell stories over time, and, yes, all artists do a version of this. But where a memoirist will make these decisions based on their own feeling of what is true, the comedian is directly basing their decisions on their audience. This orients comedians' memories not around the factual truth, but on what would work best onstage. It's an instinct that explains why there are so many dang legends in this book.

Kreischer, who as of this writing is one of the biggest touring acts in the country (thanks to "The Machine" story, which has over fifty million views on YouTube), has become a bit of a storytelling machine, with the ability to efficiently process his life as it would be best performed to strangers. To go back to Heidegger, by way of that guy on TikTok, Kreischer's view of himself as the Machine shapes how he remembers things. I've seen it happen firsthand, when, on one of his podcasts, he took the nonstory of him enjoying appearing on my podcast and turned it into an epic, filled with extraordinary circumstances and our hero overcoming adversity.[2] A simple question I asked about a time he made fun of one of my articles became a confrontation. Or even sillier: According to his telling, my interviews are supposed to be only thirty-five minutes long, but ours somehow, impossibly, against all odds, grew to be two hours. Who cares that that was the amount of time I asked, and always ask, for? The story was better; therefore, that's the way he told it. Fuck that bitch (me), this was Russia (podcasting).

I don't mean to pick on Bert. His non-truths are not harmful, as these things go. But because stand-ups seem to be just talking up there, audiences tend to take them at their word, when actually, comics are doing some combination of writing and performing. The mystery E. B. and Katharine

White felt all those years ago persists. As I said earlier in the book, comedians are not wizards; they are magicians. They are not making a rabbit disappear; they work tirelessly on a trick. All stand-up is built on a fundamental lie—that a performance is a "real" conversation—so if that's the case, what does truth in comedy even mean?

It's an important question, in these postmodern, post-truth times, in which people searching for certainty cling to whatever truth they can find. And truth in comedy is important, but not all perspectives on truth are the same. Some comedians are taking advantage of this trust by trying to get away with deception, while others are using it to explore more vulnerable work. And then there is another, younger group of comedians searching for something genuine beyond the ways comedians have traditionally learned to *perform* genuineness. Though there is a tendency to think of truth as one distinct, undeniable thing, as if it could be mathematically proven, like any element of comedy there are multiple ways in which a comedian can try to interpret and manipulate truth. In the process, these comedians are expanding the bounds of the concept "truth in comedy."

Quick summary of the history of the concept "truth in comedy." In the 1950s and '60s, "sick comedians"—your Shelley Bermans, your Lenny Bruces—became models of authenticity, inspired by the great postwar, existentialist-indebted look inward. "Many Americans were attempting to find their 'real selves,'" wrote Michael J. Arlen in *The New Yorker* about this movement.[3] "The new entertainers, in addition to playing off on these searches after identity, attempted to gain the goodwill and regard of their audiences by revealing—or, anyway, acknowledging—*their* 'real selves.'" A decade passed and Lenny Bruce begot George Carlin and Richard Pryor, both with similar legends (legend count #5 and #6) of eschewing their mainstream audience and clean-cut presentation in exchange for something more shaggy and "authentic." Late-seventies Pryor, the greatest to do it, in my opinion, modeled how various forms of truth telling interweave with each other to earn an audience's trust, mixing pitch-perfect behavioral impressions with dead-on observational comedy with an exploration of his inner self with openness about his faults and failures with challenging social critique. Then, reacting to the corporatization of stand-up comedy clubs in the 1980s, nineties comics showed their authenticity by, say it with me, "not selling out." This resulted in, for example, Bill Hicks railing against advertising, fashioning himself a sort of maverick, saying things in interviews like, "I'll continue to be me. As Bob Dylan said, the only way to live outside the law is to be totally honest. So, I will remain lawless."[4] And alternative comedians reacted to the rigid observational jokes and tight, late-night-ready five-minute sets of the eighties by trying to not perform at all, espousing the mantra of "fewer jokes; more you."

Now, the perceived culmination of a lot of these ideals—Louis C.K. If you prefer not to read about him because of his sexual indiscretions, just skip to the next section of this chapter. But he must be discussed. In the story of comedy's march to be taken more seriously, C.K. was, for nearly a decade, its avatar. And at the center of this celebration was "truth." The *Los Angeles Review of Books* called him "television's most honest man."[5] *The New Yorker* wrote in 2015, in an article about a new C.K. special, "Comedians are seen as honest populists: laughter, we think, not only feels good but teases out universal truths."[6]

Like Carlin and Pryor before him, C.K. has his own legend (legend count #7) of being awakened to the truth. After decades spent doing the same absurdist material over and over with the same result—writing gigs, but a relative disinterest from the entertainment industry toward him performing his own material—C.K. had a breakthrough after his first kid was born. Pointing out the bips and boops of the parenting marathon goes back forever—*My son is always making such a mess! My daughter is always asking for money to go SHOPPING!*—but C.K.'s frankness about how gross and boring and annoying it can be felt new, whether it was calling his four-year-old an "asshole" or revealing "I literally scrape shit out of my daughter's little red vagina a few times a day." Besides making him more popular, doing this material gave him a feeling of closeness with the audience that he had not experienced before. As a result, he established himself as someone who could see the big truths of our society. This was epitomized by his 2008 viral appearance on *Late Night with Conan O'Brien*, where he argued that people take technology like cell phones and airplane Wi-Fi for granted, saying, "Everything is amazing right now and nobody's happy."

His stature continued to grow as he figured out ways to structure jokes that would appeal to both liberal and conservative (or at minimum politically correct and incorrect) ideas of truth. He would acknowledge white privilege and find ways to say the n-word with a hard *r*. He'd defend gay marriage and combat homophobia with jokes that used the f-slur. He would say that men are the most dangerous things in the world for women, but also that women should be called the c-word if they are being one. He convinced some people he was speaking truth to power and others that no one could tell him what he could and could not do. Active and casual comedy fans with both of these perspectives considered him the greatest comedian alive and he became the model to which all other comedians must aspire and by which they must be judged.

This assessment was backed up by a few very public choices that signified integrity and independence. First and foremost, he dressed like a sack of garbage onstage, wearing a poorly fitted black T-shirt and black jeans, presenting a white male averageness. Even though the decision to not care about how you look is as much a choice as trying, it helped him sell the image of "I'm just a regular guy just talking up here." Then there was that, despite being routinely asked about it, he didn't actively discourage claims that Dane Cook, when Cook was the biggest comedian in the country, stole a joke from him, although in retrospect both jokes were built off a decades-old Steve Martin joke. Also, he announced that he was going to turn over material every year, as if he was the only comedian to write new jokes and, then a couple specials later, he announced he was going to bypass the networks to release stand-up specials directly to his audience online. But nothing did more for the public perception of him as a true artist than the arrangement he made for his FX show, *Louie*. Known in the industry as "the *Louie* deal," it involved C.K. accepting less money in exchange for the freedom to do everything in the show—star, write, direct, edit—without outside input. *Louie* influenced the proliferation of semiautobiographical comedies/dramedies about the life of a comedian *and* prestige sitcoms more interested in creating a surreal, abstract, comedic tone than hard jokes, but in terms of public perception, the fact that C.K. was doing it all by himself gave off—and there is no other way of putting this—auteur vibes.

Then, in 2017, *The New York Times* published a story revealing five accusations of sexual misconduct against him. Despite in the past having called rumors of such behavior "not real,"[7] soon after, C.K. copped to all of it.[8] And I remember feeling something breaking. "Why our perception of him changed, I don't think it's because of what he did but because he denied it for two years," the comedian/Oscar-nominated *Borat Subsequent Moviefilm* cowriter Jena Friedman said, assessing the situation. "If you are in this position of truth-teller and then you gaslight people, I think that seems to a lot of people like a bigger indiscretion than jerking off in front of women without their consent, or tanking a lot of women's careers on your path to success."[9] People understood C.K. was a creep. He talked about masturbating frequently in his act. But, as I've said, trust is essential for the comedian-audience relationship. It is impossible to carry on the same without it. It is hard to separate the art from the artist with stand-up comedy, because the art is the artist.

Yes, what C.K. did was terrible, but it also is just terribly ironic. "The most honest man" is a liar!? But really it wasn't ironic or surprising. C.K. was always one of stand-up's most gleeful liars; he just hid it behind stand-up's presentation of "I'm just a regular guy just talking up here." A fact he was, ironically, quite open about. In 2011, HBO brought together three esteemed stand-ups and Ricky Gervais for *Talking Funny*, a conversation about the trials and tribulations of being a (male) comedian. And there's a fun moment in which Jerry Seinfeld talks about his favorite of C.K.'s jokes, but in the process reshapes it to sound more like Jerry Seinfeld material. Gervais says Seinfeld turned it into a joke and that he doesn't think C.K. even tells jokes. He explains, "I just [think], *This is a man falling apart for my pleasure. This is a man spilling his heart out, telling me what a bad day he's had.*"

C.K. compared Gervais's naivete about the joke-writing process to that of his toddler daughter's and said, "I try to make it seem like, 'I'm just getting this out,' but I know all the moves." One of his favorite moves is to share a fact or a story like "Did you know that back in the third century . . . chessboards used to be round?," a premise of his from the late eighties, only to take it back with something like, "Well, they weren't. That is a big fucking lie that I just made up." As the decades wore on, C.K. was able to bring what he learned from this technique into more and more of his act. Slowly, while people were too busy fawning over him, C.K.'s stand-up reverted to its original goal of, as Marc Maron once put it, executing the will of his comedy.[10] As in, C.K. went back to focusing more and more on getting the audience to laugh at his most outlandish, potentially off-putting ideas and less on revealing something about himself. But by the point of his critical zenith, he was so skilled at manipulating the audience that he was able to exploit his perceived integrity to maximize the reach of his comedy. Maybe C.K.'s greatest talent was giving lies a sense of realism. A straddler of the alternative and club scenes, C.K. figured out how to map the aesthetics of truth onto his absurd, insensitive, and self-aggrandizing act.

You can get a sense of how C.K. viewed the truth in a moment from his 2010 appearance on *WTF with Marc Maron*. The two are debating how to discuss the dissolution of their friendship, and C.K. tells Maron it's his podcast, and he can edit it to make it sound like anything he wants.[11] It made me think of how C.K. handled his beef with Dane Cook on a 2011 episode of *Louie*. At the time it was praised for its authenticity, for giving the audience a peek behind the curtain, but C.K. wrote the entire scene and wouldn't take any of Cook's script notes,[12] despite Cook telling C.K. when he saw the script that he was "projecting some of these thoughts."[13] It's hard to know C.K.'s true thinking here, but my read is that as an artist, he was interested in his own truth, or he wasn't interested in the truth at all, but the veneer of truth that he could control. Beyond just C.K., historically and currently the veneer of truth has been dangerous for comedy, allowing comedians to cloak jokes based on harmful stereotypes in "It's funny because it's true" and spread baseless conspiracies by fashioning themselves as truth tellers.

It wasn't hard for Louis C.K. to talk about masturbating all those times, because it allowed him to seem like he was putting himself out there without ever actually being at risk. What he wasn't is vulnerable. And for there to be real truth in comedy, vulnerability is necessary.

"I believe being VULNERABLE is vital to creating MEMORABLE comedy," wrote Gary Gulman in May 2019.[14] It was a part of a series he was doing, in which he tweeted out a bit of joke-writing advice every day. It continued: "For the 1st few years just getting on stage is vulnerable. As a pro it means sharing a part of yourself that makes you uncomfortable and just as important, COMMITTING to the joke." I would soon learn that at the time, Gulman was himself transitioning from his standard mix of impeccably crafted whimsical flights of fancy and detailed observational comedy to material about his struggle with mental illness that almost ended his career. It was material that would become the acclaimed HBO special *The Great Depresh.* What I realized while watching is that if a comic is willing to forgo the gimmicks, tricks, or *moves* that give them control, thus giving themselves to their audience, there is an extraordinary vulnerability that emerges.

I think of Margaret Cho, in her 2001 special, *I'm the One That I Want*, risking professional ramifications by naming names and revealing the dark side of her experience starring in *All-American Girl*, the first American sitcom about an Asian family. There had been a lot of attention paid to the show's failures, but Cho sought to set the record straight, discussing the pressure she was put under to lose weight, resulting in an eating disorder that led to hospitalization and drug abuse. And somehow she made it all funny. In one moment in the special, she talks about coming home after having a great time on set, when she gets a call from a producer she had come to trust, who informs her in a panic that the network is "concerned about the fullness of your face" and that she has to do something about it if she wants to be a star. "I didn't know what to say to that," she tells the audience. "I always thought I was okay looking. I had no idea I was [*crescendos into a shout*] this giant face taking over America! [*smiles then switches into mock horror*] Here comes the face!" "It is also the classic tale of artists taking what moves them in life and creating something of worth about it," she said, looking back on the special's twentieth anniversary.[15] "It's just bringing an ancient way of healing into this era of comedy, politics, gender, queerness."

I think of Tig Notaro, in 2012, going from being hospitalized from a gastrointestinal infection to a breakup, to her mom dying suddenly, to being diagnosed with breast cancer and four days later stepping onstage at the Largo in L.A.

and starting her set with "Hello. Good evening. Hello. I have cancer. How are you? Is everybody having a good time? I have cancer. How are you?" What makes Notaro's performance so incredible to think about is how it's not only that these are difficult subjects to make art about, but that her actual self, with her actually sick body, was performing it. In an interview with *Slate* in 2020, she provided the perfect image of what it looked and felt like: "I felt very much like a baby giraffe trying to stand up," she said.[16] "I had never been so vulnerable or personal onstage. I had not shared my dating life. Even when I was diagnosed with cancer, I called my manager and said, 'I don't want anybody in this town knowing that I'm sick.' I was scared I wouldn't work again."

And I think of Maria Bamford, who possesses a sheer technical mastery of so many of the skills at a stand-up's disposal, but what sets her apart is the level of difficulty of the material. She is driven to talk about things that are hard to talk about. The stigma around mental illness is so prevalent that "stigma around mental illness" is now a phrase everyone is familiar with. But when Bamford was doing material about mental health in the early 2000s—like "I never really thought of myself as depressed though, as much as [*gets ironically wistful*] paralyzed by hope"—it was scary to bring up. Unlike being a perv and sexual abuser, apparently, mental illness has led to people losing work, having difficulty maintaining relationships, and struggling to be considered a full member of society. Through their work, all three of these women confront the popular idea of what it means to be fearless onstage. "Fearless" is often used to describe comics unafraid of hurting people, when it should apply to the comedians afraid of being hurt *by* people and persisting anyway.

These comedians were not motivated by trying to make

themselves feel better—that's what the doctors and meds and healthy living practices are for. Instead they are motivated to help, even if it is by offering their audience a surrogate for their own pain or by making it easier to have conversations about difficult subjects. Coming of age in San Francisco in the 1980s, Cho was influenced by ACT UP's grassroots movement to end the AIDS epidemic. "I loved the slogan 'Silence = Death,'" she wrote in her 2004 book *I Have Chosen to Stay and Fight*.[17] "I want to take it further. [Silence] is worse than death. When we never see who we are, never hear what we think about things, what we are doing as a group or what we are doing individually, then it is as if we were never there in the first place. Silence = Nonexistence." What distinguishes this philosophy from that of comics who pretend to be truthful, or even those who use stand-up as a form of confession, is a distinction Beth Lapides made to me between "getting laughs" and "giving laughs."[18] To get laughs, which I associate more with club comedians like C.K. motivated by crushing the audience, a comedian uses the audience to make themselves feel better; to give laughs, like Cho, Notaro, and Bamford, a comedian uses their truth to make the audience feel better about their own. As discussed in chapter 5, one of the things comedians can do to empower their audience is give them the vocabulary and language they need to best represent themselves. If what is so difficult about living with something or dealing with something is the shame associated with talking about it, stand-up transcends the conversation, by being able to shout a vulnerable truth. If it's mockable, it is manageable.

What Bamford, Cho, and Notaro represent is a genuine authenticity, in contrast to the popular, constructed image of authenticity. The writer and philosopher Alexander Stern distinguished between the two, calling authenticity, as it is often conceived, a sham, a self-centered pursuit bastardized by "corporations that profit off our innermost desires."[19] Where a genuine authenticity can be achieved through "resistance to self-absorption and fantasy" and "acknowledgement of our dependency on others and of the historical contingency that inhabits every corner of our lives." It's a point Notaro echoed when I spoke to her nearly a decade after her breakthrough set.[20] She told me that when she meets people who were in attendance, she feels connected to them, as if they went through something together. "What I figured out more and more as time has gone on," she told me, "[is that] I was looking for help. I certainly had friends and family, but my mother and my primary relationship were gone. It's not too crazy to think that a dark theater where I do stand-up would be where I would go for comfort, having lost those people in my life." Just as there is a closeness that comes from trusting a comedian, there is a closeness that comes when the comedian trusts their audience.

Truth is an impossible-to-achieve standard. What matters is the "search for truth," as Lapides explained to me, more than a "fait accompli, like, 'this is THE TRUTH.'" The search does not have to been done selflessly, but it cannot be done selfishly. It cannot be done alone.

In early 2017, John Early and Kate Berlant performed on *The Tonight Show Starring Jimmy Fallon*. It was quite an unusual set as late-night sets go. Going against a traditionally safe format, the duo boldly offered a new vision of what stand-up can look like and what truth in comedy can mean. They come out looking the part. Berlant, with her big vaudeville face, is wearing a purple romper, while Early, looking like a Sunday-school teacher's favorite student, complements her with a lilac turtleneck under a light gray suit. Instead of starting the set, they stop themselves so they can really "focus and take it in." They trade over-the-top pleasantries and pretend that they might make each other cry. Berlant thinks of her mother, "who put her through private school." Halfway through their time, they again stop themselves from starting their set to look each other in the eyes and say how proud they are of each other. Berlant: "I would actually argue our friendship kinda transcends heteronormative expectations of [*crosses her eyes*] intimacy." With one minute left, the set reaches a panicked crescendo. Berlant says, "It's not lost on me that not a lot of women or gay men get this opportunity." Early agrees, pained, "We let down our communities." Twenty seconds. Berlant: "There's no time for material, just go physical." Berlant pretends to punch Early, then slips into the robot. They both do the Charleston. The audience, which started off a bit confused before warming up, breaks out into celebratory applause at whatever this is.

The set reminds me of something Early said to me when I first interviewed him: "People who are performing themselves, the way that we see who they really are is in the way that performance fails."[21] To do a bit like this, where the line between real and fake is ambiguous, in front of a studio audience of tourists and the most middle American audience at home, is risky. Right away, this audience might not even register any of the performance as comedy, resulting in an excruciating four minutes of televised audience silence. However, it was still better than the alternative. "The weirdness of stand-up is that you have to pretend that it's off the cuff," Early explained on an episode of *You Made It Weird with Pete Holmes*, talking about the *Tonight Show* set. "*That* is so embarrassing to me."[22]

A few months later I was still thinking about the set, when I went to see Early perform at the Bell House, a live performance venue in Brooklyn. In the middle of his show, he asked the audience, "You know what straight men love more than pussy?" Early cocked his head and raised his eyebrows, as if he *really* wanted to know. Even I, one of the few straight men in attendance, was stumped. His face constricted and he made a fist to accentuate the answer. Lowering his voice to convey a passionate masculinity, he told us: "The truth." It was a joke on a performative idea of truth in comedy that was propped up by the previous generation of comedians and soured by C.K. An idea of truth that a younger generation of comedians, raised on the internet and within marginalized realities, has been questioning.

By this time in 2017, people had already started to remark that everyone in Brooklyn sounded like Early and Berlant. When the *New York Times* comedy critic Jason Zinoman asked on Twitter if everyone was copying Berlant, Bo Burnham, who would later go on to direct Berlant's first stand-up special and one-person stage show, replied that she was the "most influential/imitated comedian of a generation"[23] and the "Millennial Lenny Bruce."[24] He explained that she was doing "hyper self-aware deconstructive performative liberal stuff 5 years before" anyone else. Both Early and Berlant went to NYU, with Early studying theater and Berlant creating her own major called "the cultural anthropology of comedy," and together they've led a charge to blow up one specific facet of stand-up comedy—performance.

Early credits his comedic perspective to the confusion of watching his parents, both ministers, when he was growing up. "That's the person who I know very well and I'm watching them in this heightened performance," he told me when I interviewed him. "Also, as a gay person," he continued, "before you know it, you're like, *I'm trapped in a performance.* Before you know what's going on, you have a very fractured understanding of what it means to be authentic." Berlant, whose father is a respected fine artist with work in the collection of the Whitney and whose mother worked in experimental theater before transitioning to set design, credits her perspective to getting a master's in performance studies and not an M.F.A., as it is "a problem-driven, critical theory–based world, [where] you're reacting to your own performance and performance of identity and thinking a lot about the politics of watching and being watched."[25] Berlant does for comedy what Alex Katz tried to do for art with works like 1959's *Ada Ada*, a single painting that features two portraits of his wife in a blue dress that are very similar but not identical. With his work he pushed back on the idea that any portrait can capture the singularity of a person, because there is no such thing; Berlant is pushing back against the idea that there is one real self that performance obscures. As she explained to Nathan Fielder, another comedian who wrestles with the concept of truth in his work, "This obsession with the truth, and this obsession with authenticity or sincerity. This idea of a self at all, that is totally devoid of fiction, or is not a fabrication . . . feels more and more like a total fallacy."[26] Judith Butler also came up in my conversation with Early, and their influence on Early and Berlant is obvious as well. As Butler writes in *Gender Trouble*, "Laughter emerges in the realization that all along the original was derived."[27]

There is no "true" self for you to show the audience. It's why Berlant finds readings of comedy like Gervais's of C.K. ridiculous. "'Look how stripped down and raw.' It's so funny," Berlant explained to Fielder. "We know what it's like to construct a self in a performance, just existing walking down the street. So this idea that anyone is going to be on stage and *not* be an actor, or a performer, that performance is not a construction *at all*, it's so bizarre." Following this line of thinking, Berlant's and Early's work wrestles between hyper-awareness of performance and a full embrace of performing.

Berlant and Early were at the forefront of a new comedy vanguard. As the original alternative comedy movement was a reaction to a certain phoniness that Gen X comedians saw in the schtick of comedy-club comedians, the millennial and Gen Z "New Queens of Comedy," as my *Vulture* colleague E. Alex Jung named them in 2018, were reacting against the phoniness of going onstage and acting like what you're saying is authentic, whatever that would mean.[28] These comedians were not pretending that "I'm just a regular guy just talking up here." As Jo Firestone, a New York alternative comedian, writer on *The Tonight Show* at the time Early and Berlant performed, and future star of chapter 10, once explained it, "No matter what, stand-up is lying," regardless of whether you're singing a song or claiming you ran into your ex the other day.[29] If the comedian, she argued, is going to be lying, singing and dancing "feels closer to truth" because the performer is not pretending they didn't just make something up. "If we're all going to be performing and making up this persona," she explained, "you might as well put on an outfit and put on the tap shoes." Though few literally wore tap shoes, since 2015, I've seen a least one comedian sing at each comedy show I've been to. Most often what I'm seeing is a queer version of musical comedy, like Patti Harrison performing an "earnest song" that she had written for and was rejected by Dua Lipa, with the chorus "I would kill myself, if you asked me to / I would kill myself, I kill myself for you / I would kill myself if you asked me to / If you killed yourself, I would kill myself too," or the straight but queer-enmeshed Catherine Cohen singing, as a sort of postmodern Betty Boop, "Boys never wanted to kiss, so now I do comedy / Boys never wanted to kiss, so now I need all of you to look at me / Look at me, look at me, look at me ooo-OOO ohhh." Sometimes it's just Larry Owens singing "Being Alive" from the Stephen Sondheim musical *Company*, with his Obie Award–winning voice, where there isn't a joke as much as a camp reveling in too much.

This movement feels so new, so different from comedy that came before it, that I often stop to ask myself, *Where did it come from?* And that frequent question arises because these performers' influences extend beyond traditional comedians to include artists like drag queens. Part of that presence came from the widespread popularity of *RuPaul's Drag Race*, and part of it came from going to drag shows and bringing queens into comedy spaces. In 2014, Aaron Jackson and Josh Sharp were two improvisers at the UCB, who had a minor hit on their hands with their *Parent Trap*–inspired, extremely irreverent, very gay musical two-person show, *Fucking Identical Twins*, which they performed at the theater twice a month for about a year and a half (as opposed to the theater's standard three-month run). Because of a lack of queer programming at UCB at the time, and because it was a show that benefited from repeat viewings, a lot of up-and-coming gay comedians would come to every show. Quickly a joke about a "post-show talkback" at the nearby gay bar Barracuda turned into reality, with the duo wrangling a herd of queer comedians to see what they thought was the funniest show in New York at the time, a pre–*RuPaul's Drag Race* Bob the Drag Queen.[30] Looking back, Jackson and Sharp have realized that the significance of this time was felt not just in their shows (*Fucking Identical Twins* has since been developed into a feature film with A24), but in the twice-a-month gay comedy mixer they hosted, in which tastes and sensibilities could be shared and developed and inspired by its surroundings.

For years, drag queens had adapted stand-up to work in gay bars for gay audiences uncomfortable in traditional comedy clubs, so it makes sense that young gay comedians themselves would then adapt that adaptation. Drag's influence has materialized in many ways, including the use of drag vernacular and forms, like the lip sync. But it also shaped this class of comedians' comic ideals, especially in terms of the fluidity of person and persona, as well as the act of both aspiring to realness and mocking the idea that there *is* such a thing. As the comedian Guy Branum puts it, "A possible definition of camp is pretending to do a thing while actually doing it."[31] In practice, this means performance that is aware it is performance. You are more likely to see this generation of queer comedians try to fully, reverently inhabit a character and perform through them, than just as them. It's John Early performing Vicky, a confident Southern Christian housewife stand-up with the catchphrase "I'm looking for my denim." It's Cole Escola, a converted cabaret performer prone to doing monologues as tortured, self-obsessed women. It's Bowen Yang as the iceberg that sank the *Titanic* who only wants to talk about its music career. It's Matt Rogers performing as "Matt Rogers," an aspiring pop star who wears a bad blond wig to perform a song as Christine Baranski performing as

Martha May Whovier from *How the Grinch Stole Christmas*, who herself is performing a certain sort of feminine confidence in her desire to "fuck that Grinch." It's Megan Stalter's cavalcade of stilted, lobotomized influencers performed on the very platforms they inhabit.

I wouldn't suggest that this style of character comedy is a brand-new invention. You could point to a number of examples throughout the history of *SNL* or to Stephen Colbert as Stephen Colbert on *The Colbert Report*, but often these characters were satirizing a bigger ideal. The distinction here is in how dominant this style has become among sketch comedians, through the queer- and female-dominated genre of front-facing camera comedy (the name for comedic monologues made directly on cell phones for social media), and how focused this generation is on satirizing how its targets perform themselves, in ways that can only be captured by . . . performing. It is surely the influence of growing up with and on social media. Instead of building characters from observing people socializing, they are observing how people present themselves online.

Though not stated as an explicit goal, many of these performances look like attempts to find truth beyond how people have been taught to perform truth, both in everyday life and onstage. This is best captured by the podcast *StraightioLab*. Hosted by the Brooklyn comedians Sam Taggart and George Civeris, it's not a podcast by two gay men about straight culture but instead a podcast about two gay men making a podcast about straight culture. In each episode they take a topic and dissect its straightness. Topics include the very literal and the very abstract, like "Pride," "Neil Patrick Harris," "Posting About Quitting Social Media," and "Being Gay with Your Friends." In an episode titled "Celebrating Love"—as in the social media cliché way of describing weddings that was born out of the social media cliché "love is love"—there is an exchange with the guest Pat Regan that I feel captures the perspective of this generation of comics.

> **PAT REGAN:** I think gay marriage has largely been a flop at the box office . . . It's kinda because it's been couched in this celebrating love. That's not what's appealing about it. In the way that the marketing campaign for [Billy Eichner's 2022 "first gay rom-com from a major studio"] *Bros* I think failed it because it focused exclusively on its importance and not on like what was fun about it. Which, to put it in gay marriage terms, what's fun about it is that it is so silly because it's two guys or girls getting married to each other.
>
> **GEORGE CIVERIS:** Right, it's inherently funny.
>
> **SAM TAGGART:** Yeah, doesn't matter the intent.
>
> **GEORGE CIVERIS:** "They should be different but they are the same."
>
> **PAT REGAN:** Yeah, you know what wasn't a box office flop? [Adam Sandler's 2007 movie where he pretended to be married to Kevin James] *I Now Pronounce You Chuck and Larry*, or whatever.
>
> **GEORGE CIVERIS:** I mean, you don't need to tell that to us!
>
> **SAM TAGGART:** We are leading the campaign to bring that film back.

On the podcast *Couples Therapy*, hosted by Naomi Ekperigin and Andy Beckerman, Civeris and Taggart were asked how they place themselves as performers reacting to the pure irony of the nineties and the pure sincerity of the Obama era. Civeris suggested the podcast had a "sincere irony."[32] He explained, "If I am being somehow ironic in my outlook on things, it doesn't come from a cynicism. If anything, it is reacting to a cynicism of a false sincerity." Burned by comedians who didn't back up the honesty of their presentation, a new class of comedy fans have embraced comedians who are honest about the fact that it is just a presentation. To their audiences, at least, this rings true.

In 2011, Bo Burnham was twenty, but he found himself chopping it up with four legends who prayed to the altar of truth in comedy—Marc Maron, Ray Romano, Judd Apatow, and Garry Shandling—on the Showtime show *The Green Room with Paul Provenza*. Swimming in a baggy gray V-neck T-shirt, the floppy-haired Burnham looked like a stretched-out eighth grader, all torso with toothpick extremities. He remained silent for minutes at a time. Throughout, Maron and Romano were playfully dismissive of him in a boys-being-boys way, but the tenor changed after Burnham asked Shandling how he reconciled stand-up, which Burnham feels is an inherently Western art form, with an Eastern philosophical perspective. Shandling, who at that point was semiretired from comedy, focusing instead on gaining a deeper understanding of Buddhism, explained that the real answer would take too much time, but in short, "authenticity." To him, it appeared the word meant being free of ego and free of fearing societal expectations. "When I saw you onstage," Shandling said to Burnham, "I didn't see a fake moment." A curious Provenza wondered how this could be, as Burnham performs with such ironic detachment that he doesn't reveal himself onstage. It's a good question, and Burnham would spend the next decade trying to figure out how to communicate his answer, revealing his take on the truth in comedy conundrum.

Unlike the path of his friends and occasional collaborators Berlant and Early, it was Bo Burnham's unprecedented internet success that forced him to wrestle with what truth means and what truthfulness looks like at a time when honesty is equated with being publicly revealing. In 2006, at sixteen, Burnham wanted to share the new songs he had written with his brother, who was away at college, so he posted them on YouTube. One of those songs went viral, getting over 250,000 listens in a day and putting him on a path to be one of the newish platform's first breakout stars. At seventeen, he put out an album on Comedy Central Records. Having deferred at NYU, by eighteen, he was developing a movie musical with Judd Apatow. At nineteen, he released his first special. Fans have always confused artists with their personas, but it can be disorienting when the artist is still at the age when they are trying to figure themselves out (see: every child star ever). This created a tension in Burnham that he's continued to find new and more complicated ways to explore with his work. Early on, it seemed he was trying to do a contemporary version of what Steve Martin did in the seventies—making fun of show business while being show business—but as he matured, his act felt like comedy's version of Bertolt Brecht's *Verfremdungseffekt*, translated as "alienation effect," "defamiliarization effect," "distancing effect," or "estrangement effect." The goal is to force the audience to approach the show intellectually by removing aspects of theater that create a false empathy.

For Brecht, this meant having actors break the fourth wall, stripped-down staging, bright lights, loud noises, and anything that might prevent the audience from thinking they are an observer of real events taking place. For stand-up, that means breaking down the conversation illusion.

"I want you to leave my show skeptical about performance," Burnham said in 2016, when his special *Make Happy* was released.[33] There are a few ways this statement can be taken. First is that Burnham is saying the audience should be skeptical of *the* performance, because an artist should not be trusted to be telling you the truth at any moment. Like, a third of the way through *Make Happy*, Burnham tells the audience he feels his shows are too planned and wants to get better at improvising. He then asks an audience member for his name. "Rob." "I'm gonna try to make up a song about Rob . . . off the top of my head." The prerecorded track starts. "Bo had sex with [*pause*]'s mom," allowing Burnham to say "Rob" in the pause. After the bit, Burnham is defiant: "I'm not honest for a second up here. Honesty's for the birds, baby. You want to see an honest comedian, go see the rest of them, all right? [*In a stand-up comedian voice*] 'This thing actually happened.' [*Sarcastically*] Cool." This moment feels like a critique of not just truth-telling comedians, like C.K., but the authenticity fetishization in how the history of stand-up is told. The hope is that by creating distrust with his performance, Burnham also can communicate a distrust of performers, broadly. Still, this was all building to his main point, which is to be skeptical of the social construct of performance.

That's because Bo Burnham, in 2013, in front of eight hundred people, at the Edinburgh Fringe Festival, had a panic attack onstage. Then they kept on happening. The issue was not the shows themselves. The issue was growing up performing, as he says in *Make Happy*, setting up the show's closer, "Can't Handle This." An homage to the Auto-Tuned rants Kanye West did on the *Yeezus* tour, the song first makes a joke about the triviality of West's and, by extension, any famous person's problems. He sings about the size of the Pringles can and Chipotle employees' inability to keep everything inside the burrito. But then the song breaks down. In close-up, almost looking right into the lens, he sings: "I can sit here and pretend / Like my biggest problems are Pringle cans / And burritos / The truth is my biggest problem's you." He holds out the "you," while the camera slowly pans over the audience, who, in contrast to stand-up specials' history of brightly lit smiling audiences, are shown as an ominous black mass. He continues:

> I wanna please you
> But I wanna stay true to myself
> I wanna give you the night out that you deserve
> But I wanna sing what I think and not care what you
> think about it

It's a perfect synthesis of everything he had been thinking about. And I know from conversations that it shook some comics to the skeleton. It's not the adversarial relationship as conceived by the club comedians of the past: Burnham reveals something conflicting about what the comedian and audience expect out of a show. He would later tell Pete Holmes on the *You Made It Weird* podcast that the show isn't meant to answer the question of what the artist and audience should do about "this really weird, dissociative thing [of] 'I'm supposed to be honest and vulnerable with you.'"[34]

All the skepticism he's trying to create, he explains, is "the show is trying to get to the point where I can be honest . . . Before I can be honest with you," he continues, "I have to be honest about how weird this is and then we can finally get to the honest part." Easier said than done, as "the show never gets to the honest part." Echoing Early's idea of the potential of failure, he says, "To fail to be honest is honest, much more than 'my father did this' and 'my mother did this.'" If the situation is inherently fake, the only way to tell the truth is by acknowledging its falseness.

With 2021's *Inside*, Burnham took this idea and blew it up into a virtuosic meditation on how to express yourself at a moment when the self is digitally fractured, and how to connect with people when you're forced to be socially distant. Shot in his guesthouse (must be nice), with equipment always in the frame and interstitials showing him setting up shots, it all felt overwhelmingly Brechtian. Contrasting the realism of his performance and the visual proof that it was clearly staged, over and over again in the special Burnham portrays how the internet has subverted the distinction between the real and the performed. And because it wasn't stand-up, which has a built-in barrier between performer and performed-to, Burnham was able to call into question the very nature of digital performance that we all are compelled to participate in.

And then . . . the funniest thing happened. I went on TikTok, and between videos of people befriending stray cats, I saw video after video of teens analyzing *Inside*, white women showing photos from their Instagram to prove Burnham nailed them in "White Woman's Instagram," and people of all ages lip-syncing "All Eyes on Me" as if the lyrics ("Are you feeling nervous? / Are you having fun? / It's almost over / It's just begun") were a conversation between the same person at the start and end of the pandemic. I was bewildered: How could a special so pointedly *against* online performance result in so much reverent online performance? It didn't make sense, until one day when I was scrolling, I heard my voice. Or at least I thought it was me. It sounded like me, off camera, faintly agreeing with Bo Burnham, as he is explaining the reason behind the panic attacks that inspired *Make Happy*. I scrolled more. Stray cats. Tips on cooking steak. "All Eyes on Me" lip sync. Me again. This time, I could clearly see it was me talking to Burnham at Vulture Festival in 2018. I confirmed this as I was shown another video of myself later that day. And another the next day. At one point the comedian Moses Storm sent me a message on TikTok: "If you even think about Bo Burnham while on here, the algorithm will send you 91 videos of you interviewing him."

It felt bad and weird. It made me uncomfortable. I felt compelled to reply to these videos, saying "This is me!" as a way of reconnecting myself with this image of me. Though I didn't like any of this, it did make me understand the reaction to *Inside* better. A lot of people had been feeling really bad, seeing how the isolation of the pandemic mirrored the self-imposed isolation of living online. The disassociation I was feeling in this moment was what a lot of people who grew up knowing only digital existence had been feeling their whole lives. As Burnham explained to me on TikTok, "Yourself is atomized into a thousand different versions of you that are watching each other and taking inventory of each other."[35] And it made me understand what Shandling saw in Burnham all those years ago. On *The Larry Sanders Show*, Shandling's influential nineties late-night-show send-up, the curtain that separated the front-of-stage and backstage was meant as a sort of allegory for the divide between, as Apatow would put it, "what people are trying to project versus what they're actually feeling."[36] *Inside* explores what happens when it's not clear which side of the curtain you're on anymore.

Inside isn't a live performance. There are multiple takes and camera setups over the course of many months. Still, *Inside* is the special of Burnham's that connects the most emotionally with people, not in spite of its being his most contrived, but because of it. *Inside* is actually anti-Brechtian. It posits that attempts to remove artifice are actually artifice, but one can attempt to create artifice genuinely. Unlike Brecht, Burnham doesn't want to create an experience that is only cerebral. In contrast, around the release of *Inside*, it became popular for comedians to include documentary footage in their specials, as if they were scientists offering mathematical proof. "See?" they'd say. "This proves that it's real." But how people behave in a documentary to a person like Burnham is also a performance, so to call it "true" feels false. *Inside* feels true, because it's honest about being manufactured.

Burnham, as I see it, is going after the ecstatic truth, an idea put forward by the filmmaker Werner Herzog, who is known for including fictional elements in his documentaries, like staging his subjects or having them perform scripted scenes. Out of a belief that facts are shallow, and rejecting cinema verité, Herzog is after an inner, deeper truth that "is mysterious and elusive and can be reached only through fabrication and imagination and stylization."[37] It is why Michelangelo slapped a big ol' noggin and large oven-mitt hands on his *David*, knowing the seventeen-foot-high sculpture would be looked at from below, understanding that exaggeration was necessary for it to register as realistic, if not more than realistic. Part of Burnham understands that stand-ups, also often seen from below, are doing this, too, so to shoot them as if it were otherwise might *feel* dishonest.

If he is always lying, isn't that just what Louis C.K. does? Well, no. C.K. played the part of an honest man to add weight to his comedy's falsities; Burnham uses the transparency of artifice to try to convey a deeper truth. *Inside* is not a literal depiction of what the pandemic was like for Burnham (he, for one, probably slept in his actual house), but a real attempt to capture what he wanted to communicate about it. People shouldn't take it literally and leave the special worried that he is a suicidal recluse now, but rather leave it worried for people generally who might've had a hard time during the pandemic. Opposed to the self-interest of C.K.'s "truth," Burnham offers a "truth" that can help the viewer better understand themselves. The goal for Burnham, like Shandling, is never their personal truth, but truth, period.

I have one last true story about the truth. In 2020 and 2021, I volunteered weekly with a mutual aid organization, delivering groceries to those homebound during the height of the coronavirus pandemic. One day, waiting for the bags of food to arrive, we were talking about what we all do for a living. When asked, I'd do my usual spiel: writer, comedy writer, no, like a journalist, interviews mostly, yes, I've met John Mulaney. "I think my son should do stand-up, he's so funny," a nice woman in her early fifties exclaimed, thinking I'd be able to help . . . convince him, I guess. "He should,"

I said, in the spirit of giving. "He won't," she replied. "He's too afraid." I said that is common. "No, like he's traumatized." "Hmm?" "Eight years ago, when he was a teenager, he watched a woman performing stand-up on Comedy Central and the set went so poorly, she ran off the stage. So, now he's terribly afraid of bombing." I laughed, which in retrospect, was rude. I knew exactly what she was talking about.

For weeks leading up to her 2013 special, *Live at the Fillmore*, Kristen Schaal kept on posting on social media and talking in interviews about how poorly the taping went. What Schaal was referring to was that about halfway through the set, the show starts falling apart. She pulls an eyeball out of her pocket and says it's her "lazy eye" that doesn't do anything but "sits around all day." After it doesn't go over well, she grows mournful; she says it was her grandma's favorite joke and she wished the joke would've gone over better because "it's not like she can come back from the dead and punch it up." The room is silent as she tries to start her next joke, but that goes even worse. Schaal begins to look around for water because her mouth is dry. The camera cuts away to a confused audience as they look around at each other. Schaal leaves the stage. Her friend and occasional comedy partner Kurt Braunohler comes out and says Schaal was just getting water and reintroduces her, but she doesn't come out. More cutaways to a confused audience. She eventually comes back with note cards and explains that her "surreal brand of whimsy" is not as popular nowadays as "autobiographical humor, like Louis C.K. or Michael Richards." After telling some more adult jokes, a little kid in the audience STARTS TO HECKLE. And now this little girl comes walking up to the stage. She takes the mic to show Schaal how it's done. "I might be little, but you know what they say, little girls are made of sugar and spice and everything nice," starts one of her jokes. "Guess when they get to *your* age they're just filled up with bitter corn whiskey." She adds a fist pump and exclaims, "Bam! Joke sold!" Completely in shambles now, Schaal's last resort is to introduce her special guest—her "dancing, charming, disarming horse!" Only to learn the horse decided he's dropping out of showbiz, causing Schaal to absolutely lose it. She soon abandons the stage, saddened.

Watching it the first time, it was obviously a goof, but part of me nagged, *What if this is real? It can't be! But what if!?* By the time it gets to the closing bit, in which Schaal agrees to take on the role of the horse, galloping in a circle while Braunohler screams, "Kristen Schaal is a horse! Kristen Schaal is a horse! Kristen Schaal is a horse! Kristen Schaal is a horse!" over and over, I was sure it wasn't real. But it totally was. This really did happen. Yes, it is weird, surprising, fascinating for a special to go wrong unintentionally, but it is also weird, surprising, fascinating for a special to go wrong on purpose.

The result is a genuine articulation of the fear of putting yourself out there—knowing a bit can go wrong, knowing the audience might not understand—that can be captured only by actually putting yourself out there, knowing a bit can go wrong, knowing the audience might not understand. Moreover, it captured the tension Schaal felt being a stand-up comedian at all. Starting out in both comedy and performance art spaces, she'd experienced successes but also found herself feeling out of place. One example that stuck with her came early on in New York, when she performed for *Late Night with Conan O'Brien* talent scouts. "I came after people doing real stand-up, like, 'So I got divorced' . . . They were telling jokes as themselves and people were there and they understood the agreement [of what a comedy show was like]," she'd tell me years later.[38] "I went up with this [character] who wasn't speaking English [acting out movies like *Star Wars* and *Jaws* without words] and people couldn't handle it. They were just like, 'No.'" She doesn't confess this feeling of fearing rejection to the audience, but she does convey it. *Live at the Fillmore* uses the excitement of a stand-up going wrong to question if maybe there is something wrong with stand-up.

"You mean Kristen Schaal?" I asked, back in 2021. "Yes!" "That was all on purpose." "Really!?" "Yes, I've talked to her about this stuff. It was a silly idea she had." "I can't wait to tell my son!" she said.

The next Saturday, I was pumped. Rarely does having inside information about an obscure stand-up special from nearly a decade ago have the potential of changing a person's life. "He doesn't believe you," she said. "Did you tell him I've spoken to the comedian?" "Yeah." "And still?" "He thinks it was real." "But it's not." "It was to him." And that was it. We never spoke about comedy again. Arguably, no artist is creating work just to provide the audience with the facts and figures of their life; they are hoping to do the impossible by trying to make the audience really feel how their reality really feels. That includes comedians, even if it might appear they are simply reciting information. In this case, Kristen Schaal succeeded.

Now, what if I made this story up? Wouldn't it be fun? Or funny? I didn't, but what if!? Did I? No. But if I did! Would it be more or less effective? I didn't . . . It's true. Essentially. Hopefully.

7

LAUGHTER

It's 1839. You're the revered French realist historical painter Paul Delaroche, and you're working on *The Hémicycle*, the twenty-seven-meter-long panoramic depiction of famous artists chilling with each other that would become your masterpiece. One day, someone stops by to show you a photograph. It is your first time ever looking at one. Sacrebleu! There you are looking at daguerreotypes of people's gray, sooty, sullen faces, and what do you say?

"As from today, painting is dead!"

It wasn't.

But painting's role in culture had changed. Rather quickly, society no longer needed painting for representing reality. Photographs were easier and eventually cheaper to produce. Also, they were steal-your-soul accurate. Movies took this a step further, able to capture life in motion. This is the predicament described by the art critic and philosophy professor Arthur Danto's concept "the end of art."[1] No longer trapped in art's primary value system, artists soon worked to determine what even makes something art in the first place. Movements throughout the modern and postmodern eras offered their perspectives, from the Impressionists to Andy Warhol faithfully re-creating a Brillo box. Writing about what he witnessed in the sixties, Danto was not saying that art was over, just that how it's evaluated must evolve. Looking back on his own assessment decades later, Danto wrote, "Whatever art is, it is no longer something primarily to be looked at. Stared at, perhaps, but not primarily looked at."[2] Like how this book is trying to foster a deeper way of watching comedy, Danto was celebrating art that beyond being aesthetically appealing would be intellectually engrossing. For artists who embraced the freedom to experiment, the invention of photography was considered a good thing. Like Renoir, one of the Impressionist painters who indirectly benefited from this new technology. He's quoted as saying, "Photography freed painting from a lot of tiresome chores, starting with family portraits." With the invention of the photograph, artists were free to explore what being an artist could mean.

Well, welcome to the End of Comedy. Our photography was the launch of YouTube. It's not just YouTube, but YouTube was the video-content-on-demand tipping point. Soon after came Twitter and the iPhone and Facebook videos, and Snapchat and Instagram and TikTok. It's a cliché to say things on the internet are at your fingertips, but, come on, laughs are literally at your fingertips. And there are algorithms that can sense what makes you laugh and then feeds you whatever that is over and over. The idea of going to a *place* to laugh sounds downright antiquated. "Maw! Paw! I'm going down to the ol' Comedy Store, to precure me some giggles!"

"[People] don't seek [comedy] out because they need

funny content," Hannah Gadsby explained to me in the summer of 2020.[3] "That's everywhere. [Everybody's] funny on the internet." It is a point echoed by Jerrod Carmichael, who told Marc Maron on *WTF* that the internet was swallowing up the comedian.[4] The other by-product of the camera in the 1800s was that it democratized art; in the same way, so have digital technologies. It's not just an updating of the joke as folk tradition; social media has made it easier for nonprofessionals to create and distribute original, authored, performed comedy. Great! Good on 'em! Because, as Gadsby told me, "It's freed up the art form from providing this one particular service." And as with painters and the photograph, comedians are now free to explore every version of what being a comedian can mean.

This is the post-comedy era. It was an idea that I introduced in 2018 in a piece entitled "How Funny Does Comedy Need to Be?"[5] "Post-comedy uses the elements of comedy (be it stand-up, sitcom, or film)," I wrote at the time, "but without the goal of creating the traditional comedic result—laughter." If I could, I would swap the words "the goal of creating" with "the only goal being to create." None of the work that I was referring to in that piece is completely free of laughter, but there has been an evolution of goals. An evolution in how comedy and comedians are valued.

For as long as there have been comedians, if the audience was laughing, they were doing their job. But hear me out: What if the audience doesn't laugh? What if the goal is for them not to laugh? Can it still be comedy? Not to spoil this chapter, but yes. Frankly, if it's not accepted that there is comedy beyond this one function, comedy will not be able to progress as an art form, or be an art form at all. This is it. This is the moment when comedy either expands its criteria for success beyond laughter or it dies. The good news is that there are already comedians in this mode who have achieved great critical and commercial success. The bad news is that many other comedians responded to these successes by saying they aren't actually comedy. Let's settle the debate.

"When did comedies become thirty-minute dramas?" was a joke from the 2016 second season of Julie Klausner's big-jokes sitcom *Difficult People*. I laughed when I first heard it. However, I don't know if "when" is the right question. Because the answer is sort of obvious—the early 2010s. *Louie*, then *Girls*, then *Transparent*, then KABLOOM! "Why" is the question.

Part of the shift was the rejection of the sound of laughter. Specifically, the laughter of strangers at TV tapings or, God forbid, canned laughter from TV tapings gone by. "There was a sense of generational disgust with the multicam sitcom of the nineties," Kathryn VanArendonk, my colleague at *Vulture* and a scholar of television forms, posited to me. "Even for people who loved those shows, they became synonymous with emptiness and shallowness, in the way the sitcom very much was not in the seventies and early eighties." In the early 2000s, this led to a rise of two comedy formats. There was the single-camera comedy, like *30 Rock* and *Happy Endings*, which used this switch to squeeze more jokes in, aspiring to a joke density previously only seen in animation. And the mockumentary sitcom, like *The Office* and *Modern Family*, where there was a "shift from punch line and toward cringe." But the big change came, according to VanArendonk, with streaming and "the simultaneous influence of cable dramas and prestige aesthetics, which took that shift and then exploded it to the point of total generic ambiguity." They are comedies that make you think, *Is this a comedy?*

If you are still confused (and that is your right), here is a quick list of shows I came up with to orient you: *Atlanta, Search Party, Insecure, Fleabag, Better Things, BoJack Horseman, Ramy, Russian Doll, Reservation Dogs, Mo, Catastrophe, Life & Beth, Somebody Somewhere, Swarm, Master of None, Baskets, Barry, Beef,* and *The Bear.*

None of these shows are dramas. I wouldn't even call them "comedy in theory," as the critic Matt Zoller Seitz wrote in 2016. They are comedies in practice, but with fewer formal expectations. Often people will just call them dramedies, but few of these shows are simply lightly funny dramas, as they are just as likely to borrow from genres like thrillers or mystery. Premiering in 2016, Donald Glover's Afrosurrealist *Atlanta* helped pioneer genre ambiguity in sitcoms. Many episodes resemble straight-up horror, if not TV versions of the Theater of the Absurd or Comedy of Menace, with protagonists interacting with unusual characters like a Black Justin Bieber or Katt Williams playing a man who keeps an alligator in his bathroom in a way that is sort of funny, but with a lingering sense of disquieting uncertainty. "First and foremost, it's a comedy," Stephen Glover, the *Atlanta* writer and executive producer, explained upon the release of the show's final season in late 2022, before adding, "The thing I've realized from doing four seasons of *Atlanta* is stuff I think is funny, some people might be like, 'That's terrifying.' Or, 'That's very sad.'"[6] Unlike a traditional sitcom, which might have to figure out how to make the show 100 percent funny, *Atlanta* and shows like it are free to see if they can make the funny and terrifying and very sad exist all at the same time.

These shows tend to have distinct visual styles and foreground difficult ideas or subjects, but the most significant distinction to VanArendonk is how "this particular generation of comedic TV has little interest in that outlet for relief." It is taking on the meaning of "situation" in "situation comedy." Where in the past "situation" meant a predicament and a comedy of "familiar, everyday circumstances," as VanArendonk explained, "in some ways the current wave of TV comedies actually *are* situational comedies, where the entire experience of registering humor comes from latent background feeling that life is funny, not from a structured punch line." More than situation comedies, they are state comedies. State, not like "of America" but like a state of being—the characters' condition, their disposition, their lot in life. While the first season of *Russian Doll* gets some laughs out of its main character's time loop *situation*, the larger comedic tone, which carries the show through even its flashbacks to the trauma caused by living with a dangerously erratic mother, is the *state* her life is in after spending thirty-six years living with a death wish. This is not to say the approach to storytelling of *Russian Doll* and shows like it is better than a traditional sitcom, but instead that they are offering a new, more expansive take on the elements associated with the genre.

The comedy of these shows is a tone. It's a vibe. The fact that they activate the state of play makes them comedies, but they then hold you there, instead of using play to generate laughter. These shows are asking you to trust the comedic situation to mean it is a comedy without there being laughs, *the* traditional way comedies proved they were doing their job in the past. If you do laugh, it's not like a big sitcom laugh from a big sitcom joke. It's often not at any one gag, but a big exhale after a buildup of too much bewilderment and mirth.

Whatever you call these shows, their popularity and critical acclaim has echoed through all of comedy. Since the post-comedy boom, it's become much harder to get big-joke comedies on the air, which has altered the goals many comedians had for the types of work they wanted to make. And it has created a market for this type of comedy in other forms. I am referring to stand-up comedy, in which the act of forgoing laughs is more noticeable, radical, and controversial.

Let's talk about *Nanette*!

In 2016, after a lifetime of searching, Hannah Gadsby finally got a diagnosis that stuck—autism spectrum disorder. And with it, they realized they needed a break. Their touring schedule was taking too much out of them. The expectation of their audience was too daunting. They needed to "quit comedy." At first this meant quitting how they approached their comedy career, but, as they worked on the show that would become *Nanette*, it developed to mean quitting the form's conventions. They wanted to change their comedy; instead, they changed comedy. If I may, I would like to tell you how.

Underneath the fury and the heartbreak of *Nanette* was a deceptively simple, elegantly composed piece of stand-up comedy. A visual thinker, Gadsby would later tell me they saw the show before there were any words.[7] With *Nanette*, they pictured a series of callbacks, interlocking like an action hero holding on to the ankles of another who's holding on to a ladder attached to a helicopter (my metaphor, not theirs). "A callback is, of course, when you pepper a little joke up top and then later on when you keep referring to it, it gets funnier and funnier," they explained. "Out of context, it's not necessarily funny. It's just building a language with an audience. With *Nanette* I did that, but instead of making the callback funnier, I made it devastating." As they called it, a "gay comic 101" joke early in the special—about a drunk threatening them for hitting on his girlfriend, only to stop when his girlfriend says, "It's a girl!"—later reveals itself to be a traumatic event they hid from the audience. Though it appears in the moment that Gadsby has abandoned comedy, the reason the audience feels safe enough to hear the brutality of their experience is that it is told to them through a traditional stand-up structure.

In the special, Gadsby blames jokes for having only a beginning and a middle—no end. "I froze an incredibly formative experience at its trauma point and I sealed it off into jokes," they tell the audience. "And that story became a routine, and through repetition, that joke version fused with my actual memory of what happened. But, unfortunately, that joke version was not nearly sophisticated enough to help me undo the damage done to me in reality. Punch lines need trauma because punch lines . . . need tension, and tension feeds trauma." But this doesn't mean *Nanette* doesn't have jokes. It has a ton, particularly at the top of the show. That was by design, as Gadsby wanted to give the audience the thing before taking it away. But it's not as if at any point *Nanette* stops being funny. The audience members just stop laughing when Gadsby needs them to, when the show ceases being about the immediate release. Regardless of passages of the special that are quite serious, as a whole, conceptually, *Nanette* is very funny. There is a fundamental, knowing, ridiculous irony to quitting comedy by way of doing comedy. This juxtaposition is not laugh-out-loud funny, like the first portion of the show, but think-about-it-later-smile-and-go-"huh"-to-yourself funny. You might've already left the show when the irony hits you, so you're not going to make the laugh noise, but it tickles the same part of the brain as when you do.

Gadsby could've done an hour of laughs, as they proved with their next special, 2020's *Douglas*, but they withheld them in *Nanette* because they wanted to withhold the relief that many people come to comedy for. This was the work of a very intentional and capable comedian. To entertain people for an hour as a comedian without laughter is difficult and demanded someone with Gadsby's skill as a storyteller and thoughtfulness when it comes to constructing shows. There are plenty of unfunny one-person shows being performed at black box theaters across the world, but Gadsby was deliberate about doing *Nanette* at a comedy festival, where its ideas would be most challenging. "I broke the contract," they'd later say, referring to the fundamental comedian-audience transaction of comedian says something to make the audience laugh and the audience laughs.[8] "I betrayed people's trust and I did that really seriously, not just for effect." This aspect of *Nanette* is what I found most challenging the first time I saw it, at New York's SoHo Playhouse, nearly a year after the special was filmed and months before it would be released on Netflix. I admired the show, but part of me resisted its abandoning of stand-up fundamentals. My thinking was that Gadsby's story and message were compelling, important, and provocative, but *couldn't they have integrated it more into traditional stand-up?* After it premiered on Netflix and garnered the response it did, I got it—if *Nanette* were "better," it would've been worse. Meaning if *Nanette* had better adhered to the value systems of a stand-up comedy special, it would be less impactful. *Nanette* is punk. Gadsby demands your attention by withholding much of the enjoyable distraction of a good stand-up set. It's rare for stand-up to show and not just tell, as it is an art form where the artist is directly addressing the audience, but this is what is so brilliant about *Nanette*'s construction. Gadsby didn't just do an hour of jokes about quitting comedy—they found a way for the audience to feel what happens when comedy is removed.

And by not offering the audience relief, they demand that the audience take responsibility for doing the work of processing. This has always been the facet of *Nanette* that stuck out to me because of how unusual my first time seeing it was. As I've said, the show starts with lots of laughs, but slowly gets closer and closer to the truth, before finally building to a powerful revelation of hurt. At the end, Gadsby offers a big, closing message, which is meant to be a sort of a guide for the next steps for them as well as the audience and comedy itself. And in the middle of this section, when everyone is most connected, a woman in the second row got up and left. Maybe she was overwhelmed or triggered or maybe she had to pee really badly. "Sorry. Thank you," she told a gobsmacked Gadsby. Gadsby froze for a moment. Unlike in the special, at this show they were defiant. I don't remember their exact words, but the tenor was "I gave you my story, what the fuck are you going to do about it now?" Earlier in the run, this was how the show would end, as the show as a whole was combative, but as Gadsby worked on it, and filmed it, it became much more about taking care of each other's stories. Though tonally different, both the ending I saw and the ending of the special aren't an answer, but a call to action. Gadsby sacrificed themself (rhetorically, as they kept on working), and they motivated masses to spread their message. I do think this is part of the secret of the special's incredible popularity. Also, you don't get many comedy specials that appeal to both comedy fans and people who hate stand-up.

And the popularity, with Gadsby's social media following growing sixfold after *Nanette* went up on Netflix, is a distinction. Of course, there have been intimate one-person shows and comedians who critiqued comedy in their work before, but *Nanette* became an international lightning rod in a way no hour of stand-up ever had. It's the most revolutionary piece of stand-up of my lifetime. Comedy and comedians changed directly as a result. Beyond the direct inspiration and the expansion of what counts as comedy, the nature of show business is such that if something is a huge hit, it leads to other projects in the same vein getting made. And it all self-perpetuates, as the supply of people working this way meets a sudden demand from the industry.

Gadsby does not take credit for any of this. "Artists don't invent the zeitgeist! They respond to it," as they say in *Nanette*. In the fall of 2017, *The New York Times* and *The New Yorker* released reports of Harvey Weinstein's history of sexual assault and predatory behavior. In response, Alyssa Milano shared her own experience with Weinstein and encouraged people who were survivors of sexual harassment or assault to share their stories with the tag "me too," a phrase created in 2006 by the activist Tarana Burke to encourage empathy for sexually abused women of color, and a movement was started that would quickly spread across industries and countries. This included comedy. For years prior, women in comedy were asked what it was like being a woman in comedy, but often you could tell that the person asking the question didn't want the whole truth, but instead some version of "hard, but worth it." After the *Times* released its report on Louis C.K.'s history of sexual misconduct, finally there was a more welcoming space for the whole truth of how men in comedy take advantage of their relative power. Though Gadsby doesn't say the phrase "me too" in *Nanette*, its spirit is in their work. Take this section:

> Do you know what should be the target of our jokes at the moment? Our obsession with reputation. We're obsessed. We think reputation is more important than anything else, including humanity. And do you know who takes the mantle of this myopic adulation of reputation? Celebrities. And comedians are not immune. They're all cut from the same cloth. Donald Trump, Pablo Picasso, Harvey Weinstein, Bill Cosby, Woody Allen, Roman Polanski. These men are not exceptions, they are the rule. And they are not individuals, they are our stories. And the moral of our story is, "We don't give a shit. We don't give a fuck . . . about women or children. We only care about a man's reputation." What about his humanity? These men control our stories! And yet they have a diminishing connection to their own humanity, and we don't seem to mind so long as they get to hold on to their precious reputation. Fuck reputation. Hindsight is a gift. Stop wasting my time!

The audience isn't cracking up, but the rhythms still sound like stand-up and maintain comedy's ability to give its audience ammunition for difficult conversations.

Of course, a lot of great work was made in the wake of the MeToo movement. *Nanette* was *Nanette* because of creative decisions Gadsby made. Namely, the willingness to withhold some laughs. Catharsis can feel hollow to an audience when easy relief from your state isn't really possible, so by forgoing laughs, Gadsby gave a portion of their audience what they were looking for—the feeling of being understood. Through an accidental by-product of their own shifting relationship to comedy, Gadbsy tapped into an international shift in what audiences wanted from comedians, and it wasn't just laughs.

Nothing against laughing. I love to laugh. Your hahahas. Your little hehehes. Your hohohos. Oh, wait, no, that's Santa Claus. But you get it. It is nice to hear laughter. Sometimes someone at a comedy show has a cute, distinct laugh and all the comedians can't shut up about it. Love that. But it is a limited criterion through which to consider an art form. It is particularly limited when you take the art form and film it, introducing myriad options for sound design and visual storytelling. Although for decades, the stand-up special, prioritizing laughs, was shot as straightforwardly as possible, there is a new class of comedians looking to reshape the priorities, push the boundaries of the form, and make the special special.

"What the Hell Happened at Jerrod Carmichael's HBO Taping?" read a headline on the comedy news website *The Interrobang* in December 2016.[9] I was surprised. First, I didn't even know Carmichael had a new special in the works. Second, by the time a comedian films a special, the thing is bulletproof. Especially a comedian of Carmichael's caliber. I'd seen him live and found him uncommonly present, giving off an easy demeanor that stood out from a lineup of comics shouting for our attention. And yet "jerrod carmichael's hbo special taping was like watching two trains collide . . . you just kind of watch hopelessly," wrote one attendee on Twitter.[10]

The next day, *The Interrobang* released a dispatch from the show from Jeffrey Gurian.[11] Gurian, a dentist in his sixties who moonlights as a stand-up and comedy journalist, called it "the strangest, most unusual performance I've ever seen." Gurian described Carmichael "openly wondering where he should start, complete with prolonged silences, which occurred several times during the course of his performance." Gurian complained about the lengthy winter wait outside to get in, how Carmichael went way over time, and how he spoke softly to the point of inaudibility. The most unusual aspect of the show was that Carmichael kept on repeating the same jokes over and over again, getting worse and more confused reactions each time. After specials come out, most stand-ups drop the material, because audiences grow tired of jokes they've heard before, and yet here Carmichael was repeating material from his special while recording it.

And then in March 2017, the special came out. Named *8*, and directed by Burnham, it was something else. By that point in my life, I might've watched three hundred stand-up specials, give or take fifty, and this undeniably looked and sounded and felt different. Together, Burnham and Carmichael were able to create a feeling of intimacy through a use of loving close-ups and thoughtful silences. While in *Make Happy* Burnham redid parts of his set without the audience present to get shots he couldn't get otherwise, with *8*, he and Carmichael took it a step further. Instead of removing the audience, they manipulated them to help establish their desired tone. All of those things Gurian complained about—the awkwardness, the quietness, the silences—were used to great effect. With HBO's *Crashing* and the film *Funny People*, Judd Apatow figured out the best way to make a great comedian seem like they're a struggling upstart is to have them perform the jokes over and over until the audience's performed response evaporates and all that's left is discomfort. Where Apatow was trying to capture the feeling of struggling, Carmichael and Burnham were trying to remove the feeling of control stand-ups often use to milk laughter. It is the stand-up version of what was happening in the post-comedy TV shows at the time, with Carmichael and Burnham creating a feeling of uncertainty.

Throughout *8*, as Carmichael sets up jokes, the camera is in tight close-up, panning around his head, as if it's an examination, echoing Carmichael's own inward focus. "I want to be a better Black person. I don't know how to be," he says, searching. Capturing post-2016-election feelings of existential dread and dissolution, Carmichael looks down, as if he's trying to find the words, but all he can find is hopeless and shameful apathy. Looking up, he doesn't offer the audience the relief of certainty. "I really don't." The silence is broken by a sneeze. Carmichael says, "God bless you," and the audience laughs, appreciating the feeling of being acknowledged. "I don't want to be a court jester to you for an hour," Carmichael said when *8* was released.[12] "That's not why I got into it." "My job is to articulate my point," he said in another interview around that time.[13] "Hopefully you laugh at the end or at least feel something." By that measure, though unusual for a comedy special, *8* was a success because it made people feel . . . bad. For Carmichael, like Burnham, *that* is more genuine. You might come to a comedian for answers, but certainty is not a realistic expectation. Months after the election of Donald Trump, it was more honest to not know. Tremendously influential on the aesthetics of specials in the years that followed, as well as a bit of a legend (legend count #8) because of how badly the taping went, *8* rejects the stand-up special as a transaction with the audience. Instead it argues that it is a collaboration with them, even if the people in the audience are unaware of their contribution.

Then, in 2018, Carmichael, taking a break from stand-up and focusing on directing, experimented with removing the audience altogether. For a special entitled *Drew Michael*, Carmichael shot the comedian Drew Michael on an empty set, with glowy, hip-hop music video lighting and no audience. "This May Be the Most Polarizing Comedy Special of the Year," read the *New York Times* headline.[14] Because even after *Nanette*, it was still shocking to watch a stand-up on TV without hearing the sound of laughter at all. Carmichael, however, thought it made sense for Michael and his act. Experiencing hearing loss at a very young age, but not getting hearing aids until his early twenties, Michael has a very different relationship to the audience's feedback than most comedians.[15]

Michael's ambivalence toward audience feedback would only be intensified when, a few years into his stand-up career, Michael saw a stand-up he opened for destroy the audience in a way he had never seen before, doing some of the worst, hackiest comedy imaginable. "*I don't even want these laughs*," Michael remembered thinking while watching the set, he'd later tell me.[16] "*Okay, laughter isn't the metric, because I have seen shit that I think is terrible murder.*" These two experiences resulted in Michael's developing an inward-directed performance style that Carmichael felt would be best captured with him alone talking to the camera. At its best, the lack of laughter both heightened the feeling of intimacy and helped convey the self-centered, masturbatory nature of stand-up that Michael was hoping to condemn in the special. While Michael would acknowledge it didn't always work, as there was some disconnect between the concept and the material, he was proud to participate in such a gutsy attempt at showcasing stand-up in a different way. And in the years since, Michael has found other ways to experiment, directing his own work and doing things like closing a special, 2021's *Red Blue Green*, by reading a seven-minute version of a "Why did the chicken cross the road?" joke that plays more like a dramatic monologue, where instead of laughter, you hear a bittersweet musical score.

When Carmichael returned to stand-up in early 2022, he used many of the same techniques he learned in *8* and *Drew Michael*, but now with the hope of celebrating the audience-comedian relationship. Also directed by Burnham, *Rothaniel* is a revelation. It is revealing. The headlines were that Carmichael came out as gay, which he did. It's not a bait and switch, but it is clear Carmichael was not motivated just to tell people who he sleeps with as much as to capture the feeling of coming out when part of you doesn't want to. As Carmichael later joked on *WTF*, the synopsis of it could be "Man who's afraid of heights jumps out of an airplane on HBO."[17]

Rothaniel was shot in a small Greenwich Village jazz club, with Carmichael sitting down, wearing a baggy red polo that left his neck exposed. The special gracefully flows between three acts, in a structure that has similarities with *Nanette*, in how he starts with the laughs before taking them away. The first twenty minutes are a hilarious, *One Hundred Years of Solitude*–esque summary of the history of infidelity by men in his family—his father, in particular. "My father . . . had me and my brother, with my mom, aaaand I know he had four kids with a bitch named Vernita," goes one joke. "It's not that I hate her name. It's just that it sounds like a villain in a Tyler Perry movie." The telling of those secrets leads Carmichael to confront his own. The pace slows, as he lets the reactions of his friends and community speak for themselves, be they fully supportive or begrudgingly supportive. Next thing you know, ten minutes have passed and no one has laughed. Almost akin to the sort of free-associative therapy sessions he had been taking part in since his last special, the first two-thirds are a performance of what he is feeling in a way that makes him and the listener comfortable, before he gets to the genuinely challenging part—his mom's inability to accept his sexuality. This is not structured like a story. There are no jokes. He's just there. As is the audience, so they start asking him questions like "Do you think without your mom's approval you'll be okay?" and "You think a lot of the guilt is your dad's guilt?" Again, there's uncertainty. Again, this moment that feels genuine to the viewer at home was manipulated by the filmmakers. Based on conversations I had with people who went to tapings of the set, of which there were four, some believe Burnham edited together genuine audience questions that happened in the moment with questions from Q&As they did at some of the shows. By this point, Carmichael and Burnham know uncertain truth can play realer than unquestioned authenticity. They were also trying to re-create the organically conversational shows Carmichael had performed leading up to the taping, which would demand certain manipulations because audience members tend to be on their best behavior at special tapings and might be less likely to speak up unprompted. Essentially, the goal was to capture visually what Notaro described in chapter 6: an artist needing help, abandoned by some of their support systems, and the graciousness of the collective in offering encouragement. This was only possible because Carmichael was not always searching for a laugh, to let either him or the audience off the hook.

Though *8* and *Rothaniel* are tonally as radically different as two specials can be, they are similar in that the focus of the performance was on the finished product, the special. The goal, for Carmichael and Burnham, is to make specials that are works of art in and of themselves, and not simply documents of a tour that just finished. *Rothaniel* came together in months, starting with Carmichael having an idea and wanting to capture how it felt before it was formed. Instead of building an hour, minute by minute, and filming whatever you got after a couple years, Carmichael, along with Burnham, is set on flipping the order of things, conceiving of the *idea* of the special first and then using live shows as essentially preproduction. Instead of prioritizing the audience in front of them, they're trying to maximize the emotional impact of the filmed piece, through performance and visual storytelling. Specials like these will change how stand-ups approach their work, and already have, but the change will happen slowly.

When Carmichael was on *WTF*, Marc Maron was warm but grumpy. He was Marc Maron. It was sort of the same way he was when Drew Michael was on. Maron said that "as a comic," when he watched *Rothaniel*, his reaction was, "He hasn't really worked his shit out yet,"[18] as in the material wasn't ready, not that Carmichael wasn't. Maron also wished the show had a closer. Carmichael responded that he didn't want to give the audience one just because it is what is expected of comedy. "The resolution of the special is the lack of relief," he explained, because that was the truth of the story he was telling. Maron understood, somewhat. Frustrated by some of the discourse around the special, Carmichael explained that part of him feels that if not giving people relief and laughs means it is not comedy, then fine. Just call it something else. But then he remembers he is doing all this because he loves stand-up. "My true intention is to expand the art form," he told Maron. "I don't want to see it die." He added, "I don't think comedians know that they are dead. These are ghosts." For Carmichael, salvation comes from breaking down and rebuilding the audience-comedian relationship in service of a more dynamic finished product. For comedians, this means embracing that they are free of needing to perform whatever their version of Renoir's family portrait is. They are free to make art. And, for the audience, it demands they not expect a family portrait from comedians, but look at what they're making as art, and embrace the opportunity to experiment in new styles of play.

Is this comedy? That's the question I found myself being asked more and more since 2017. People would say to me that *The Bear*, FX's pressure-cooker depiction of an ascendant Chicago beef sandwich joint, was too stressful to be a comedy. And *Rothaniel* is more of a one-person show. *Nanette*, of course, is a TED Talk. It's a critique levied at much of the comedy I've been talking about in this chapter. And it was at the core of the critique of my original post-comedy piece. While most comedians just laughed off the pretentiousness and a few were complimentary, some reacted very negatively. Before he was disgraced for allegedly courting and grooming teenage girls (though he kept touring), Chris D'Elia took a screenshot of the headline, "How Funny Does Comedy Need to Be?" and tweeted "Lmaooooooooooooo wut."[19] Joe Rogan, with an editor's eye for concision, tweeted "LOL WUT."[20] Bert Kreischer ragged on it on the *Bonfire* podcast, with hosts Big Jay Oakerson and Dan Soder. (As alluded to in chapter 6, this is the exchange I ended up asking/confronting Kreischer about.) "To say comedy doesn't need to be funny," started Soder, "so it doesn't have to be the thing that it is?"[21]

It is an argument I didn't understand until years later, when I saw a chair made of fabric pinned to the wall of Denmark's Designmuseum, hanging there all floppily. Obviously "a chair," but one that couldn't be sat in, it was a comment on the very idea of functional art, the name for art that has a definitive utilitarian purpose. This refers to things like furniture, but could comedy be thought of as a functional art? Obviously, all popular arts, and fine arts, have some sort of use, be it to entertain or inspire or distract or provoke thought. The range of uses historically available to other art forms is broad. Comedy's aim, however, for so much of its history, has been to fulfill the audience's acute need—laughter—meaning all other functions were secondary. This is why so many people, on both sides of the microphone, have had such a hard time accepting this post-comedy moment. For most comedians, making people laugh is the reason they exist, so to suggest comedy doesn't need laughter is an existential threat. For a lot of audience members, laughter is why they are drawn to comedy at all. It's like if you come home after a hard day at work, needing to rest your weary bones, and your only chair is made entirely out of fabric and pinned to the wall. When I told my comedian friend J. F. Harris this idea, he joked that, just like a chair that doesn't fulfill its function, comedy that doesn't fulfill its supposed function is uncomfortable.

Something similar happened with architecture in the latter half of the twentieth century, with the postfunctionalists like Peter Eisenman, who pushed back on the "form follows function" ethos. Eisenman only cared about how his constructions (the few that were built) worked aesthetically, without regard for buildability or, even more, livability. The architecture scholar Andrew Ballantyne wrote that Eisenman "[enhanced] the reputation of his building by letting it be known that it was hostile to humanity."[22] Meaning he asserted the art of building over its usefulness. The function, beyond personal expression, is not to the people, but to the art. None of the comedy makers I've written about are anywhere near as anti-humanist as Eisenman, as, at the end of the day, they are all partly motivated to connect with their audience more honestly. That said, they are similarly unwilling to provide certain services that people assume they'd provide as comedy makers, with the goal of expanding what counts as comedy. Though you cannot sit in the chair pinned to the wall, anyone who sees it still thinks *chair*. And while, truly, no one would ever suggest all chairs be pinned to walls, it does expand how one thinks of them.

The point is that it is outside the norm. The point is questioning what comedy is. It is avant-garde and conceptual and unusual and possibly off-putting, but it is still comedy. It is comedy that asserts that comedy is an art form, period.

I am arguing that comedy doesn't need to make people laugh. When you rewatch your favorite episode of your sitcom for the seventeenth time, you are likely not going to laugh, as you've heard all the jokes before. Then why rewatch? Because you are experiencing comedy, even if you are not laughing. Just as a scary movie doesn't demand you scream nonstop or at all to feel scared. Comedy is not the art of making people laugh—that is the craft. Comedy is the art of manipulating funny; funny is that which generates mirth. This can be a comic working their ass off until everyone is crying with laughter or it can mean giving the audience the funny only to take it away as a point of narrative contrast. It can be an intense TV show where there are no laugh lines, if there is a feeling of mirth. I am not contradicting what I wrote in chapter 3 advocating for the value of funniness. Post-comedic works are not superior to their laugh-riot counterparts, as many critics have suggested. It's about asserting that comedy is an art form that can house multiple value systems at all. What makes comedy such an interesting art form to follow—and hopefully to create—is its malleability to artist and medium. I would never restrict it by holding it up to any one standard of what it is. I don't care if you like *Nanette*, but it is important to me that people accept that it is comedy. To deny that *Nanette* is comedy is to deny comedy's potential as an art form. It is especially silly for comedians, who only can benefit from an extended leeway in what they do.

The definition of comedy already had been expanding for about a decade by the time *Nanette* came out. Because, if you think about it, that episode of *The Bonfire*, a comedy podcast released at the time by Comedy Central, was an act of post-comedy, as its hosts Oakerson and Soder were producing a piece of comedy where the goal was not to create laughter. In this case, the primary intention seemed to be to convince their audience that they were right and that they were unimpeachably doing stand-up correctly. It's why the most successful post-comedian is Joe Rogan. LOL WUT? There is no comedian in this country bringing in a larger audience for not being funny than Joe Rogan. He had the number-one comedy podcast on Apple until he made a deal to be exclusive to Spotify, yet, if someone laughs listening to *The Joe Rogan Experience*, it is incidental. Trying to get LOLs from *JRE* is like when you're trying to get meat out of a Maryland blue crab: It's in there, but you also know there is other shellfish that is much easier to eat. Several times a week, eleven million people download upward of three hours of Rogan bullshitting about things he read, while giving platforms to people spreading a wide range of information, from the accurate and thought-provoking to the paranoid and insidious. Often it's the sound of stoners googling. Obviously, there are podcasts that are trying to be as funny as possible, just as there are plenty of comedians aspiring to wall-to-wall laughs. Realism never went away. There are still habitable buildings.

Countless comedians throughout history have pushed the boundaries of what is acceptable to say. It's why the comedian who *Nanette*-era Gadsby most reminds me of onstage is Patrice O'Neal—the equal parts feared and revered comic's comic who was known for pushing the audience's limits on topics like race and gender—because both found killing overrated and wouldn't let the audience's desire to have a nice night out deter them from sharing the parts of themselves that others might be uncomfortable with. Post-comedy is also about pushing boundaries; however, it is less focused on what a comedian can say and more on how they can say it and how the audience might respond. Come on! This matters so much to me. Just let me have this one. I promise no one is trying to take away your laughs.

The eighties were ending, and by that time, Andrew Dice Clay was used to killing arenas of people with "a sharing of anger and rage at [underdog] targets," as George Carlin once put it.[23] It was the day after Christmas and Clay wanted to do a set where he could be his offensive, grotesque, silly self, free of expectations. He dropped in, late at night, at New York City's Dangerfield's. There weren't that many people there, and of those who were, a bunch left as his set progressed. After a joke (?) in which Clay asks a woman whose date went to the bathroom if she's "wearin' drawers under those pants," only to then tell her boyfriend when he returns that she was coming on to him, an audience member screamed for Clay to do one of the dirty nursery rhymes that made him so famous. Clay dismissed him. "The show's not about laughter. It's about comedy. You don't have to laugh to enjoy it." On March 14, 1990, a recording of the nearly two-hour set was released, with the title producer Rick Rubin gave it: *The Day the Laughter Died*.

On March 13, 2020, almost exactly thirty years later, President Trump declared Covid-19 a national emergency. It was the day the laughter died. It was the day laughter could kill. Like, actually kill other people. The virus was transferred person to person, via the expelling of airborne particles. Laughing involves opening your mouth a whole bunch. I didn't ask for this. When I wrote about post-comedy, it was not a letter of recommendation. But in 2020, it started to feel like a monkey's paw wish.

Less than two weeks later, I watched my first stand-up show on Zoom. Maria Bamford was quick to adapt. Besides being a genius, Bamford, maybe more than any comedian I know, has a wide-eyed understanding of what it means to perform. She filmed one special in a living room, for just her parents. Another special has her performing jokes for audiences of different sizes, from a small theater to a bunch of people in her living room to four people on a bench outside her home to alone in the mirror. That first time, Bamford did some new material, sitting down, holding a computer mic, with her face up close to her laptop camera. She had learned on an earlier show that laughter would be untenable, as Zoom couldn't prioritize sounds, meaning any noise the audience made would cut off her mic. She'd finish a joke and in the moment of silence, where laughs used to go, I'd scroll to see five hundred faces smiling to themselves. At the very end, Bamford unmuted everyone and asked us to scream. Listening to the glitchy cacophony that sounded like a room full of robots laughing so much that they're short-circuiting, I cried. Soon, stand-up—the ever-malleable, cheap-to-produce art form that it is—jammed itself into whatever shape it needed to in order to fit a wide variety of digital broadcasting platforms, many of which made audience feedback impossible. But performers kept on doing it and people kept on logging in. It was about comedy. You don't have to laugh to enjoy it.

Two months later, George Floyd was murdered by a police officer named Derek Chauvin. At the height of the worldwide protests that followed, Dave Chappelle recorded a set in front of a masked, distanced crowd on a farm near his hometown of Yellow Springs, Ohio. That night, the show was called *Dave Chappelle & Friends: A Talk with Punchlines*, but when it was released as a special on Netflix Comedy's YouTube channel, it was called *8:46*, because, as Chappelle howled:

> This man kneeled on a man's neck for eight minutes and forty-six seconds! Can you imagine that!? This kid thought he was going to die. He knew he was going to die. He called for his mother. He called for his dead mother. I've only seen that once before in my life: My father, on his deathbed, called for his grandmother. When I watched that tape I understood this man knew he was going to die. People watched it, people filmed it, and for some reason that I still don't understand, all these fucking police had their hands in their pockets. Who are you talking to? What are you signifying? That you can kneel on a man's neck for eight minutes and forty-six seconds and feel like you wouldn't get the wrath of God.

Chappelle, wearing all black, moving between hunching over on a stool and standing at attention, moves his voice between reflection, a cry for help, and a pained scream. It is powerful. It is full of power. A gifted comedian, he masterfully jumps between personal and historical parallels, providing the audience information but also conveying exactly what the moment felt like to him, personally, in all its hurt and terror. Overwhelming to behold, this nearly thirty-minute jeremiad is not funny at all. Those are Chappelle's words: "This is not funny at all." No one laughs. No one wants to. *8:46* has been watched over thirty million times on YouTube.

But is *this* comedy? It's as close to a sermon as it is to stand-up, but sermons don't air on a YouTube channel called "Netflix Is a Joke." I am not arguing that giant media companies get to decide, but that *8:46*, whatever it is, is a piece of work in conversation with the history of comedy. Part of its power comes from the fact that it is a comedian doing it. The subtext of the performance is *This is how serious the situation is: A comedian can't be funny.* It reminds me of a time Robin Williams was asked if he got laughs when he started out and responded, "You have to. There is very little stand-up tragedy."[24] So, is it comedy? I don't know. Honestly, it is up to you to decide for yourself. Do you want to allow comedy to include moments in culture like this? There is no right answer. This isn't math. It's art.

8

THE LINE

The splash zone always terrified me. Watching Comedy Central in the 1990s as a nervous little boy, seeing Gallagher with his Sledge-O-Matic (big wooden hammer) smashing unsuspecting watermelons, shooting shards of green flesh and pink guts onto the plastic ponchos given to audience members sitting in the first few rows, I retched in disgust, imagining sitting there, hoping nothing got on my face. And what if something did!? How would I be expected to laugh!? And if I didn't laugh, would Gallagher clonk *me* on the head!? That's what I had going through my mind when my friends first suggested we sit in the front at the Comedy Cellar. Comedians there weren't making as much of a mess, but, from past trips, it was clear to me that the audience that hugged the stage was similarly in the line of fire. The comics would talk to you, and by "talk to you" I mean make fun of you.

The Comedy Cellar had been open for twenty years when my friends and I started going in the early 2000s. I had never been to a comedy club before, but I could tell the Cellar had seen better days. Online ticket promos only managed to half-sell rooms. I had first heard of the place from watching *Tough Crowd with Colin Quinn*, a comedic sociopolitical roundtable show that was modeled after the debates that would happen at the infamous comics' table in the back of the restaurant upstairs, the Olive Tree Cafe. Picture a rectangle: That was, and still is, the shape of the long and thin cellar. The ceilings were low. The wall behind the six-inch elevated platform they call a stage was brick, just like the comedy clubs on TV. Pretty quickly I picked up on the fact that though the crowds in general were fairly diverse, the front row was extremely diverse, be it in terms of age, religion, gender, sexual preference, or race. This gave the comedians options if their material wasn't working.

"Look at Harry Potter over here." That's what I would get. I had not read *Harry Potter* or watched any of the movies, but I got what they were trying to say—I had brown hair and glasses. I should say they didn't just say "Harry Potter." No, that's not funny enough. "R******d Harry Potter." Now, that's funny. "Gay Harry Potter." Funnier! Honestly, as a group of four guys, it was a lot of gay stuff. It blurs, but I'm pretty sure Lisa Lampanelli called us the "United Nations of f*****s." I forgot this, but one of my fellow UN representatives remembers Lampanelli touching another's leg and making some sort of Black penis joke. He also told me he always thought her act was kinda racist. I had no idea. I had not asked my friend at the time. I'm sure I laughed. Maybe I thought this was funny, maybe it was the pressure of the crowd, maybe I was scared she'd notice and go after me next. I know I was not offended. Why would I be? I was not gay, but I also didn't know why I would be offended if I were. But, also, in general I didn't get offended. This is not a point of pride as much a proof of privilege. None of the slurs Lampanelli threw around—and she threw them *all* around—applied to me, and everyone else seemed to be laughing. I guess she'd call people "kikes," but by 2002 that wasn't a word that meant anything to me. Frankly, in retrospect, I was desensitized.

And if I thought I was desensitized, it was nothing compared to the comedians. Upstairs at the Olive Tree Cafe, the regulars would be mercilessly and endlessly roasting each other. Add to that, Manny Dworman, a larger-than-life surrogate father to a lot of the comics, demanded that those who sat at the infamous table engage in intense debate over the major topics of the day. Dworman would even, according to Andrew Hankinson's oral history *Don't Applaud. Either Laugh or Don't. (At the Comedy Cellar.)*, assign comedians books on the given topics.[1] Hollywood wasn't calling yet and the internet wasn't what it would become, so the comedians who defined the culture were always around, fermenting in their sensibility, and trying to impress the comedians in the back with how far over the line they could go.

The comedians I most associate with the club at that time were *Tough Crowd*'s most regular guests: Patrice O'Neal, Keith Robinson, Jim Norton, Robert Kelly, Rich Vos, Greg Giraldo, Nick Di Paolo, and the very occasional woman like Judy Gold and Lynne Koplitz. Though to the right of *The Colbert Report*, which would eventually replace *Tough Crowd*, calling this group conservative is too broad. The show's comedy was more defined by the aggressive, reactionary bravado with which the panel engaged in topical issues and, more than anything else, an approach that valued personal expression over how other people might respond.

Their line was whether a performer was funny or not. "Don't applaud. Either laugh or don't," were the instructions Quinn gave the audience before tapings.[2]

Quinn, whom I'd interview years later, likes to push back on the idea that comedy should never punch down by saying comedy is not punching at all, it's "play fighting."[3] To his point, in my experience of going to live shows, audience members can't control what they laugh at, so, in the moment, the direction up or down of the punch matters less than the force behind it. If a comedian in a marginalized group made a joke about wishing that Dick Cheney, an undeniably elevated target, died after a long, painful battle with cancer, a lot of people wouldn't laugh, just because the darkness overpowers or, at least, distracts from the playfulness. In contrast, in my experience, audiences love a joke that is based in a positive racial stereotype. In *Don't Applaud*, Quinn explained that his perspective comes from his childhood: "Where I grew up was very multi-racial and very open as far as the way people spoke to each other. If you were funny, you said whatever you wanted and that was it." At least at that time, it was not being offensive to be offensive, as much as a belief that being overly sensitive was disingenuous.

In this mindset, it would be offensive *not* to talk about a certain race, religion, or sexuality. According to the professor Beck Krefting, the dominant club-comic perspective is rooted in a conservative revulsion against the push toward multiculturalism and faith in a neoliberal "belief that social equality has been achieved and thus any failing on the part of individuals to succeed or obtain the American dream signals a personal failure rather than impugning institutions that favor certain identity categories."[4] To someone like Lampanelli, being an equal-opportunity offender is an inclusive response to diversity, as that particular approach theoretically treats everyone equally. Lampanelli retired from stand-up in 2018, but when she was doing it she'd recall Black people coming up to her saying she didn't do enough Black jokes and Jewish people saying she didn't do enough Jewish jokes, "because people know by making light of it, that's how you include people, that's how you include your friends."[5] And it is not just the Queen of Mean, as she was known; this is the dominant perspective of comedians who "make fun of everyone." Keegan-Michael Key and Jordan Peele made a similar argument in 2014: "To not make fun of something is, we believe, itself a form of bullying. When a humorist makes the conscious decision to exclude a group from derision, isn't he or she implying that the members of that group are not capable of self-reflection?"[6] You could read this perspective as a desire to bring more people in, but you can also read it as the price outsiders need to pay to be included.

The audiences loved it and continue to love it. Just as all forms of comedy have been supercharged by a generation of comedy nerds and the internet, the politically incorrect have maybe benefited the most. It would be easy to say these fans are all conservatives and bigots, but that lets half the political spectrum off the hook and ignores the reality of who is going to the Comedy Cellar most nights of the week. The comics might be much more open minded in alternative-comedy Brooklyn, but regardless of the diversity of the lineup, the audiences are often not as diverse as, at least, those at the Cellar. You can't say offensive jokes are "not funny," or punching down is "never funny," because people are laughing.

Ironically, the best explanation I've ever seen for this phenomenon was by two academics. In 2017, Lauren Berlant and Sianne Ngai pushed back on the idea that people laugh at the politically incorrect because of detachment, suggesting that the reason is actually proximity. In a comedy space, they write, ideas and beliefs and people are close to each other, "in a way that prompts a disturbance in the air."[7] "People can enjoy that disturbance," they continue, "and one thing they can enjoy in it is that it feels automatic, spontaneous, freed-up. Pressed a little, the enjoyment is not always, hardly ever, unmixed; but in the moment, the feeling of freedom exists with its costliness."[8] Audiences are happy to pay admission to be in a room where they don't have to worry about what they are worrying about. John Waters said in 2022, "I want movies to disturb me."[9] And, similarly, there are people who want comedy they know is wrong. Academics writing about comedy like to throw around the words "carnival" and "carnivalesque," referring to a space free of social order and expectation, where one can enter a state of play. Louis C.K. describes it as a game he plays with the audience, where he's "gonna astonish you with how much I shouldn't be saying this."[10] As I've said earlier in this book, the job of the comedian is to turn an audience of strangers into a group of friends. And, at the Cellar, this is how friends talk to each other.

I mention all this about the Comedy Cellar because it is, based on who performs there, the most important comedy club in the country (with the Comedy Store close behind). And as such, its perspective on speech, offense, and the line represents the conventional wisdom—"*reeeeeelax*, we're just joking around here"—that has dominated since the beginning of comedy. And good for them. I'm glad people are having fun. So much fun that these comedians and their fans are at the ready to fight anyone who dares to suggest approaching it differently. However, sometimes I feel that those who fight to protect it do so less like warriors and more like helicopter parents so worried about comedy getting hurt and comedy moving beyond them that they stunt its development. To openly allow for critique is to take comedy seriously, and taking it seriously will allow it to evolve and mature. I want to be crystal clear, because people are violently sensitive about this stuff: It's not just about this word or that word. It's about understanding how the line works and how it maybe doesn't.

Let's push back on the conventional wisdom a little bit. You know, what the hell. Push its boundaries. We'll start with a line comics like to quote George Carlin saying: "I think it's the duty of the comedian to find out where the line is drawn and cross it deliberately." Now, he didn't say exactly that. What he really said is a bit softer: "I like to find out where the line is, sort of. Sort of, sense where the line is drawn. And then deliberately cross it. And drag the audience with you. And have them happy that you did it. That's the key. Once you get them over there, they say, 'That was good!'"[11] When you see the full quote, the word "deliberately" changes meaning. It feels like a lot of comics interpret it to mean "on purpose." That a comedian must cross the line because fuck the line. But based on how Carlin's spoken about these issues in other places and his own work, it reads like "with intention": A comedian should cross the line because of a specific experience they want the audience to have.

Maybe it is a simple fact that people like to have their boundaries pushed, or maybe pushing the boundary is a way to talk about subjects too sensitive to discuss anywhere else. Either way, it is a very different mindset. It suggests an openness to feedback, where the shortened version of the quote presents a self-centeredness that could easily lead to defensiveness.

Defensiveness is why I stopped going to the Comedy Cellar. It's seeing a comedian I used to love twenty years ago tell a joke about how cabdrivers smell bad and then spending the rest of their set complaining about the fact that people didn't laugh. Audiences, they say, are too sensitive or too woke or whatever the new word the right co-opts to describe young people who care too much. What comes up most often is political correctness, a term that's been knocked around so much it has lost its initial definition, but essentially it means avoiding certain behaviors out of desire not to insult or discriminate against the marginalized. And this amorphous term is, as Steve Harvey told the audience of *Family Feud*, "killing comedy."[12] Tracy Morgan agrees: "I think PC is killing comedy."[13] So does Lampanelli, who wrote an op-ed with the headline "How Political Correctness Is Killing Comedy."[14] One more, from Adam Carolla: "Nothing kills comedy quite like people who are constantly offended."[15] If political correctness or people being offended is killing comedy, no one told comedy, which seemingly is more popular than it has ever been, both in terms of live ticket sales and the paychecks some of these embattled comics are getting for their specials. That means either it isn't harder, or its being harder is a good thing.

Here's a question—when is nowadays? As in, "You can't say anything nowadays." Like, is it the last week, year, decade? Well, let's take *Blazing Saddles*, the 1974 comedy western, which both its director, Mel Brooks, and its fans often say "couldn't be made nowadays," likely because of how many people in the movie, from the bad guys to sweet old ladies, call the Black sheriff (played by Cleavon Little) the n-word. Brooks himself has only been saying it couldn't be made nowadays since the early 2010s, as far as I can tell. That said, he has been saying it a lot! Fans, or at least bad-faith actors co-opting the film for their own goals, have not just been saying it for longer; they've been singing it. I cannot believe this is true, but, in the year 2000, the one-hit-wonder pop-punk band SR-71's second single was a song called "Politically Correct," and closed with this triplet: "What happened to make us so afraid / You couldn't make a Mel Brooks movie today / I saw *Blazing Saddles* yesterday." So nowadays is about twenty-five years ago? Well, the comedy historian Kliph Nesteroff notes that the same year *Blazing Saddles* hit theaters, 1974, its cowriter Richard Pryor was arrested in Richard, Virginia, for using the same sort of "obscene" language he wrote into the film.[16] If, in the police car, Pryor said, "*I* couldn't make *Blazing Saddles* nowadays," he'd be right. So maybe nowadays is fifty years, give or take?

You freaking wish. As documented in M. Alison Kibler's *Censoring Racial Ridicule: Irish, Jewish, and African American Struggles over Race and Representation, 1890–1930*, around the turn of the twentieth century, there were protests and debates about "racial comedy," which at that time referred to impersonators of Irish, Jewish, and African American people.[17] One story involves the vaudeville comedian Joe Welch, who in 1909 faced backlash for his offensive Jewish character. In response, he made this slippery slope argument: "If we take the Hebrew character from the stage, the stage would lose much . . . The Irish, or some of the Irish, [are] loudly demanding the effacement of the Irish comedian. As yet we have not heard from the Germans—yet if any race on the face of the globe has been offensively caricatured it is the German race—we may even hear from Booker T. Washington insisting that the negro shall cease to be impersonated. Should things keep up . . . the stage would be without characters and without comedy."[18] As long as there have been marginalized groups of people trying to gain a foothold in American society, there have been attempts to push back against certain comedic portrayals and, in turn, comedians and their xenophobic supporters who fought to maintain the status quo.

But language evolves. There are a ton of words you can't say anymore because no one would know what the hell you're talking about. You can't say "smoking grass" without being met with blank stares. So you shouldn't be surprised that people might not love your using of slurs they don't hear in any other context. But it also goes both ways. Lucy couldn't tell Ricky she was "pregnant" on *I Love Lucy* in the fifties, where now it has become commonplace for stand-ups to not only say the word but actually *be* pregnant in their specials. People say "bitch" so much on television now, it is actually kind of weird. No one could say the word "gagatondra" before 2021, because no one had ever said it before, but then Gottmik said it on *RuPaul's Drag Race*, with a string of giant red latex anal beads hanging from her head, and now it's out there to say until it becomes too played. Though I do think it would be hilarious if in, like, 2030, a comedian says in an interview, "Ugh, you can't even say 'gagatondra' anymore!"

Back to Carlin and words you can't say where and when. In May 1972 he recorded *Class Clown*, a breakthrough album for him creatively, which featured a routine that would become his signature, "Seven Words You Can Never Say on

Television." Shit, piss, fuck, cunt, cocksucker, motherfucker, and tits. "Those are the heavy seven," he jokes. "Those are the ones that'll infect your soul, curve your spine, and keep the country from winning the war." One of the words was "piss." Piss! Two months after recording the track, Carlin was arrested for doing the routine in Milwaukee.[19] He'd go on to be arrested six more times for it. By 1977, Carlin performed the joke in his first HBO special, saying these words on television. He'd say them again on television in 1978. And then for a third time in 1983. If Carlin were still around, you could imagine him updating the routine as "Seven Words You Can Never Say on Television Anymore." Maybe he'd change the words. Maybe he wouldn't. But I'm sure he'd be doing it on Netflix and getting paid twenty million dollars for his trouble. Would people complain on Twitter? I don't know, this is a fake thing I made up. Probably. But it wouldn't matter.

Because, today, the people who say they can't say anything anymore are often found saying it during a performance they earned tens of thousands of dollars for, on their podcast they make hundreds of thousands a year on, or the special they got paid millions for. Unlike Carlin, unlike Pryor, you know where they aren't saying it? A jail cell. They were two of many comics arrested after or during performances until obscenity laws started getting overturned in the 1960s and '70s. In 2021, while comics in the States were complaining about their free speech being under attack in tweets while using the bathroom, in the privacy of their own home, Vir Das, the biggest English-speaking comedian in India, recorded sets that criticized the government and religion on a secret stage, in the middle of the jungle, on top of a mountain, out of fear of getting arrested, as his country's vice president was calling for his jailing.[20] That's being like Lenny Bruce, in a way a comedian throwing his name around because they also perform in the Village isn't.

An anti-PC comic could argue that the other side underestimates how many people are fine with politically incorrect jokes in the present day; however, those comics underestimate how many people have had a problem with it all along. On *WTF with Marc Maron*, Nesteroff shared one powerful anecdote from comedy history, involving Will Rogers, often referred to as the Jon Stewart of his day, known for speaking out on sociopolitical injustice with a folksy charm.[21] In 1934, Rogers was hosting the Shell-sponsored *Shell Chateau* (cool name) radio show and he introduced a song by referring to it as "a real n****r spiritual." While he was still talking, throwing in three more n-words, the board was lighting up with complaints. This transitioned into a Shell boycott by Black organizations and Rogers's movies being pulled out of Harlem. Shell asked Rogers to apologize. Rogers, according to Nesteroff, did not do that, instead chastising the protesters for being "too quick to attack." You can imagine how the rest of this speech went: "I meant no ill will." "I'm not a racist." "I can't be a racist, because I was raised by darkies." The protests expanded. Editorials and letters were written. But because it never reached the white press, Rogers never talked about it again and Shell let it pass. "Those grievances have been lodged for ages, but were willfully ignored," Nesteroff explained to Maron, as long as the marginalized "did not have the purchasing power or the influence in the body politic to have their voices heard."[22]

Enter the internet. Free speech has been democratized. People have always been free and able to have and vocalize their opinions, but what they lacked was a platform. Now people have a platform and the potential for reach. It is still just a complaint. A thousand people saying you shouldn't say something doesn't mean you can't; it just means you can't without these thousand people bugging you. Still, these thousand or five thousand or ten thousand people don't actually have any power to stop you from doing anything; all they can do is put pressure on the networks or streaming services that might air your stuff. If a comedian's work is removed from a streaming service or no longer rerun on a network, that's because the companies consider the comedian's work less valuable than the time it would take to deal with the response. It's why networks with commercials are more likely to do something, because advertisers have the least stomach for any conflict.

Look, I'm sure it sucks to have a lot of people say you are bad. Anytime anyone has disliked something I did, it made me really sad, and I considered quitting being a writer. Writing this chapter is already making me nervous, based on the right-wing media ecosystem's history of stirring up anger around political correctness.[23] But I accept that freedom of speech does not mean freedom from consequence, and it definitely doesn't mean freedom to be famous without anyone saying something about it.

Because that's the other thing with the internet: The access to the platforms goes both ways. You can't say anything anymore? People are literally saying the worst possible shit constantly. Whatever word you think you can't say, search for it on Twitter. The *true* statement is that you can't say whatever you want and still be mainstream, Hollywood famous. Most comedians acknowledge that most audiences get it. That's because you can make homophobic jokes, but you can't make homophobic jokes and then host an award show where gay people make up like 50 percent of the audience. Also, that's not even true! Kevin Hart could have hosted the Oscars. He stepped down instead of apologizing. And then when he apologized, the producers begged him to come back. That's because, as of this writing, a comedian can, depending on their level of stardom, say whatever they want and still be famous and get work. The real line that matters is between not famous enough and famous enough for a major media company president to sit through an uncomfortable town hall answering questions about you.

In 2019, I was booked to do my podcast live at Comedy Central's short-lived San Francisco festival, Cluster Fest. The room, I was told, fit one thousand people, which is a lot of people to watch two people talk, especially when one is me. The other was Anthony Jeselnik, who sometimes gets called "stand-up's prince of darkness," which accurately captures his over-the-top, cartoon-villain persona. After the interview, he thanked me for letting him go "full Kanye." By that he meant talking tons of shit about how much better he was than every other comedian.

When I asked what motivates him, he said, "I hope people try to be like me," referring to writing very dark jokes with punch lines that hit like sharp right turns, "and fuck their whole lives up."[24] He was frustrated by comedians who pursue his style of dark joke-telling lazily, without a consideration for how different audiences might react. When I asked him then about political correctness, he responded that without it "I wouldn't have anything to do." To him, asking if political correctness is killing comedy is akin to asking, "Is football ruining the NFL?" "No," he continued. "You need the fucking thing to play the game. You need to have it. I love political correctness. I love it. I support every piece of it. I don't care if they go too far. It's the only way I get to do what I do." Jeselnik, who compared himself to Al Swearengen from *Deadwood* in the interview, does not care to be a hero for the cause as much as an antihero who works with the cause for largely personal gain. To a comic like Jeselnik, political correctness both establishes the line and intensifies it, turning it into an electric fence.

"Comedy helps us test or figure out what it means to say 'us,'" write Berlant and Ngai, meaning that in practice, comedians and their given audience are always in a conversation over the norms of the given show. They continue, "Always crossing lines, it helps us figure out what lines we desire or can bear."[25] This is how it works: Imagine a cliff. Wile E. Coyote. Straight drop. Infinite fall. The line is like the edge of the cliff. Now imagine a child playing (aww). Ten yards from the edge, you might not register you are even on a cliff. Three yards from the edge, you would. You might tell this kid to be careful. But you wouldn't be freaking out. Three feet from it, you would. Three feet on the other side of the cliff would be the worst thing you've ever seen in your life. I'm talking about, to quote Hannah Gadsby, "tension." By playing closer and closer to the edge, you build up more and more tension and thus it's a big relief when the punch line releases the tension. Now, a comedian like Jeselnik won't just walk up to the edge and walk back. That would be boring. He walks up to it, stands on one foot, hops, jumps off, only to catch himself on the ledge and pull himself back.

Look at this joke from his 2015 special, *Thoughts and Prayers*. I will lay it out with commentary in such a way that it is evident to you how he pushes the audience closer to the edge of appropriateness and then pulls them back, only to push them again.

> [*Coming off a joke in which he is a serial killer, he starts by demanding the audience not tighten up. His tone is defiant, if not menacing.*]
>
> I hate sensitivity. I hate it.
>
> Even when little kids get sensitive, that makes me mad. [*This gets a smattering of laughs*]
>
> I got a six-year-old nephew. I asked what he wants for his birthday. He said, "Uncle Anthony, I want you to get me a Barbie doll." [*Jeselnik pauses and in the silence you can feel the audience be like, "Oh no"*]
>
> I said, "Fuck you. [*There's an instant, loud laugh and Jeselnik smiles a little bit*]
>
> "You six-year-old piece of shit." [*Another big laugh, after which Jeselnik's body language softens, as he tries to bring the audience back in*]
>
> And don't get me wrong. Don't get me wrong, I don't care if he plays with dolls. He can wear dresses if he wants to. [*You hear titters that suggest the audience is softened, as Jeselnik's performance grows almost earnest*]
>
> But I'm not getting him a Barbie doll. You see, Barbie dolls give little boys unrealistic expectations . . . [*There's a huge laugh, in which you can hear a few women in the audience cheer. Jeselnik smirks with self-satisfaction, before returning to the menacing body language of the start of the joke*]
>
> . . . of how easy it's gonna be to tear off a head. [*Jeselnik and the joke get an applause break*]

Political correctness is great because it makes the line clearer, if the comedian cares to look, better allowing them to twist and turn the audience around it. It's pretty obvious in a joke like this, but there are some comedians who are able to toe this line at length. Bill Burr, a stand-up uniquely respected by all types of comedians, will start with a ten-full-yards-past-the-line premise, like saying that fat actresses posing on the cover of a magazine are not "brave," lose the audience, and figure out how to pull it back minutes later by clarifying that what he's actually talking about are his anger issues and his frustration with the type of parts he gets offered in Hollywood as a bald redhead, so by the end you are safe and sound and understand better how his brain works. But all of this demands people be offended. If not, how can you say that you're being edgy? If you are saying supposedly offensive things and the audience is instantly all on board, it is not a comedy show, it's a rally.

Jeselnik used to say there was no line, but as he got older and better at comedy he realized "there are a million of them." Everyone has a line, according to Jeselnik. But really everyone has a million. "My dad suffers from psoriasis," Jeselnik told me. "If someone made a joke about psoriasis, I wouldn't laugh."[26] A point Jeselnik referenced Colbert making—which I've also seen attributed to Steve Martin—is that when you're young it's easy to make jokes about cancer, but things change when your friends start dying of cancer. There are a million lines per person and they shift with time, sometimes along with society, sometimes not. When I asked Jeselnik about cutting a joke about hate crimes from his act after the Pittsburgh synagogue shooting, he told me he didn't want to see it in a white supremacist's tweet one day. Fans sometimes ask him, "Why do you not make rape jokes anymore?" To which he answers, "Because I had a fucking special where I did five of them and then I read the [Jon Krakauer] book *Missoula* and I was like, 'I don't think I think this is as funny as I did back then.'" Does political correctness make comedy harder to do? Sure, in the sense that it would be easier to run for a touchdown if you didn't have to worry about holding the ball, but that's the game. It's what makes it more exciting than watching a bunch of men sprinting with helmets on.

A comedian trying to navigate eight quadrillion lines (one million per person times eight billion people) brings to mind that one scene from 1999's *Entrapment* where Catherine Zeta-Jones's butt tries to avoid lasers in order to steal a painting. That said, as I see it, there are four kinds of lines, four ways in which people get offended. Here they are:

Discomfort

This isn't about any one topic as much as an approach. Paul Mooney was known for this. Hours-long shows, where he would just beat his audience over the head with his perspective and ideas. Marc Maron told me that what he learned from opening for him is that Mooney was defying the white audience members to fight the part of themselves that might think, *When is this n-word going to shut up?* (Though they'd actually use "n****r" in their head.)[27] Maron would then try to do the same with Judaism. This also can include someone like Andy Kaufman spending a set reading *The Great Gatsby* or Ziwe playing the same song over and over and over and over (up to thirteen times)[28] again until the audience (at least the members who hadn't walked out) sings along with what she deems to be an appropriate amount of passion, both of which challenge not a sociopolitical belief, but the audience's understanding of what a show is. There is a righteousness to discomfort. The comedian Aida Rodriguez, who likes to push her audience past their worries about certain words, like using "homeless" instead of "unhoused," in order to actually confront the issues, told me about the influence of opening for Mooney early in her career. "Not being able to have conversations that are uncomfortable has become part of the unhealthy environment that we live in now," she told me.[29] "If we don't have the uncomfortable conversations, we won't move forward, because we're not unpacking." I wanted to start with discomfort because I believe most comedians who upset large numbers of people think they are doing some version of this, when they're more likely doing one of the following.

Taboos

You know the things you are not supposed to talk about at dinner parties—sex, death, money, religion? Those things. Sex and religion were the big ones for a while. It is what Lenny Bruce got arrested over. However, because of him, both of those topics have become normalized to discuss onstage, though they still undeniably have juice, like when performed by people whose sex life is less culturally accepted, like women and queer people. Death is not for everyone. Other than jokes in which dogs get hurt, I don't think there is a topic with a higher bomb percentage. I get it: Death can be tragic. But laughing at it is also how some comedians and audience members process tragedy. Beyond that, for those who think about death often, maybe because they have lost someone close to them, they know what it feels like to not be able to talk about it. To hear it discussed, to have someone else push through their discomfort, is titillating. I feel that. On the other hand, cursing seems unremarkable to me, but your *f*'s and *s*'s still bother people enough for there to be a *thriving* market for comedians who don't curse. Conversely, there are also some TV shows whose "comedy" is just a lot of cursing. Honestly, of all these topics, money might be the hardest, as it creates a divide between the performer and the crowd. I once saw Maria Bamford openly discuss how much money she got paid for the show we, the audience, were currently at, and the audience was dumbfounded, unsure how to respond. But Bamford knows from her history performing about another societal taboo, mental illness, that it might not always be easy to talk about, but the reason you push those boundaries is to normalize the conversation, hoping to make it easier the next time.

Politics and Political Issues

This one is kind of obvious. If a comedian talks about loving guns, a person who believes in gun control might complain. If a comedian talks about hating guns, a person who loves guns might complain. This category also includes jokes about politicians. Kathy Griffin and Donald Trump's severed head. Michelle Wolf at the White House Correspondents' Dinner: "I actually really like Sarah [Huckabee Sanders]. I think she's very resourceful. She burns facts, and then she uses the ash to create a perfect smoky eye. Maybe she's born with it, maybe it's lies. It's probably lies." Katie Rich, a writer for *SNL*, getting suspended for tweeting, "Barron will be this country's first homeschool shooter." There are not examples of similar reactions to comedy about Democrats, despite what conservatives suggest. Because for how much the conservatives shout about free speech in comedy, for some reason they get the most butt-hurt when that free speech is used to mock them. It is very important to distinguish "politics and political issues" from "groups," the category that follows. Because the distinction has blurred as conservatives continue to obsess over identity politics. A joke about a transgender person is not the same as a joke about Mitch McConnell.

Groups

Though the previous three are just as common, this is the one that gets most of the attention. This includes the marginalized—women, people of color, members of the LGBTQIA+ community, the disabled, the unhoused, etc.—but also groupings like victims of sexual assault. Much of the debate around rape jokes, for example, seems to be a discrepancy between defenders who felt they were joking about a taboo and their critics who felt the jokes were ultimately mocking a group: survivors. Religion is complicated, because talking about religion is a taboo, but religious people are groups and religious people often react as such. Considering there is a perception that all complaints about content come from the left, I want to make a distinction between the nature of these complaints. Daniel Sloss, a popular Scottish comic, had an anti-religious joke work for years in the U.K., but when he performed in America for the first time, someone pulled a gun on him. Not all types of groups are so politically fraught. Gabriel "Fluffy" Iglesias is one of the highest selling stand-ups ever, appealing to the widest audience possible, by swearing to never discuss three things: religion, politics, and, on an equal level to those topics, sports. In the 2016 documentary *Can We Take a Joke?*, Jim Norton complained about being heckled by a Journey fan. So, yeah, groups don't always mean the marginalized. Jokes about "straight white men" are structurally the same as jokes about gay people, nonwhite people, or women to some straight white men oblivious to power structures.

That said, though the structure of the jokes might be the same in many ways, how they are received by the group is greatly impacted by the group's station. As Kibler noted in a particularly illustrative example, Jews and African Americans in the early twentieth century "linked misrepresentation to the denial of civil rights and vulnerability to violent attack," whereas Irish Americans, who were in less danger of harm or disenfranchisement, saw the fight against offensive portrayal "as a way to advance their interests, particularly the goal of Irish independence."[30] This presents a flaw in the equal-opportunity-offender argument: If all people are not equal, your insults cannot be received equally. Comedy has an ability to strengthen in-groups and, often, comedians do so by making jokes about out-groups. And, relatedly, if a person of the out-group wants to be part of this in-group, the test to see if they can hang, if they are "one of us," is laughing at the joke.

Though all four are lines that can be crossed, the degree to which the audience member is offended is more influenced by how they feel about the person telling the joke. Take this Anthony Jeselnik joke:

> Who was it who said, "The first million is the hardest?"
>
> Was it Hitler?

This does not offend me. I am Jewish, but my family was in the U.S. before World War II, so maybe that changes things. Maybe not. Also, I'm a few generations removed. The Comedy Cellar's longtime booker Estee Adoram was born in Poland, into a Holocaust-survivor family. She wouldn't like the joke. As she told Lena Dunham in a 2018 interview, she doesn't like Holocaust jokes because they hit a "very raw nerve."[31] Probably the biggest factor for me is that I like Anthony Jeselnik and more importantly I trust him. I trust him not to be anti-Semitic, because of my knowledge of him and my understanding of how his comedy works. Adoram might be fine if Dave Attell told a Holocaust joke, because he's Jewish and she's been booking him for decades. For both of us, I'm sure there are other comedians who, if they told that joke, we would be really troubled.

Comedians are in the business of creating the feeling of "it's safe to laugh" that people get naturally from our friends and family, so if the audience similarly trusts them, they offer them similar grace. Like, my absolute favorite joke-joke is a rape joke,* because when my bubbe first told it to me, in a

* A nun passes away and finds herself up in the clouds. There, she is greeted by an angel—halo, wings, the whole nine. "Welcome to heaven. We are so happy to have you here. Follow me." So she does. A few minutes pass and the nun hears in the distance the worst screams she's ever heard. Just terrible, awful screams of pain. "What is that?" the nun asks. "Oh, they are just drilling the holes for the wings," the angel says, smiling. That seems reasonable enough, so they keep on walking. Another few minutes pass and then the nun hears even louder screams than before. Just horrible, bloodcurdling screams.

half-hearted whisper that quickly turned into a proud Brooklyn boom, I laughed with my full heart, with the concept of offense never crossing my mind. There is no bigger factor in offense than your relationship to the person telling the joke.

Let's say you have a joke about a sensitive subject that has worked before. If people on a given night aren't laughing, it's not because they are too sensitive. It is because they do not trust *you*. You have not sufficiently created a situation in which it feels safe to laugh. And for certain members of marginalized groups, or people with friends or family of those groups, it might be harder to get them to laugh because the safety for these people is under attack. I've been in rooms with all types of people with all types of comedians and they were all able to laugh, so it's not a *them* problem.

At the same time, the comedians need to trust the audience. If a stand-up tells a joke and the audience doesn't laugh because they are offended, they can either take this information in and adapt, or push people away. You can make a career of offending crowds, saying whatever you want, and your audience will eventually be made up of exclusively the people who like what others find offensive. It's harder to try to walk the line than to draw a line in the sand, so that you only have to speak to the people on your side. Ultimately, this is still about "either laugh or don't,"

"What is that?" the nun asks. "Oh, they are just drilling the holes for the halo," the angel responds calmly. The nun nods and continues to follow the angel.

After a few more minutes, the two arrive at the Pearly Gates. Saint Peter greets the nun, "You lived such a good and wonderful life. Let me welcome you to heaven." The nun thinks and responds, "I think I'm going to pass." "What?" Saint Peter says, shocked. "You know the alternative: Hell. You'll be raped. You'll be sodomized."

The nun pauses for a second. "At least I have the holes for that."

but what not laughing looks like has evolved with this new generation of comedy fan, who is as invested in the art form as the comedians themselves. These fans feel an ownership, so that when they don't laugh, they want to say something.

There are hecklers, but primarily they'll say something on the internet, where the majority of the discourse around these subjects is held. It's become common for an audience member to have a negative experience at a comedy show, then take their negative feeling and express it online. For a while, comics complained about this amorphous blob of blogger bogeymen, but for the last few years it has become just ordinary "social media." Now, I am not going to defend Twitter, but I am also not going to spend precious word count on it. (Especially since by the time you're reading this, Twitter might not exist anymore.) Some comedians will complain about how young people are offended too easily, when it's really just people on Twitter, and they can't tell the difference. Gilbert Gottfried liked to say, "The internet makes me feel sentimental about old-time lynch mobs. At least lynch mobs had to put their shoes on, go out, get their hands dirty, and deal with other people." As a joke, it's funny enough. As an argument, it is ridiculous. Because the thing about lynch mobs is they actually lynched people. Especially after Chris Rock and then Dave Chappelle were physically attacked while onstage, more and more comedians started conflating reasonable criticism with violent threat. The threat of political correctness to comedy was treated by some literally, if only to further make the case for their own cool dangerousness.

Though I acknowledge that Will Smith's response to Chris Rock does show that there are audience members who react physically when their lines are crossed, that episode said more about the state of Will Smith than about comedy. Still, since I have you, reader, I will say, if you are at a regular comedy show, don't slap the comedian. And if possible, don't heckle. I have a problem with heckling, especially when someone is working on new material. Comedians need to be able to figure out material with an audience. It is how they find out where the line is. That said, if a comedian says something so awful that it makes a person heckle, it probably gives them a good sense of where the line might be.

The bigger issue with a certain sort of powerful comedian crying that their free speech is under attack is that it overshadows the comedians who are *actually* in danger, and what a real threat looks like. In *Don't Applaud*, the author speaks to Liza Treyger, a millennial comedian who's a regular at Comedy Cellar, about an interaction she had with an older comedian who said, "You have to admit, you girls are the worst audience members."[32] She didn't admit that, telling the author that she replied, "No, girls are the best audience for me and old white dudes are the worst." She continued, "They get mad at my material for sure. I have the worst trouble with dudes threatening to kill me, coming back to shows the next day, trying to ruin my bit, folding their arms." And yet when you hear someone saying that free speech is under attack, it's never examples like this. It's not the 2022 viral video of Ariel Elias getting a beer can thrown at her head because an audience member felt they could tell, just from her act, that she had voted for Biden. These reactions to Treyger and Elias, though extreme, are rooted in the same intense subjectivity (mixed with Hitchensian misogyny) discussed in chapter 3. They reflect the belief that "comedy must be funny to *me*." Considering there are people out there behaving this way, if there is to be a vigilance around protecting free speech in comedy clubs, ideally it would be to protect vulnerable comedians from people who are offended that they get to speak freely, and not to discourage audience members from having their own reaction to material that, again, is designed to be offensive. But that isn't how the conversation goes, because historically, it's not been about free speech for free speech's sake, but about maintaining the social order of who gets to say what.

Accordingly, here is the issue with the concept of "Either laugh or don't": It assumes that all jokes are told and received in a vacuum. And I understand certain comedians' and certain audience members' desire for that to be the case, just as most desire for there to be equality among all people. The carnival sounds fun as hell—partying, wearing masks like an extra in *Eyes Wide Shut*—but comedy is not treated as the carnival in other ways, as shown by the entire book you are currently reading. The fact is that, even though a comedian making fun of Journey might feel the same to a Journey fan as the same comedian making fun of, say, Jews to a Jewish person, how this comedy then interacts with society is different. And, inasmuch as there's a desire for comedy to have a social value (which the cast of *Tough Crowd* shared by presuming people would care about their opinions about the issues of the day), it demands self-awareness and critical thought from comedians and audience members. The carnival is an aspirational standard that starts with understanding. I believe most comedians and audience members get this intuitively, and, in practice, most comedy shows feature comedians who get "it" and audiences who get "it," and comedy is better for this understanding. Because stand-ups write their material in public, with the audience, for a future audience, all types of comedy demand that both groups listen to each other.

What follows is a story about what it looks like when they don't.

The first time Dave Chappelle crossed a line of my own was at that same Comedy Cellar show where Lisa Lampanelli called us "United Nations of f*****s" that I mentioned earlier. It was 12:45 and we were paying our bill. In the middle of making plans to catch the 1:16 train back to Long Island, the host informed us that there was a special guest. "Dave Chappelle!" The audience energy shot from negative ten to positive ten million. This was the summer of 2003, after all, and the first season of *Chappelle's Show* had premiered just months earlier, turning him into the biggest comedian in the world to, at least, the people in the club that night. The other thing about it being 2003 was that cigarette smoking had just been banned in bars, a fact Chappelle reminded us of, as he started smoking, sitting on a stool placed right at the front of the already low stage.

And then he just talked, mostly to the audience, sometimes to the staff or comedians who were going to the bathroom, a few times to Neal Brennan, the cocreator of *Chappelle's Show*, who was standing in the back. In the decades since, my friends debate if he was high or drunk or neither. He was loose and comfortable, taking long pauses, going on tangents without a joke in sight. We didn't laugh much, but you couldn't say we weren't entertained. Around 2:30, he fantasized out loud about what his life would be like if he were to get Oprah pregnant, a premise that would go on to become a *Chappelle's Show* sketch in its second season.

Eventually out of cigarettes, Chappelle asked if he could

bum one from anyone in the audience. One passed to our table and my friend Kurt stood up to hand it to him. When Kurt sat down, he accidentally spilled his drink all over himself. Chappelle's face dropped. He felt badly. Hoping to diffuse the embarrassment, Chappelle asked what he was drinking. Without thinking, Kurt responded with the truth, "Sprite," making it clear he was under twenty-one. The audience laughed. "You could've said anything. Vodka. Gin." Chappelle then did that thing he does onstage when he laughs and hits the microphone against his thigh. "One Sprite, please!" It was 3:15. The last train of the night was at 3:31. He'd stay on for another forty-five minutes. After, we spent hours waiting for the first morning train and talking about what we'd just experienced. Gentle as line-crossing goes, that performance pushed the boundary of how late I wanted to stay out and, more importantly, expanded my understanding of what a comedian could do onstage.

In retrospect, this was one of the last times either Chappelle or I would be able to have such an experience. In February 2004, the second season of *Chappelle's Show* was airing on Comedy Central, and with the first season newly out on DVD (on pace to being one of the bestselling TV shows on DVD ever), it was becoming a world-conquering phenomenon. I couldn't go anywhere without hearing a (white) person saying "Yeaah!" or "oKAY!" in the style of Chappelle's Lil Jon, or "I'm Rick James, bitch!" in the style of Chappelle's Rick James. And I was me; imagine being Dave Chappelle. Months after those impressions aired, Comedy Central renewed *Chappelle's Show* for two seasons in a deal worth fifty million dollars. By that summer, his frustration and stress started coming to the surface. There was a report of him leaving the stage in front of four thousand fans in Sacramento, only to come back to tell them, "You people are stupid."[33] "You know why my show is good?" he asked the Sacramento audience rhetorically. "Because the network officials say you're not smart enough to get what I'm doing and every day I fight for you. I tell them how smart you are. Turns out, I was wrong." In response to many "I'm Rick James, bitch!" screams, he told the audience the show was ruining his life. He had to work twenty hours a day and it destroyed his ability to do the "most important thing" he does—stand-up. This is what it looks like when the audience doesn't really listen to the comedian. The rest is legend (legend count #9).

Chappelle has an ear for mythmaking, for honing the truth in a way that makes it feel larger than real life. And from how he's talked about it in some interviews and from accounts of comedians I've talked to with some knowledge of the situation, it seems Chappelle brought that same spin to the story of why he left *Chappelle's Show.* As Jason Zinoman documented in his ebook, *Searching for Dave Chappelle*, Chappelle had long admired Bobby Fischer and would occasionally talk about what it would be like to vanish while on top.[34] So, at the height of *Chappelle's Show*, he vanished. The story is that it was because someone laughed at one of his sketches the wrong way, but that was the last straw on a very stressed back.

The infamous sketch involves a pixie, played by Chappelle in blackface, that would pop up any time a Black person felt the stress of racism. Chappelle finds himself on a plane, having to order the fried chicken, and the pixie pops up. While he was filming as the pixie, a white person on set laughed the wrong way. "I know the difference between people laughing with me and people laughing at me, and it was the first time I ever got a laugh I was uncomfortable with," he'd tell Oprah in 2006.[35] He realized at that moment that though there were a lot of people who understood what he was trying to do, "There's another group of people . . . the kind of people who scream 'I'm Rick James, b——!' at my concerts . . . they're going to get something completely different." When he tells Oprah he doesn't want Black people disappointed in him, she shoots back, in a way only Oprah can, by saying, "You didn't want to be disappointed in yourself." Chappelle pauses and with a charming smirk responds, "You know what, Oprah, you're right." That's why he left.

In that same interview, he told Oprah, "I was doing sketches that were funny, but socially irresponsible," and leaving the show, he was implying, was an act of social responsibility. Walking away from all that money afforded him an integrity he never received for anything he had created prior. This building of a legend peaked with Rachel Kaadzi Ghansah's beautifully written, heartfelt 2013 write-around profile in *The Believer*. Maybe one of the most poignant, thoughtful things ever written about comedy to that point, it went on to get nominated for a National Magazine Award. This passage captures exactly where the national consciousness was with Chappelle eight years after he left his show:

> Chappelle did such a good job of truth-telling, on every subject, that nobody knew what to do when he just stopped talking. In no way did his quitting conform to our understanding of the comic's one obligation: to be funny. To talk to us. To entertain us. To make us laugh. We aren't used to taking no for an answer, to being rejected, especially not by the

> people who are supposed to make us smile. Especially not by Black men who are supposed to make us smile. And yet Chappelle did just that.[36]

This, of course, wasn't exactly true. Chappelle didn't stop making people laugh. The opposite was true. He kept performing stand-up, competing with Dane Cook in the late '00s to break the record for longest stand-up set ever performed, doing shows in the four-, five-, six-hour range, making a lot of kids miss their trains home. From accounts that would come out here and there, these sets were in the style I witnessed that one late night. Chappelle was reconnecting himself with who he truly was as an artist—a nightclub comedian. When comedians talk about Chappelle's greatness, despite the controversy that will be coming in a paragraph or two, it is greatness in this form: being in a room and playing with an audience; finding all the little lines, crossing them deliberately, earnestly explaining his real position, only to undercut that again with the dumbest joke of the night. In his sets during this period, he was able to present all the paradoxes that make up a single person.

Then he "came back." First, in 2014, he did a run of sold-out shows at Radio City Music Hall. I went to one, and it was one of the most joyous stand-up experiences of my life. "It Took 10 Years, but Dave Chappelle Finally Weeded Out All of His Terrible Fans" was the headline I wrote (oops), because no one screamed, "I'm Rick James, bitch!"[37] I did note that a section about the competing allegiances of Black queer people was the weakest. Still, when Chappelle released two specials on Netflix in March 2017, I was excited. "Dave Chappelle's Netflix Specials Will Remind You Why He's One of the All-Time Best Stand-ups," my headline read at the time, and I stand by it.[38] I also wrote, "Chappelle's absurdity can lean toward glibness and offensiveness when it comes to jokes about LGBTQ issues. Some of it comes from a position of support, but it's hard to defend a joke like, 'Turns out "Q" is like the vowels, that shit is "sometimes Y." It's for gay dudes that don't really know they're gay, you know, like prison f*gs, who are like, "I'm not gay, n***a, I'm just sucking these to pass the time."'" My opinion was representative of the critical consensus, but, based on what came next, it would appear that Chappelle would mostly focus on the negative.

Over his next four hour-long specials, Chappelle tried to bring in his detractors with one hand, asking for understanding, only to push them away with the other, denying them the same. More and more of each set became focused on women, gay people, and transgender people. *Yeah, but he isn't being malicious.* Maybe you could make that argument for the first specials. But if you do something and people tell you it hurts them and then you do it again anyway, that is malice. *Well, they're "just jokes."* Regardless of my feelings on the implication of "just jokes" (don't like it!), as the specials went on, they clearly weren't. In *The Closer*, he very plainspokenly said, "Gender is a fact" and "I'm team TERF." Frankly, it's hard to make a "just jokes" argument about the comedian behind *8:46*, a special without any. *Well, he's just speaking his truth. He is working through his feelings in public and it is brave.* I would be more sympathetic to this case if he were working through his feelings, but instead it appears he's doing the exact opposite, which is *defending* his feelings and his unwillingness to evolve. *Well, he's speaking THE truth.* No, he's not. *Okay, fine, all he's doing is revealing the darkness spinning around his mind and allowing the audience to judge for themselves.* But isn't that exactly what the backlash is? People judging for themselves? *Wow, that's a great point. I, a rhetorical device, free of societal pressure not to change my mind, have evolved my thinking on this issue.*

Chappelle closes *The Closer* by directly asking the "LBGTQ, L-M-N-O-P-Q-Y-Z" to "stop punching down on my people." It is unclear if he means comedians or Black people or both, but the implication is that their criticism is an unfair attack. With this, and throughout the special, he shows the limits of the punching-up and punching-down framework. The argument against punching down makes sense on its surface—comedy should attack those in power, not the marginalized. There's another George Carlin quote that often goes around when this conversation bubbles up. Sharing what he finds unusual about Andrew Dice Clay's act, Carlin tells Larry King: "Comedy traditionally has picked on people in power. Women and gays and immigrants are kinda, to my way of thinking, underdogs."[39]

Based on the examples earlier in this chapter, you can't say that comedy historically doesn't pick on the disempowered. What is more accurate is that comedians themselves traditionally were underdogs and, presumably, as such, would relate to their brethren. Though modern comedy, with minstrel shows, was invented as a way to subjugate and dehumanize first enslaved African Americans and then a new wave of immigrants, it was the subversion of the form by those groups that defined the American comedic perspective of the outsider. This is how you get observational comedy and the ideas of truth telling, as both suggest looking from the outside and/or below. This attracts performers who feel like outsiders, people who feel marginalized. Undeniably, often they are. The issue is that when some comedians start seeing success, they can't or are unwilling to clock the power shift. Besides how difficult it is sometimes to parse who is exactly up and down in a given scenario, a certain sort of comedian has started to play the victim. This is still about the line. Some comedians use self-deprecation as a way of knocking themselves down a few pegs, closer to the status of the audience, and freeing themselves up to take shots without seeming cheap. But these days more comics try to get the audience to think they are being oppressed as a way of justifying their sloppy provocations. Chappelle's alphabet joke is an attempt to prop up the opposition, painting the queer community as some sort of massive conspiracy, as a way to distract from the fact that he is the one given twenty million dollars to use his large platform to exercise an agenda.

It's an agenda he shares with a group I refer to as comedy's bad little boys. These stinkers spend most of their sets complaining that audiences are too sensitive, too politically correct, too woke, too not like them. Ricky Gervais is their king. Joe Rogan their pope. Bill Maher is their president. Given a two-hundred-million-plus subscriber platform from Netflix, they say they are being silenced. Their jokes involve introducing a word they are not "allowed" to say, sheepishly asking if they should say it, and, when the audience all agrees, saying it. Very cool, edgy stuff, giving their audience exactly what affirms all their preexisting opinions. They name their special something like *Triggered*, as Rogan did, cosplaying as iconoclasts, self-mythologizing their own victimhood. Without struggles of their own, they charge toward targets in their minds, like Quixote and his windmills.

Defensiveness, which has taken over Chappelle's act, is just not compelling art. And it's played out. I brought this up to Tom Segura, a bad little boy–adjacent comedian who copped to dabbling in some bad word humor in the past, but now feels it is tired. He explained to me, "Going 'Hey, you know what I found you're not allowed to do?' And then talking about that. It doesn't seem like that's really much interest to you then."[40] People want to see what an artist thinks is interesting, not what the artist thinks the audience wants or especially what they think some unrelated group of outsiders doesn't want. This reflects the main creative problem with intentionally politically incorrect stand-up: It focuses the audience on *what* the comedian says and not *how* they say it, undermining the artistry of the performance.

Chappelle thinks he's helping. Malice? No, it's tough love to teach trans people that they need to be less sensitive. "I've never seen somebody in such a hilarious predicament not have a sense of humor about it," Chappelle says in *Equanimity*. This brings to mind Lauren Berlant's idea of "humorlessness," which they were working on before their untimely passing in 2021. Part of their work on the subject included the question of who gets to *not* have a sense of humor. "If you already have structural power," they explained in an interview, "humorlessness increases your value," whereas "the privileged demand that the less privileged not be humorless."[41] Alluding to the idea of the feminist killjoy, popularized by the feminist scholar Sara Ahmed,[42] Berlant continued by saying, "If the person who names the problem is a kind of subject like a feminist, a person of color, a politicized queer, or/and a trans person, the privileged devalue them because they're used to being deferred to and not tortured by a refusal of recognition." How dare trans people "inconvenience other people's casual relation to language, nature, taxonomy, gesture, and concept" by asking to be addressed by their preferred pronouns and names. Comics like to say people who are offended just want attention, just want power, and it's like, duh, because they don't have either, but the comics can't understand that because they have both. It would be one thing if comedians combated humorlessness with humor, but instead their reaction is more humorlessness. Chappelle is offended that people are offended.

I was talking with a rather prominent comedian (they didn't want to be named because of the troll armies Chappelle and the like have inspired) after an interview and, after being sure no one was around to hear, he told me a joke he'd been playing with:

> A lot of rich and famous comedians are very concerned about how sensitive audiences are. But no one is more sensitive than a comedian. One of these guys talks about sensitive audiences and calls 'em "bitch-ass." But I happen to know he's more sensitive than any of us. More sensitive than me. I won't say his name, out of professionalism, but listen to how sensitive this comedian, who shall remain nameless, is . . . Okay, he quit *Chappelle's Show* . . . because someone on the crew laughed the wrong way at a joke. And I get it! I get it completely, but don't call me sensitive because I'm not laughing at your transphobic hate speech.

It's a point I'd see a lot of people make—Chappelle, of *all* people, should get it. He is clearly sensitive and that's nice and good, but it means he knows the impact of hearing someone laugh at you, instead of with you. And he knows that by putting it on TV, you give up control over who sees your work. Again, as he said to Oprah, there's a group that gets what he's trying to do and another that is going to get something completely different.

A comic as good as Chappelle, or even a bit worse, should know the difference. "There were a lot of jokes about my girlfriend and you hear the misogynists laugh a little louder," Jeselnik explained in 2019.[43] "If I talk about race, racists laugh a little louder." As a result, Jeselnik transitioned away from jokes about groups. I bring this up because in *The Closer* Chappelle tries to talk about, from his perspective, the *actual* injustices facing trans people. "North Carolina passed a law once," he starts. "They said a person in North Carolina must use the restroom that corresponds with the gender they were assigned on their birth certificate." At that moment, you can hear, faintly, multiple members of the audience say, "That's right." Someone loudly wooos. He rebukes them in the moment, saying, "No American should have to present a birth certificate to take a shit at Walmart, in Greensboro, North Carolina," but he can't deny they are there, laughing at him describing being uncomfortable being in a public restroom with a trans woman who "hikes her skirt up" and "pulls a real live, meaty dick out!" Comedy might not be able to change minds, but it strengthens opinions.

Though there is an instinct to treat sides on these issues as a binary—pro-trans versus anti-trans—more likely all potential viewers of *The Closer* exist on a spectrum of opinion, and as a result, they each are impacted by Chappelle's material differently. Take the above trans bathroom joke, which continues with Chappelle saying he'd prefer if a trans man was in the bathroom next to him. "I would feel better if it was a man with a vagina that backed up to the urinal next to me," he says. "I wouldn't even think about that. I'd just be like, 'That's funny. This guy is peeing out of his butt for some reason.'" Though the direction of the joke is against North Carolina's bathroom bill, how it is received will vary based on each audience member's prior thoughts and feelings. A trans person or a total ally will have different opinions about the joke itself, but their stance on trans issues would very likely not be impacted at all. Audience members who obliquely support the trans community but feel some trepidation or confusion around the topic might find relief from their worry about this issue, in a way that moves them in the direction of unqualified support. Conversely, for audience members who aren't outright bigoted but are confused, skeptical, or generally weirded out by transgender people, Chappelle's dehumanizing fascination with the biology of the trans community can resonate and reverse any soft allegiances they were forming. For the unrepentant transphobe, Chappelle, just like the satirists of chapter 5, is giving this audience a vocabulary to talk about trans people—he is giving them ammunition. It's hard to prove anyone ever heard a joke and then went out and committed a hate crime, but people repeat jokes they like. It deems certain speech allowable, and worse, it encourages people who are less funny, who are more oblivious to context, to try to walk the same line, and that will result in vulnerable people feeling bad and more vulnerable.

Chappelle believes this is funny, but, as he said to Oprah about the sketch that made him leave *Chappelle's Show*, is it socially irresponsible? It depends on how responsible a comedian is for the people who don't understand them, to people laughing the wrong way. However, now Chappelle has ostensibly switched sides, deciding to not worry about it. It is a perspective he talked about when Bill Burr was on *The Midnight Miracle*, the soulful podcast Chappelle cohosts with the rappers Talib Kweli and Yasiin Bey.[44] Burr tells a story about when he first started doing material about going to see his wife, who is Black, up in Harlem and realizing he was the last white person left on the subway. "The whole joke was just me being scared and describing the neighborhood and my experience," Burr told Chappelle. But in Florida, a white man came up to him after a show and said about that joke, "Man, I like you; you ain't afraid of Black pussy." Burr found it liberating how far away people's interpretations can be, and it made him decide it's not his job to "babysit" the audience. The fear is that by babysitting, by spoon-feeding your material to less savvy audience members, it might come off as you not respecting the intelligence of the people who get it. At its best, it can result in stand-up that is more complicated and paradoxical. But, often when a comic gets to a point where their audience is on board with everything, the result can be the opposite. It's hard to find the nuances when the audience is laughing at any word you say.

Laughs lie to you. Sometimes audience members laugh because they're scared. Hannah Gadsby tells a story of seeing Jim Jefferies, ever a bad little boy: "He's just hating lesbians—just really, really hating. I'm sitting there, I just felt so unsafe. But I found myself laughing because I was scared."[45] And there are people who laugh, as in the Drew Michael story, in chapter 7, because of the overwhelming comedic force of the comedian. Watching *The Closer*, I felt bad for members of the audience who were maybe trying to work through their own feelings about a changing world. I pictured audience members completely on the fence laughing at a cruel joke about transgender women and having to resolve their cognitive dissonance by thinking, *Well, if I laughed, I must agree.*

Chappelle is funny. As I argued earlier in the book, if people find you funny, you're funny, and, undeniably, people find Chappelle funny in this moment. He's the biggest comedian in the country. And I do get it: Chappelle is an exceptionally charismatic master of the craft of making people laugh, even at things they don't agree with. But how good Chappelle is technically at stand-up is hindering how great he could be. In a room, Chappelle might be as great as he likes to say he is. He can be silent onstage and the audience gets pulled in. It's a superpower few have ever possessed, and he is undoubtedly its omega level. He can talk for long stretches without jokes, telling stories earnestly, if that's the type of story it is. He can be stupid when the audience needs that. And, yes, he can find a small room's line and cross it deliberately as few have ever done. But all this ability to connect with the audience, to ride their energy, to manipulate them, has slowly become hell on his material. By focusing on sensitive subjects, Chappelle pumps his jokes up with so much artificial tension that, when combined with his undeniable charisma, it means he doesn't have to do much to get huge shock laughs. The danger and relief for a comedian can become addictive. In an interview with David Letterman, Chappelle compared himself to Evel Knievel; like a stuntman, with each special he chases the rush.[46] As mythmaker, he determined this was noble, as if he's the only one to dare "go there." In reality, he was just attracted to what was already hot. Less a truth teller than a clout chaser. A lot of his supposedly edgy jokes had been done before. Bigotry is hack.

What has happened to Chappelle's comedy is best illustrated by a bit in *Equanimity*, in which he talks about how great at joke writing he is. To prove this point, he tells the audience, he wrote a joke punch line first, pulling "So I kicked her in the pussy" out of a fishbowl of random punch lines. (Neither here nor there, but this is surely a lie. Chappelle is *very* good at making lies seem true.) After a nearly five-minute childhood story about a friend inviting him to have dinner at his house, the friend's mother sadly informs little Dave, "We'd love to have you. It's just that we weren't expecting company. And I'm afraid . . . there's not enough Stove Top stuffing . . . for everybody." Chappelle pauses. "So I kicked her in the pussy." Playing off the tension of "when is he going to say it," he gets a big laugh for the sharp turn. It was a pretty clever, interesting journey this first time, but in recent years a noticeable portion of his jokes have followed this formula, following long buildups with an unrelated, shock punch line. Predictable to anyone paying close enough attention, it makes both the slow buildup, where he occasionally tries to sneak in some sort of message, and the inevitable twist so incredibly boring. It's like a sleight-of-hand magician who, no matter the fancy shuffling, always pulls the four of clubs as the prestige. Then you realize the entire deck is made up of fours of clubs. He used to be better than that. This is what it looks like when a comedian doesn't listen to the audience.

Of course, based on the venues he's playing, Chappelle is bigger than ever, despite all of this, so maybe it doesn't matter. But I do think time will tell. Chappelle wants to be seen as the, or at least *a*, GOAT. That is the reputation he has among his peers, again largely for his mastery of the live audience. But to younger comedians and younger, savvier comedy fans he is becoming a "relic," to quote a piece Danielle Fuentes Morgan wrote about *The Closer*.[47] From her experience teaching classes on African American comedy, she observed, "To younger audiences, he is out of step not only with the comedy of the moment but with the zeitgeist in general." After *The Closer*, Robin Tran, a trans stand-up comedian, tweeted:

> I think they should keep the Chappelle special up on Netflix forever with a CW for transphobia. It should stay up even 10 yrs from now when he's begging to have it taken down because he's ashamed of it when most of society has moved on. He should own it like a scarlet letter.[48]

As discussed in chapter 4, nothing moves the line like time. Eddie Murphy, a mentor to Chappelle, was maybe the biggest stand-up comedian who ever lived, but no conversation about his back catalog leaves out the hard-to-watch homophobic material. Over the years, Murphy has expressed regret, releasing a statement apologizing in 1996[49] and telling *CBS Sunday Morning* in 2019 he cringes when he watches it back.[50] Still, he said he tries to consider it "within the context of the times." What gets lost in the conversation was that at the time people also had a problem with the jokes. There were negative reviews and protests after 1983's *Delirious*. The *Los Angeles Times* review stated that Murphy's jokes "not only celebrate ignorance but are dangerous."[51] This is saying nothing about the gay people in the audiences, who didn't have a platform at the time, like Twitter, to voice their opposition. And yet Murphy doubled down in 1987's *Raw*, a special that otherwise would be considered his masterpiece, featuring some of the best character stand-up ever performed. I suspect, nowadays, he wishes he'd listened.

9

CONTEXT

One more thing about Dave Chappelle. Part of the reason for the late-career controversies is that he cannot comprehend how his material sounds outside the cult of personality he built for himself. I've seen Chappelle live two other times since that 2014 Radio City "comeback" and I noticed a trend, through all these shows, where the farther my seats were from the stage, the less loudly the people around me laughed. This is probably the case with most comedians I've seen in large venues, but it was particularly noticeable with Chappelle how proximity influenced the impact of his presence. I am not surprised, then, that when you put these shows on Netflix, with people now watching at home, as far as ever from the stage, there is backlash.

Well, shouldn't they have not watched, as Chappelle and his supporters would argue? The issue is that on Netflix, the audience is far removed from who Chappelle thinks he is, which is just some comic; many people will automatically consume his work because he is a major culture figure, or more likely because the algorithm recommended it. It's certainly frustrating for Chappelle, but the wound is self-inflicted. The comedian can control the content and they can also control how it's presented. Famous comedians, after touring in one hundred three-thousand-seat theaters full of fans, will release specials that are documents of the tour without considering how to create a filmed experience comparable to the energy in those rooms, or how to ensure their material translates to people unfamiliar with their work. The result is an echo chamber. Once a comic gets arena-level huge (especially if there are other entertainment industry distractions), it has been shown over and over again, it is impossible for them to write material as good as the stuff that got them there. If you watch a big comedian you've never heard of, it might not even register to you as comedy. It's like listening in on a group of friends laughing at an inside joke you weren't invited to be part of.

This is to say, comedy is an incredibly context-dependent art form. All art is created in a certain context, obviously, but the results are far less drastic if you remove that context. If a man in a painted-white William Shatner mask jumped out at you with a big knife, as in *Halloween*, you'd probably scream in horror. If you saw a woman wearing a wedding dress diarrhea-ing in the middle of the street, as in *Bridesmaids*, you'd probably also scream in horror. Unlike pornography, you do not know something is comedy when you see it. Often stand-ups are booked to perform in college cafeterias, and to those eating, unaware they are at a show, it registers as someone talking loudly in the corner. Younger or lesser comedians are dependent on the space they perform in to create the context, so they work to fit themselves into the house style. But when a comedian's vision refines, the goal is to get the audience to exist in the context *they* create. Brian Regan explained it to me like this: "The difficulty in doing stand-up comedy is not knocking down the pins, it's setting up the pins."[1] It goes back to the idea that comedy is about artificially creating the feeling of funniness that you experience with your family and friends. It's about creating that state of play. As a comedian builds a fan base, the audience is there less to see the comedian's material than to see their funny friend.

Problems arise when you take that roomful of buddies, film it, and place it in a different context. Worse when you're talking about streaming services—platforms with algorithms that create contexts around the individual viewer and not the comedian. And even worse because these performances live on the internet. Online, all of comedy's main forms of context—when a joke was made, the venue it was made in, and the identity of the person who made it—can be removed. Can comedy continue to exist in a land of no context? Probably, but, as we've seen, there are going to be growing pains. Comedians have changed to adapt to the contextless context of the internet. As have audiences. There is no going back.

Before we get to the internet, I want to talk a little bit about how context works in other comedy media. In his 2017 special, *Thank God for Jokes*, Mike Birbiglia tells a story about going to the doctor. Birbiglia, you see, was feeling pins and needles. *Where?* you ask. His urethra. *When?* "The moment I would ejaculate." Anyway, he gets some jokes off about that. What is important to us now is how the story ends. Birbiglia tells the doctor he is a comedian, to which the doctor replies, "If you're a comedian, how come you're not funny *now*?" Birbiglia in the present explains to the audience, "What I wanted to say was, 'I'm gonna take this conversation we're having and then repeat that to strangers. And then that's the joke. You're the joke . . . later.'" Which reminds me of a quote from Lauren Berlant: "The person who doesn't get the joke becomes a joke."[2] To expand this idea, Berlant and Ngai write, "The funny is always tripping over the not funny, sometimes appearing identical to it."[3] It is common for someone to say, "There's nothing funny about [insert topic the person is sensitive about]." And that's true. There's nothing inherently funny about anything, except poop, as Sam Richardson argued in chapter 3, but that's where comedy comes in. It creates a context that puts a comedy frame around a topic, transforming it right before the audience's eyes.

Man gets hit in the nuts with a football. A tragedy, at least to that man. But on *America's Funniest Home Videos*, with Alfonso Ribeiro's voice-over saying, "Ooooh, that's *got* to hurt"—comedy gold. There is a reason that as I write this, the only show MTV airs anymore is the fail-video commentary program *Ridiculousness*. A comedy frame can turn an assault into a hilarious prank and a touching portrait of male friendship, as the *Jackass* gang has proved. Similar but different is the meteoric rise of enjoying bad movies. What was once a pastime of small, alternative film nerd scenes in major cities has become the focus of many comedy podcasts, including the very popular *How Did This Get Made* and *The Flop House*, that in a way turn bad dramas into brilliant comedies. Speaking of bad dramas turning into brilliant comedies, the real housewives of the *Real Housewives* extended universe, totaling 145 women across eleven American franchises, are not comedians making a comedy, but a large portion of the franchise's audience consumes them as such. Though there are recaps, podcasts, and live readings, the *Real Housewives* audience doesn't really need a comedian to transform the work into comedy. Born out of a necessity to recontextualize a popular culture not made for their perspective, camp is maybe the most richly developed comedy frame.

The clearest example of how context is built and upheld to create comedy are roasts. Beginning at New York's Friars Club in 1949, roasts created a space to say things about a person you'd never say to their face. Things you wouldn't even say at a comedy show. "We only roast the ones we love" is a popular refrain and a nice story, but, in my opinion, it's bullshit. Love is not what makes roasts work. When Nikki Glaser said to Ann Coulter at the 2016 Rob Lowe roast, "The only person you will ever make happy is the Mexican that digs your grave," it was not out of love. It worked because roasts are a context. Everyone at a roast has consented to participate, knowing the rules, believing that they will enjoy the experience. There is an understanding that what is said would not be said otherwise. It's as if at the end of the show, everyone joins together to scream, "Not!" The context, then, is upheld by the form. It is incumbent on the roasters to understand the vocabulary of the medium, because if a joke is too cruel or not cruel enough or not clearly structured as a joke, the tenuous comedy frame could rupture. It is why roast jokes are the most jokey sounding of any jokes you hear in contemporary comedy.

How context is created is best understood by studying scripted comedies. A given TV comedy or movie might have some jokes, but most often the comedy is coming from a character interacting with the context the writers created through the setting and tone. Let's say you are at the office and your boss (let's call him Michael) asks their receptionist (let's give her a name, how about Pam?) what they are doing for lunch. And Pam responds, "My mother's coming." To which

Michael, who, again, is her boss, responds, with a little laugh, "That's what she said." You would not think this was funny. You might think it's harassment! But when you are watching *The Office* and Michael is Michael Scott (played by Steve Carell) and Pam is Pam Beesly (played by Jenna Fischer), you would. Why? Because of the context in which the exchange happens. You are meant to know: 1. This is fake. 2. Michael Scott is supposed to be stupid, needy, out of touch. 3. Pam thinks Michael is creepy yet harmless. 4. The show's perspective is such that most of the things Michael does are wrong. What the American version of *The Office* realizes that the British original didn't is that Michael's wrongness and his humorlessness are relatable. "We are all combover subjects," Berlant wrote, referring to the not-funny funniness of a person with a combover.[4] Meaning we all try and hilariously fail to cover up our desire not to be laughed at. It also means that a person living in one context (hair looks good) interacting with the reality of another (hair doesn't look good) is funny.

The Office was moderately popular when it originally aired, but it became a sensation on streaming. In the late 2010s, years after the show wrapped up its original run on NBC, it became Netflix's most popular show and remained there until it moved to Peacock in 2021. Over a twelve-month period ending in July 2018, Netflix subscribers watched *The Office* for 45.8 billion minutes, absolutely dwarfing the streamer's most popular original, *Stranger Things*, which was watched for 27.6 billion minutes.[5] My generation of Must-See TV comedy nerds liked *The Office* just fine. It got better ratings but didn't capture the zeitgeist like the more critically acclaimed *30 Rock*, *Community*, and *Parks and Recreation*. But it has become a way of life for those born digitally native. This is best captured by the Gen Z icon Billie Eilish, who once said, "When I wake up, I put on *The Office.* If I'm making a burrito, I turn on *The Office.*"[6] She ripped audio from a season 7 episode, directly from Netflix, for her song "My Strange Addiction" and used to open her concerts with the show's theme song.[7] She is a curious case, but hardly unique. At this point, you can't swing a dead cat on a dating app without hitting a profile that name-checks the show. It's hard to say for sure why the show connected the way it has, but my theory for why the show has thrived on streaming is because it is a comedy about contexts. In particular, in how it uses cringe.

Cringe is what happens when contexts collide. Over and over on the show, a character who exists in their own world says or does something in the implied real world of the show that is deliciously uncomfortable. The more earnestly the Dunder Mifflin employee is in their own context, the greater potential for cringe when they interact with a different context. In her 2018 book *Cringeworthy: A Theory of Awkwardness*, Melissa Dahl describes the everyday, interpersonal cringe as "the intense visceral reaction produced by an awkward moment, an unpleasant kind of self-recognition where you suddenly see yourself through someone else's eyes."[8] As a comedic force, the audience is the one that has the recognition, as the character remains un-self-aware of how they are being perceived. In the above scene, Michael is living with a different understanding of the rules of the situation than Pam and the rest of the office. When Jim looks to camera, he is communicating the bounds of his own context. With a little mug to the audience at home, via the audience of the show's fictional documentary, Jim's saying that Michael is the joke . . . later.

It turns out that both Jim and Michael were the joke . . . later, on Twitter, on Instagram, in text threads; gifs of Michael saying, "That's what she said" and of Jim turning to the camera became two of the most popular memes from the show and, considering the show's standing, two of the most popular memes, period. As a result, scenes from *The Office* are found removed from their original context interacting with spaces without a context of their own. This is how comedy interacts with the internet. How do you do, fellow kids? I am here to talk about memes.

Save the occasional cat who wanted to haz cheeseburger, in 2007, the first meme I ever saw featured an image of the rapper Xzibit, who had hosted the MTV show *Pimp My Ride*, in which he would take rides (cars) and pimp them (put a lot of wild stuff inside, like a snake terrarium and a CAT scan machine). The image was a simple, sweet picture of Xzibit smiling, with a caption that read "YO DAWG I HERD YOU LIKE CARS SO I PUT A CAR IN YO CAR SO YOU CAN DRIVE WHILE YOU DRIVE." I understood the reference and acknowledged it was humorous, I guess. This was an image macro, I would learn. What made it a meme was that people iterated on it. There were tons of follow-ups. Xzibit's face Photoshopped onto a picture of a toaster oven inside an actual oven with the caption "YO DAWG I HERD YOU LIKE BAKING SO WE PUT AN OVEN IN YO OVEN SO YOU CAN BAKE WHILE YOU BAKE." Xzibit's face Photoshopped onto an image of a hand holding a yo-yo that has an image of a dog holding a yo-yo Photoshopped onto it, with the caption "YO DAWG I HERD YO AND YO DAWG LIKE YO YOS SO WE PUT YO DAWG IN A YO YO SO YO CAN YO YO YO DAWG WHILE YO DAWG YO YOS, DAWG." Nearly fifteen years later, a meme is a TikTok where someone mimics the way the actress Julia Fox said "Uncut Gems" one time in an interview. So, yeah, they range.

At the risk of sounding cringe to my younger readers, though they can be comedic or interacted with comedically, I have a hard time considering memes in the same way as I do the work of comedians. It's complicated because, as Limor Shifman argues in her 2013 book *Memes in Digital Culture*, the internet "[erodes] the boundaries between top-down pop culture and bottom-up folk culture."[9] A joke-joke—as discussed in the first chapter, the things comedians don't really tell anymore—is the closer analogue to how memes function in that they are similarly passed around free of their originators. Many originators, like Ms. Fox, were not intending to create a meme. Yes, people make memes, but, by design, they reach people through third parties, resulting in meme aggregators, whose feeds are like rapidly curated joke books, becoming the ones who tend to build the massive followings instead of the creators. That said, just like the tradition of jokes shaping people's expectation of comedy for much of its early history, memes influence people's expectations and interactions with comedy today.

Maybe the most memed work of comedy in recent history (at least based on the internet the algorithms created for me) is *I Think You Should Leave*, the Netflix sketch show from Tim Robinson and Zach Kanin. *I Think You Should Leave*? More like *I Think You Should MEME*, am I right? This guy knows what I'm talking about [*points to no one*]. Brian Eno is famous for remarking in an interview about the Velvet Underground's debut album's outsized influence compared to how many albums they sold: "I think everyone who bought one of those 30,000 copies started a band!" Netflix doesn't regularly release numbers, but *I Think You Should Leave*'s perceived popularity is swayed by the fact that seemingly everyone who watched it made a meme or fifty. There's the image of Robinson screaming "Figure out what you do" to Chunky, an aimless game show mascot. There's the image of Vanessa Bayer, out to brunch with her girlfriends, trying to think of an Instagram caption with the subtitle of the dialogue at the bottom: "Sunday funday with these pig dicks." There's a gif of Ruben Rabasa, the charismatic eighty-something Cuban actor, in a car focus group, dabbing. There's a gif of Rabasa, in that same focus group, waving his hand in front of his nose and saying the car should be "Stinky." There's a gif of Rabasa responding, "Oh my god, he admit it!" to Paul, his focus group nemesis, agreeing to the fact that he did in fact love his mother-in-law.

These memes facilitate multiple types of communication. First, they are used to signify and foster a shared understanding. Posting, retweeting, or even seeing memes like those from *I Think You Should Leave* has, as Shifman writes, the "sweet scent of an inside joke."[10] Communicating through them is a "love language," as *The New Yorker* wrote after the phenomenon continued for season 2.[11] To be on social media sometimes feels like floating in the careless void of space; recognizing and getting a meme provides a comforting sense of belonging. It speaks to how unique it is to consume comedy through social media, where the play is less a state you stay in, like the comedy discussed thus far in the book, but a periodic spike when something with comedy energy passes your eyes.

But more than that, people use both the words and images of a meme, as well as its shared cultural association, to talk online. While fans' repurposing of material has always been built into comedy, from one-liners siphoned from favorite borscht belt comics to kids repeating *SNL* quotes and voices at each other, online memes can be easier, richer, and more vital. A meme could convey information like how excited a person is that it's Friday (dabbing gif) or what they think of your bad tweet (stinky gif). When Zion Williamson, an NBA player known equally for his unprecedented athleticism and his bulky frame, remains on the injury list, I Think You Should League Pass—the Twitter account that applied *I Think You Should Leave* memes to NBA news, to the tune of sixty thousand followers—will post Robinson in that game show sketch telling the producers, "We just gotta figure out, like, what Chunky's deal is."

Still, no meme transcended like Hot Dog Man. (If this were a tweet, you'd reply with the "Oh my god, he admit it!" gif). In the sketch, a hot dog car crashes into a Brooks Brothers. After some commotion over who did it, a man yells, "Somebody call the cops. We need to find that driver." "Yeah, come on, whoever did this just confess," agrees a man in a hot dog costume, adding, "We promise we won't be maaaad." Instantly, everyone knows he is the driver, while Hot Dog Man keeps on acting like he is on the same side as the angry mob. When the cops arrive, Hot Dog Man—who, again, is wearing a hot dog costume—says about the hot dog car that has crashed through the front of the store, "We're all trying to find the guy who did this." That's the meme that somehow perfectly captured a political time in which siloed media circles allow people to say the right thing in one space while causing the problem they are speaking about in another. On the afternoon of the January 6 insurrection, the *New York Times* op-ed columnist Jamelle Bouie tweeted the meme in response to House Minority Leader Kevin McCarthy's statement, "This is my saddest day as a member of Congress."[12] When ExxonMobil tweeted, "We're all in this together! Glad to be a part of the Oil and Gas Climate Initiative—working collaboratively toward solutions to mitigate the risks of climate change," the U.S. representative Ilhan Omar posted the meme.[13] Robinson's attempts "to avoid embarrassment or consequences through outright denial of reality," explained the comedian Kath Barbadoro about the politics of Hot Dog Man, "feels uncomfortably reminiscent of how this past year has played out."[14] It is important to remember this reading is most definitely not what the original sketch is about, but what happens when others placed it into this context.

To take it a step further, as a whole, *I Think You Should Leave* was not created with the hopes of it being memeable. Neither of its creators is especially online. However, there were some formal decisions that made the show work on social media. First and foremost, *ITYSL* uses a lot of close-ups that both maximize the potential of Robinson's expressive face and create an image-macro-ready mise-en-scène. Many of *ITYSL*'s early sketches, including "Hot Dog Man," started as failed ideas from when Robinson and Kanin worked on *SNL*. Free from the time constraints of that show, Kanin and Robinson could write overlong, overstuffed shooting scripts. This allowed them to try out many more alternative jokes and lines (or "alts") for characters, so in the edit they could pick the perfect earworm lines, which later became ideal for the caption in a screenshot. It's a bit Sketch Writing 101, but Kanin and Robinson are masterful at quickly setting up the comedic dynamic (aka the game) of the scene that results in a cavalcade of punch lines, paying off like a broken slot machine. Also, unlike at *SNL*, Robinson and Kanin were free to cast as many perfectly imperfect out-of-step oddballs as they wanted to, each of whom stand out when they pop up on a feed. Lastly, like *The Office*, the show's expertise is a character out of context. At *SNL*, sketches often feature an unreal weirdo in a normal setting or a normal person in a weirdo setting, but Robinson's characters feel and act like they are from another dimension entirely in which they are a normal person.

Because all the *ITYSL* characters—be it those played by Robinson, by the show's unknown weirdos, or by the occasional guest stars Patti Harrison, John Early, and Kate Berlant—are defined by their context, it allows those meming the show to carry their contextual weight onto the context-neutral space of social media. In that space, *ITYSL* memes are then free to move from something fellow fans recognize to something people can use to communicate, detached from knowledge of the show. This is the case with all memed comedy. This is how it works. At the top of this section, I asked, "How do you do, fellow kids?" referencing a much-memed moment from Tina Fey's NBC sitcom *30 Rock*, in which Steve Buscemi plays a private investigator who was part of a "special task force of very young-looking cops who infiltrated high schools" and greets his classmates saying, "How do you do, fellow kids?" The joke of the show is that this character is existing in a context where he thinks he, a Steve Buscemi–looking man, could pass as youthful. When this first became a meme, users were likely bringing the show's context to social media, placing whatever they might be responding to on social media into the context of *30 Rock*. In 2011, I might've tweeted "me joining Snapchat" with a "How do you do, fellow kids?" screenshot attached, as a way to commiserate with fellow, formerly cutting-edge *30 Rock* fans about our impending obsolescence. Over time, however, as the meme became more commonplace, its original association faded as people associated the image with its usage as a meme. Considering *30 Rock* was never a huge hit during its original run, like *The Office*, and that over a decade has passed since the episode aired, it's likely most people don't even know what the image is from. The meme carries the context of the joke, without the context of the show, allowing it to be freely placed in whatever context the user needs.

What's lost is authorship. Every comedian I've talked to whose work has been turned into a major meme has been positive yet befuddled about it. This includes Robinson. But there's a tension. This uneasiness was best captured by Taylor Tomlinson, a stand-up who has amassed more than 2.2 million followers on TikTok through posting stand-up clips and acting as a sort of older sister to the app's Gen Z users. In a 2020 TikTok that has over two hundred thousand likes, she starts by genuinely addressing the camera: "Okay, my absolute favorite thing about TikTok is all these people working so hard on their videos." This makes her laugh. "Only to have a super-hot girl lip-sync their video and they get like a billion likes." Her laughter crescendos to the point of near crying. "And the original person gets like a hundred. It's so unfair . . . like life." It being TikTok, over 150 people used the audio from her video to make their own videos, turning it into a meme. They included @thebrookehargis, a creator who has amassed around seven hundred thousand followers by lip-syncing stand-up routines, shifting the joke to a visual format that would connect better to the app. Where most stand-up clips are shot wide, with the comic looking out to the audience beyond the camera, Hargis is up close, making direct eye contact. To be fully transparent, Tomlinson's video got over one million views and Hargis's over ninety thousand, but that gap is the exception. In 2022, Hargis posted a video of herself performing a joke Nick Kroll had posted about people being mean to their mothers. Her video got 1.4 million views, the exact same as Kroll—again, the person whose joke it actually was. That's weird!

How icky this feels to you is a bit of a Rorschach test, if Rorschach tests determined how old you are. Someone older might see this as corporate-sanctioned theft; someone younger might think the idea of owning is capitalist cop behavior. As a millennial, I sit somewhere in the middle. It would be easier for me to embrace the internet as a utopian marketplace for the free exchange of ideas if it weren't overrun by cynical actors taking advantage of the lack of accountability. In 2019, my colleague at *Vulture* Megh Wright attempted to expose this disconnect between ideals and reality by reporting on Elliot Tebele, the man behind FuckJerry, maybe the most well-known meme aggregator on Instagram, who claims to have made millions by posting without crediting the original creators.[15] Creating an online movement with #FuckFuckJerry, Wright found examples of FuckJerry, or members of his network of aggregators, taking tweets from comedians, removing the identifying information, then using them in sponsored posts that have likely earned him tens of thousands of dollars.

In 2015, I interviewed The Fat Jewish, Josh Ostrovsky, after he sparked a similar backlash among comedians and comedy fans. In what was by far the most annoying conversation I've ever had in my entire life, Ostrovsky tried to pay lip service to caring while displaying a compulsive need to self-promote.[16] I tried to hold him accountable for stealing, and he attempted to plead the "I was drinking a daiquiri nude and looking at the internet" defense. He didn't care about crediting; he didn't even care about the memes. He just wanted to be famous.

Both Ostrovsky, to me, and Tebele, in a 2019 statement, acknowledged what they did was wrong, while also using a similar excuse. "The internet was a different landscape then," said Ostrovsky.[17] Tebele wrote there were not "well-established norms" with memes.[18] And both said they would be better about crediting going forward. Though I remember him doing so immediately after we spoke, as of this writing, The Fat Jewish usually does not credit. I wouldn't say FuckJerry gives people credit, and he definitely does not give them compensation, but now, at least, he doesn't crop out the names of the handles he gets him memes from, maybe 50 percent of the time. But no one is really keeping track anymore. The internet moved on, but, looking back, what stuck with me was not the comedians and their followers who complained and joined in. And it wasn't even the meme aggregators themselves. It was the people who defended them. I was stupid for caring, for taking this seriously. They're "just jokes."

Not that again. While all these technologies claim to be a step forward for communication, removing comedy from its context and turning comedians back to anonymous contributors to the great American joke book is a step backward for the art form.

Irony on the internet is like rain on your wedding day—not nice. Honestly, it's actually kind of like ten thousand spoons when all you need is a knife. You're just looking for a person who gets it in a sea of people who don't. This frustration stems from what is unique about irony in comedic speech. In the book *Irony's Edge*, the postmodern literary theorist Linda Hutcheon argues that the audience doesn't just "get" ironic speech, they "make" it. "Irony isn't irony," she writes, "until it is interpreted as such."[19] It is the fundamental dynamic between the comedian and their audience I've discussed throughout the book, but even more so. The audience does not just get to determine if something makes them laugh, but what the meaning of that thing is. Let's say Comedian X intended to make an ironic racist joke. Some people's brains will receive it as intended to make fun of racism. Some actually bigoted people will make it an actually racist joke. There might also be some people who already thought Comedian X was racist, based on reputation, and will also interpret the joke as racist.

To avoid this ambiguity, there is a theory that gets passed around the internet from time to time, both ironically and earnestly: "Satire requires a clarity of purpose and target lest it be mistaken for and contribute to that which it intends to criticize." Similarly, Hutcheon was worried that making the interpreter consider the literal meaning as well as the ironic created an "edge"—as in a sort of dangerous pointedness—on ironic speech, a lingering remnant of whatever you didn't want to communicate (in the above case, Hutcheon would argue the audience who got Comedian X's joke still experienced some feelings of bigotry). The good news is that research has shown that people understand the nonliteral meaning without having to internalize the literal, on the condition, as the professor Raymond W. Gibbs Jr. has studied, that the person is "given sufficient context."[20] The bad news is that "sufficient context" is not happening on the internet. Like *Atlanta* or *Reservation Dogs*, the state comedies of chapter 7 that ask you to trust you are watching a comedy, or a comedian like Anthony Jeselnik, in chapter 8, who depends on your trusting he isn't actually evil, comedy on the internet is also testing the audience's ability to trust that something even is comedy, without the full information necessary to know for sure. This raises some very basic, very deep questions about how comedy (if not all of culture) continues, if the levels of trust and context they once depended on are impossible to restore.

Over the last decade there have been comedians who explored these concerns and who have been able to use the contextless chaos of the internet to help them better communicate themselves. Playing in the comedic genre of prank, they use ambiguity to heighten the power of their satire. What follows are two of the best examples.

The first happened in the fall of 2019, when America was in the thick of the Democratic primary. In November, a video came out of Pete Buttigieg supporters doing a choreographed dance to Panic! at the Disco's "High Hopes." Being from Indiana, Buttigieg sure knows how to produce corn. Pretty quickly non-supporters called this cringe and people made fun of it. Then, in December, Nick Ciarelli and Bradford Evans, with Twitter account bios saying they worked for the Mike Bloomberg campaign and photos of them with clean haircuts and passable suits, posted a video of a room of people doing a hastily choreographed dance to Maroon 5's "Moves like Jagger," but with "Bloomberg" dubbed over the name of the Rolling Stones' lead singer. I'm a longtime friend of Evans's and a fan of the sketches and pranks he and Ciarelli put up on Twitter, so this had me laughing and laughing. I retweeted it, as did many of the comedians I follow. But so did Ted Cruz[21] and Eric Trump.[22] Sebastian

Gorka, a former Trump official, Fox News contributor, and all-around right-wing ghoul, quote-tweeted the video with the caption "Apparently NOT a parody."[23] Maggie Haberman, who at the time was maybe the most prominent political reporter in the country, quote-tweeted it with a question mark. She was let in on the joke and quipped butt-hurtedly, "All the best parody has to be explained," almost paraphrasing the "clarity of purpose" theory above.

What Haberman was suggesting was that Ciarelli and Evans should pander. The counterpoint to this request is it's nice to talk to your people in a way only they get. When you're in a foreign country, hearing someone speak your dominant language can feel like home. Hutcheon argues that irony doesn't simply create an in-group and an out-group, but that "discursive communities make irony possible in the first place."[24] Ciarelli and Evans's audience knew the nature of their tone, and by communicating this shared understanding, they helped create the ironic language of "Moves Like Bloomberg." However, people got confused. In contrast, attempts to be obvious, so that everyone will understand, often read to people in your group as condescending, unsophisticated, or distancing. This was particularly a problem during the 2020 election cycle. After being burned in 2016, many people across the liberal spectrum, from supporters of Sanders to supporters of Biden, wanted you to know exactly what candidate a piece of comedy supported.

The tension between the pleasures of ambiguity and the conscientiousness of transparency result in something I refer to as the pandering paradox, where a comedian with reach has to decide if making their point of view clear to people unfamiliar with them or less fluent in a given issue is worth having their comedy appeal less to the people who are familiar with them. It is the Adam McKay conundrum. For years, McKay made beloved comedies with a sneaky progressive message that likely was so subtle that many, many people didn't even catch it. So then he pivoted to making movies with an obvious message that the right avoided and many on the left found condescending. There is also a version of the pandering paradox that comedians of marginalized communities have to navigate once they find large platforms: To make any appeal to the mainstream might read as cynical pandering, but if they try to make work speaking only to their community, the mainstream is likely to get the wrong message. Yeah, it sucks.

Ciarelli and Evans got around the pandering paradox problem by building the confusion into the joke. The goal was to make something that would be clearly a joke to anyone who knows them and anyone who spent more than three seconds looking into who they were. Yes, they changed their photos and bios to photos of them wearing suits from when they were clean-cut teens, but they kept up all their old tweets. Meaning if any of the people who took the video as sincere scrolled at all, they would see Evans and Ciarelli posting other videos and promoting the live show at which the video was clearly shot. Their hope was that the video would reveal the ridiculousness of the modern political media ecosystem—both campaigns' silly pandering, as well as the reactionary, knee-jerk laziness and lack of online literacy of social media activism. Fooling the upper reaches of the political establishment was not the plan, but it further proved their point. "It's fun for us to build a pretend world around our comedy," Evans, who went on to work with Ciarella at *The Tonight Show Starring Jimmy Fallon*, told me over email. "It occasionally has the effect of tricking more people into thinking our comedy is real, which can be funny and scary but mostly funny."

Where Evans and Ciarella were attempting to critique how social media is used, Jaboukie Young-White, my second example of someone who effectively used online ambiguity for their satire, has a more nihilistic, burn-it-all down perspective. Young-White embraces the chaos of metamodernism, a time in which "everything is sincere and ironic at the same time." He achieved this by going to war with Twitter's blue checkmark. I got my blue checkmark by replying to an email with one word, "sure," one day at work, but, to those who grew up online, it can be an actual status symbol. As Young-White explained on Twitter, because most people, like me, get it by being associated with a mainstream media organization, it is a tool for "white coastals to pick and choose who can get into 'the club.'"[25] And though all it really symbolizes is your proximity to whiteness, it is often used to claim authority.

To point out the checkmark's arbitrariness, Young-White has multiple times changed his profile picture and bio to look like that of another account, knowing the blue checkmark would then make anything he tweeted from it seem real. He changed his account to Cats Movie in 2019 and tweeted, "The cats in Cats (2019) will have realistic spiked penises."[26] He changed it to FBI in 2020 and tweeted, "Just because we killed MLK doesn't mean we can't miss him."[27] These tweets would temporarily get his account suspended, but what finally got Twitter to remove the checkmark was Young-White changing his account to CNN and tweeting, "BREAKING: Joe Biden is not DEAD. He just getting some dick. We've all been there."[28] "A lot of those tweets were so farfetched, but people wanted them to be true so bad," he said afterward.[29]

"They liked it and didn't look twice at it." Young-White feels like he's succeeded if more people look at tweets and stop to ask themselves, *Is this real or am I getting got right now?* By pushing the chaos to the most absurd, he makes it clearer for more people just how chaotic things are. And as Twitter has grown more chaotic, with Elon Musk buying the platform in 2022, Young-White's method of satire has become a go-to form of resistance. After pronouncing "Comedy is now legal on Twitter"[30] when his purchase went through, Musk soon after started to ban people who tried to pose as someone else without marking it as parody. In response, countless accounts changed their picture and handle to pose as Musk.

Though these methods seem incredibly modern, they are ultimately playing into a history of satire that dates back millennia. This is what *The Onion* argued in 2022, when it filed an amicus brief to the Supreme Court in support of an individual who was arrested by local law enforcement for creating a parody Facebook page for the police department that eventually arrested him.[31] *The Onion*, of course, knows a thing or two about people seeing their work as the real thing they're parodying. "Parodists intentionally inhabit the rhetorical form of their target in order to exaggerate or implode it," the brief argues, "and by doing so demonstrate the target's illogic or absurdity." And with that comes tricking the audience into thinking they are seeing a genuine version "and then allowing them to laugh at their own gullibility when they realize that they've fallen victim to one of the oldest tricks in the history of rhetoric." Their argument is backed by legal precedent that says parodical text is protected by the First Amendment, as one ruling they cite suggests, "notwithstanding that not everybody will get the joke." Another cited ruling argued that parody just has to be plausibly understood by a "reasonable reader" of "reasonable intelligence and learning," who "can tell the difference between satire and sincerity." The ignorant or oblivious comedy consumer can't dictate what satirical speech is protected, but they also can't be stopped from interpreting it obliviously or ignorantly. This issue will always go back to how much a comedian cares about the people who don't get it. The internet has heightened that tension, as at least a live audience would be somewhat selecting; now ironic speech is flying all over, all willy-nilly.

Comedy's growing pains on the internet are examples of a culture in a transition. This is not a comedy-exclusive story. The human brain did not evolve to process this number of people communicating with one another. Young-White's satire—and this goes for Ciarelli and Evans's work as well—is trying to do a lot of what Jon Stewart's *Daily Show* did, which is, through comedy, to show people how to process all the information coming at them. It hopefully doesn't just appeal to reasonable readers but helps create more of them.

It must be stated that the context most comedians had to perform in before the modern internet wasn't exactly chill, either. A lot of this book is combating certain conventional wisdom that comedy clubs fight to uphold. And a lot of the reason comedy is as popular as it is now is that it has been able to reach fans who avoided the traditional spaces. There is no better example than Ali Wong.

Wong had been a comic for a decade before her first special. She performed a ton and got some TV work, but none of it resulted in building a significant fan base. And part of that was due to the context in which she was performing—comedy clubs. Though the standard is shifting at a glacial pace, at comedy clubs, regardless of the lineup, the audience is still expecting a straight male orthodoxy. Many people who go to comedy clubs don't research who they are going to see first, which only further exacerbates the assumption that the comedian will be a certain sort of dude doing a certain sort of dude humor. With these norms, if you are not a straight man, there's the fear, or reality, that you will be called out and made fun of for being different. Over the last thirty years, a handful of women have broken out from the comedy-club scene, though really so, so, so, so few, but even those who did had to adhere to the expectations of these rooms. Wong got booked on the road, but, at best, she was playing to people expecting the orthodoxy, not her potential fans. As the legend goes (legend count #10), before her Netflix debut, she couldn't sell a weekend of shows at a club in San Francisco, her hometown. The venue had to put the tickets on Groupon.

Then, on Mother's Day weekend in 2016, *Baby Cobra* debuted. I've talked to a lot of comedians and people in the industry over the years, and they had never seen anyone blow up like Wong did then. Her social media following grew fourfold after the special was posted on Netflix. The aforementioned potential fans, clearly, *did* want to watch stand-up, but they needed it to be in a context where they felt safe or, especially in the case of pregnant women, a context where there wasn't a two-drink minimum. Wong's next booking at that same San Francisco club sold out in minutes, but that was nothing, because she had jumped to being a large-theater act seemingly overnight.

It makes sense. Why would her potential fans go to a comedy club on the off chance an Ali Wong would be there, when realistically they had never seen anyone like her before in those spaces? It's why Wong notes in the special, "It's very rare and unusual to see a female comic perform pregnant, because female comics . . . don't get pregnant." Adding, dramatically, "Once they do get pregnant, they generally disappear." I would not suggest that there had never been a pregnant comedian before, as there had been plenty. Laurie Kilmartin, who once was one, said she saw a number of comics pregnant in the '00s: "Judy Gold, Sherry Davey, Lisa Landry, Cory Kahaney, Kerri Louise twice." Two of these (Landry and Kahaney) filmed half-hour specials while pregnant, but they weren't showing at the time and they didn't say anything about it. Joan Rivers appeared on *The Ed Sullivan Show* nine months pregnant but was told by censors she wasn't allowed to say a word acknowledging it.[32] Kilmartin herself had done a TV set pregnant, but it wasn't widely seen. Netflix didn't create too much context, since everyone's homepage is algorithmically built around themselves, but it gave Wong a reach beyond the context she'd been working in.

But it's not just Netflix; the reason Ali Wong became Ali Wong is that she's Ali Wong. Wearing red cat-eye glasses and a skintight, eight-dollar H&M dress featuring both black and white stripes and a floral pattern, which has since been sent to the Smithsonian, she figured out a way to create a context in a context-free space that could magnify her already immense comedic talent. In an industry where having a kid is a preexisting condition, being pregnant in a special had a tremendous, transgressive power that created an exhilarating tension, as her pregnancy remains unaddressed for the first two-thirds of the special. Encouraging her female audience to anally stimulate their male partners when they go home that night is already subversive, but to do so while confronting the culture's Virgin Mary picture of pregnancy is sacrilegious. When she finally does talk about pregnancy, her current state helps in another way. Two years prior, Wong had had a miscarriage, but struggled in talking about it onstage. It was Kilmartin who gave Wong the advice that the audience needs to know the comic is okay in order to laugh. With the special, as she said in an interview at the time, being pregnant while doing that material was how she communicated she was okay.[33] That's how she pulls off a daring bit like this:

> Most women won't let their husbands watch when they're going through a miscarriage. I sat my husband down in front of me while I sat on the toilet, and I was like, "You look. You watch the whole thing." And he felt so bad for me. And I used it as leverage and held that shit over his head for a month and got him to do whatever the fuck I wanted him to do for thirty days. He took me to see Beyoncé. He bought me a bike off of Craigslist. That's my miscarriage bike, and I love it very much. For thirty days, I finally had the marriage I always wanted.

As Wong discusses in *Baby Cobra*, the point of a joke like this is for more women to talk about miscarriages and other potential challenges of pregnancy, so they won't feel so bad if they go through it. *Baby Cobra* felt like a revolution, not just because Wong found a way to discuss the potential horrors of pregnancy, but that she found and made people ready to listen.

In the years since, as Netflix's stockpile of specials and big-name talent they could tap into has grown, their ability to break new stand-ups has slowed down, with Taylor

Tomlinson and Nate Bargatze probably the biggest exceptions. Instead, comedians have had to turn themselves over to other algorithms—YouTube's, Instagram's, and TikTok's. Comedian-destroys-heckler videos became a bit of a cliché, often performed by unheralded comedians in the 2010s, but in the 2020s it became essential practice for working stand-ups to post topical jokes, unfinished material, and crowd work on every platform. Andrew Schulz is the comic many will cite as being the first to conquer the formula, as he realized that the more he fed the algorithms, the better his clips did. As a way of maximizing content, he began focusing on crowd work, providing him an endless supply of content. "100 clips is 100 ways of discovering me," he claimed.[34] "An hour on Netflix is one." Schulz's platform of choice was YouTube, but the comedian Nimesh Patel found similar success following the same formula on TikTok, as did Matteo Lane on Instagram. Online followings grew, as well as in-person audiences. More and more comedians followed suit, kicking and screaming and talking shit about everyone else doing it. Again, it must be stated that it works. But at what cost?

In the summer of 2022, the comedian Matt Ruby wrote a post on his Substack after an Instagram Reel of his went viral, garnering over 1.3 million views.[35] The joke, which he himself didn't think was that good, hinged on the idea that the phrases "people of color" and "colored people" are basically the same, yet one is racist. With its success, it became clear that a large reason for its virality was that it made people fight in the comments. Social media platforms are looking for engagement, not passive enjoyment, so someone's hating your joke and saying so is more valuable than their just liking it. Ruby couldn't get past the fact that this was the exact opposite of why anyone, including himself, gets into comedy: "People in a room together unified in laughter." Furthermore, Ruby was fearful that, without any context, audiences online would just see "some dude with a shaved head prattling on about racialized language," and reject him as some sort of alt-right comic or, even worse, embrace him as some sort of alt-right comic. Also, he noticed, as anyone who is paying attention to which comedy blows up on social media has, that being a hack works. Being a hack works everywhere, but in the real world, comics try to avoid being labeled as such by good comedians and smart comedy fans. The algorithm is not so discerning.

It's somewhat ironic that crowd work, which is supposed to be the most in-the-moment a comedian can be and has notoriously been hard to capture on film, has become the main source of this social media content. And it's the easy stuff, as mentioned in chapter 4, that goes viral. But, having spoken to young people about viral content ("How do you do, fellow kids?" etc.), it makes sense to me that what is popular would be the easy stuff. An Instagram Reel or TikTok does not demand the attention necessary to blow someone's mind with brilliance. It favors the quick hit of a person doing a cool trick. It gives the person scrolling a dopamine rush to see people interacting with each other positively, which stands out after a pandemic kept people apart.

A bigger concern than having to scroll past average content to get to the good stuff is how stand-up clips transform the live space into an online content creation space, with venues like the Comedy Cellar filming every set for their comics to use as they please on social media. But then I remember that it's not as though comedy clubs were so great before. And it's not as if—as some comics have worried—these new audience members who come to shows because of social media are acting like they think they're supposed to talk to the comics throughout the set. The truth is that social media has brought a lot of people out to shows who have never been, and it has given comedians an opportunity to teach new fans how comedy could be, without having to play into the previously existing orthodoxy of the comedy club. Comedy is so cheap and its practitioners are so desperate for face time with an audience that the form adapts to new technologies quickly. When the technology is itself adapting at an accelerated pace, stand-up adapts more quickly than people are able to process, but, knowing the history, stand-up always ends up in the same place: stage, person, stool, mic stand, mic, audience.

Are you scared? Like, does all of this feel a bit scary? Like, does it feel like I am inviting AI comedians to perform mathematically perfect comedy for mathematically perfect AI audience members, while our human bodies are jammed into pods to provide the energy source to power this interaction? If so, I am sorry. It is natural to focus more on how things change than how they have been able to stay the same. Live comedy has evolved formally and conceptually, but zoomed out, it's the same gig. And at the same time all these platform shifts have been happening, there have been comedians, especially the post-comedy inclined, who have been working with directors to give their specials a more fully realized context. Using interesting camerawork, editing, and lighting, you're able to give the audience at home a story or a sense of time and place, making it harder to mentally break comedy down into 0s and 1s.

There is Wyatt Cenac's 2014 special, *Brooklyn*, and Mike

Epps's 2022 special, *Indiana Mike*, both of which focused on the places the comedian currently or previously lived. Katt Williams never lived in Jacksonville but when he filmed his 2018 special, *Great America*, there, he opened with eleven transcendent minutes of specific observations and jokes about the city. Mo'Nique's 2007 *I Coulda Been Your Cellmate!* and Ali Siddiq's 2018 *It's Bigger Than These Bars* similarly use setting to focus their context, using prison not just as an attempt to establish edgy cred, but to help articulate their own stories and experiences.

Still, the example that sticks in my head is Lil Rel Howery's 2019 HBO special, *Live in Crenshaw*, which up to this point is the richest marriage of stand-up performance and visual storytelling I've seen. It started with its director, Jerrod Carmichael, coming to Rel with the idea of a special set in Susan Miller Dorsey Senior High School, in the Crenshaw neighborhood of L.A. Rel is not from L.A. originally, but the high school gym's eastern and western walls are all glass, allowing Carmichael to shoot the special using natural light. Carmichael starts the special off with an L.A. youth step team and the vocalist Akua Willis singing the Black national anthem, "Lift Every Voice and Sing," followed by a step performance. *Crenshaw* was meant to feel like a civil rights rally. "I felt like I was opening up for Dr. King," Rel would say.[36]

Rel is one of the great character stand-ups working, and throughout the set he tells a multilayered story about going to and paying for his uncle Larry's funeral, in which he plays multiple characters, from his older uncle who's giving him compliments before asking for money ("Denzel Washington, who? Denzel, who? How about Lil Rel Washington, you know what I'm saying?") to his cousin Reggie, Larry's son, who can't read well but is asked to give a reading anyway, to the pastor who pulls off a eulogy for the deceased, despite not knowing him, that is so impassioned that Rel's impression of it alone gets the audience standing and cheering in affirmation. The revelation: Over the course of the hour, the sun sets. By the end, it's nighttime, and though only an hour has passed, it feels like a whole day. Rel in spotlight recreates some comically bad recent concert experiences, like Tito Jackson performing only his parts of Jackson 5 songs. The audience members, whose faces you have grown familiar with, are now cast in shadow, and you, at home, feel like you are one of them. It is impossible to not feel teleported into that moment. It defies you to try to clip it. Social media cannot compete with what it feels like to go through this journey in its entirety.

By actually capturing the electricity in the room, Carmichael and Rel extended Rel's family to include the people there and beyond. Rel said at the time that he chose not to shoot the special in Chicago, where he's from, to show "a lot of people are the same everywhere."[37] "The gymnasium represents a lot of the old spots I did early in my career," he said about the venue.[38] "Like those gymnasiums, Masonic Halls, random places I did comedy on the chitterling circuit." He added, "When you hear the word 'Crenshaw' you automatically think Black and real." Rel, who grew up going to marches and rallies, deeply understood that the most fulfilling context for your comedy is one you work to build and foster with others. As he explained on Instagram at the time: "I did it to pay homage to the people I performed in front of, to the community."[39] Community is comedy's closest context.

10

COMMUNITY

By 2012, Bill Burr had established himself as one of comedy's premier ranters. So, the comedy world was primed for when he absolutely went off on the alternative comedy scene for making doing comedy too easy:

> It basically distilled all of the horror out of attempting to be a comedian . . . No heckling, no drunks, no obnoxious behavior, no aggressiveness from the [crowd]. Every fucking reason that it takes balls to be a comedian, every fucking reason why people who wanted to be a comic but never fucking did it, you've removed from that situation and you've just created this fucking comedy womb.[1]

He continued, moving on to the audiences at these shows: "It's not even a crowd. It's like a fucking radio station. 'I only perform to hipsters, ages eighteen to twenty-four, who wear skinny fucking loose jeans and have black frame glasses.'" Burr believed these comedians were like "specialists," like long snappers on a football team, who can only play one position; so when these comics end up performing at a comedy club and their jokes don't work, "they act like the crowd is dumb." He was echoing a common point made by successful club comedians that "real comedians" can play in any room. Similarly, "real comedy fans" can enjoy comedy anywhere, as they don't worry about being offended. Now, Burr was not responding to the alternative comedy scene described in chapter 2. He expresses a begrudging respect for its early members because they got their start in clubs. Also, twenty years had passed since that first wave in the 1990s. Besides there being more comedians who were able to start and stay in the alternative comedy world, there had since been two major forces that reshaped that scene—improv and podcasting.

From the early nineties through the 2010s, improv grew from a Chicago phenomenon to a national craze. Let's take a step back and run through the timeline real quick. In 1955, Paul Sills and David Shepherd cofounded the country's first improvisational theater, the Compass Players, as an outgrowth of Sills's work developing improv techniques at the University of Chicago. (Mike Nichols and Elaine May would go on to become the troupe's most famous alumni.) Soon after, in 1959, Sills helped found the Second City, the school and theater that would house many of the biggest names of comedy for the next few generations (Bill Murray, Tina Fey, Chris Farley, Stephen Colbert, Steve Carell, Aidy Bryant, Keegan-Michael Key, Sam Richardson, Tim Robinson, and so many more). In 1981, Del Close, a former Compass Player, and Charna Halpern founded the Improv-Olympic (iO), which pioneered longform improv, where entire shows are built from one audience member's suggestion. After performing at iO and Second City, Amy Poehler,

Matt Besser, Ian Roberts, and Matt Walsh formed a sketch group together called the Upright Citizens Brigade and as a unit moved to New York City to try to get a TV deal, bringing longform improv with them. After live performances around the city, people would ask the UCB 4 to teach them how to do what they were doing. Classes turned into a school, which turned into a theater. In 2003, the UCB had five hundred students. In 2015, they had twelve thousand.[2] In the past twenty years, the country went from having a few improv theaters, most of which were in Chicago, to hundreds. Most colleges now have at least a team or two. There's improv on cruise ships. There's improv as corporate team building.

And a communal aspect was built into improv from its birth, which was not at a theater, but a community center. In the 1920s, Viola Spolin, who wasn't a comedian or a theater director but a social worker, was inspired by the play theorist Neva Boyd to develop the earliest forms of what would become improv as a way of facilitating communication among immigrant children.[3] Her son, and improv's first true believer, was none other than Paul Sills. It's a story captured in Sam Wasson's 2017 book *Improv Nation*:

> Growing up watching his mother transform mere humans into founts of inspiration, Sills had seen goodness burst forth from so many kinds of people so many times that—without devolving into a cheerful individual—he had started to cultivate something like faith. Not in God—though, unlike his mother, Sills hadn't ruled out the possibility—but in something godlike that manifested from the communal experience.[4]

Improv was to be church that worshipped community through play (to this day, improvisers say they "play" with one another, instead of perform) and expected its parishioners to uphold the laws of the religion, namely support and trust. For improv to work, for the improvisers to be able to make up a whole show on the spot, the audience needs to be involved, giving them direction, saying, "yes, and."

In the 2000s and 2010s, as the definitive alternative comedy spaces shifted from one-off bars to UCB Theatre locations, the norms of those rooms impacted stand-up shows that were performed there as well. Stand-ups, for example, would be listened to more closely and supported more when they took creative risks than they would at a traditional comedy club. In 2020, after all the major improv theaters started experiencing discontent in their community for a variety of reasons, but most prominently the fact that performers at some were not being paid at all, the effects of the pandemic resulted in a few major theaters being closed. Burr didn't know any of this was going to happen when speaking back in 2012, but what he was grumpy about then—an exceedingly supportive audience-comedian relationship—has persisted. Part of this chapter discusses where alternative comedy is at the moment. Though the UCB is no longer at the center of where alternative comedy is right now, its influence on the scene's community engagement is apparent.

Now—podcasts. It was at a UCB Theatre that I first heard the term "podcast." It was 2009, the year comedians and comedy fans first embraced the medium in large numbers, and I was attending a weekly comedy show at the UCB L.A. called *Comedy Death-Ray*, when the host introduced Marc Maron by saying, "I really hope to be on his podcast one day." After the show, I went home and learned

Maron had a podcast called *WTF* that had started that year. I also learned that there was a podcast version of *Comedy Death-Ray* that had also started that year. In the next few years, following these two shows (*Comedy Death-Ray* would change its name to *Comedy Bang! Bang!*), I was able to witness a new sort of comedy fan.

There is an intimacy to the podcast listening experience. It can feel like a private conversation you are silently a part of, which translates to fans who genuinely care about the lives of their favorite comedians. The nature of the traditional stand-up comedy dynamic, in which a non-invested audience member goes to see a comedian they've never heard of and didn't look into beforehand, demands the comedian win over the crowd by doing broader jokes with the hope of getting to more nuanced stuff. Podcast audiences are invested upon arrival. "The one thing the podcast affords me is a type of candidness that transcends comedy," Maron would tell me over a decade into doing *WTF*, adding, "These people know me."[5] It goes back to what we've been talking about throughout this book about comedy creating the feeling of friendship. Considering how many relationships are virtual now anyway, podcast hosts feel like friends you hear from often.

With *Comedy Bang! Bang!*, I saw how comedy fans transitioned from "worshipers of a top-down product," as Jamie Lauren Keiles wrote in their piece on podcast fans for *The New York Times Magazine* in 2019, to "creators and stewards of a shared, bottom-up identity."[6] *Comedy Bang! Bang!* is the most consumed piece of improv comedy ever. Though the creators don't work off audience suggestions (instead improv comedians are interviewed as made-up characters), there are several places for the fans to impact the show. They do fan art. They animate clips. Each episode starts with Scott

Aukerman reading a new catchphrase submitted by a fan. For years, Aukerman would play the party game Would You Rather?, with fans coming up with the scenarios guests had to decide between (for example: Would you rather all your haircuts end up looking like a loaf of bread *OR* every piece of furniture you sit on turns into wet sponges?). Every episode ends with a segment called "Plugs," where the guests plug their upcoming projects. Each week, the segment opens with Aukerman playing a new, fully produced theme song, written and performed by a fan, and closes with him playing a fully produced fan-made remix of an ending song originally performed by frequent guest Ben Schwartz. Fans maintain the wiki and interact on both the *Comedy Bang! Bang!* subreddit (27,800 members) and the general subreddit for the podcast network that grew out of *Comedy Bang! Bang!*'s success, Earwolf (38,700). Though the latter is meant to represent all the shows on *Comedy Bang! Bang!*'s network, it is just as likely to discuss podcasts with similar sensibilities and adjacent talent, creating the fans' own bottom-up podcast network. This behavior is not at all unique to *Comedy Bang! Bang!* and its devotees. Popular comedy podcasts don't foster fan bases; they build communities. To Burr in 2012, these fans were just nerds. But now, more than ten years in the future, that is just what a lot of comedy fans look like now.

Burr recorded the aforementioned rant on his podcast, *Monday Morning Podcast*, which helped him build his own fan base in ways not unlike the ones I described above, but with fewer nerds. And similarly, as alternative comedy has developed over the last few decades, so has club comedy. In the rant, Burr spends time complaining about "the amount of shots that over the fucking years that [alternative comedians] have taken at club comics, like we're all a bunch of hacks over there, you know, talking about airplane food." Looking back, Burr's rant is one of the earliest examples of what would go on to be occasionally referred to as comedy's civil war. The expression is a bit overblown, when you consider how little the sides of comedy interact contentiously, but it does reflect the fact that there are two visions for what comedy can be, being supported by a newly empowered fan base. When combined with algorithmic content bubbles, the divide represented by alternative comedy and club has intensified. Even as these terms become somewhat meaningless, with so much of the fan-comedian relationship happening online, these communities have become more of themselves. By understanding how these sides interact with their community, you get a glimpse at the role comedy currently has in our culture. Over the last twenty years, America has had a significant drop in church membership,[7] as well as declining participation in parent-teacher organizations, unions, women's groups, and fraternal organizations.[8] People are searching for community and comedy has proven adept at creating and fostering it.

Buried in his rant are Burr's fair points about the homogeneity of the alternative rooms that still persisted in 2012, even if they weren't the points he thought he was making. Because even though these spaces espoused equality and progressivism, their lineups were still pretty male, largely white, and very straight. Hannibal Buress's *Comedy at the Knitting Factory* (which was eventually hosted by Will Miles, Clark Jones, and Kenny DeForest, and then Marie Faustin, Aminah

Imani, and Sydnee Washington) and Phoebe Robinson and Jessica Williams's *2 Dope Queens* did a lot to diversify the lineups and audiences of New York City alternative comedy, but it wasn't until the late 2010s that it felt like the entire community was starting to really live up to its promise.

The year was 2017. "Wild Thoughts" was burning up the charts, and a young Tiffany Haddish was showing Jada Pinkett Smith how to use a grapefruit when giving a blow job in *Girls Trip*—and I felt like I didn't know who the cool up-and-coming comedians were in Brooklyn anymore. I looked at some upcoming calendars and then I saw a show listed at Gowanus's Littlefield with a funny name and *fifty* performers: "'LAS CULTURISTAS' LIVE: I DON'T THINK SO, HONEY!"

Five minutes into the hosts Matt Rogers and Bowen Yang's banter that started the show, when my mouth wasn't producing laughing sounds, it was absolutely agape, beguiled. There was something about these guys. They were plugging their sponsor—Spoke, a podcast-discovery app—and Rogers looked distraught. Imagining not having Spoke "makes me really emotional," he explained, "because there are a lot of young gays out there discovering *Las Culturistas* who wouldn't even know who Amanda Peet was." He asked Yang, "Who else, bitch? Who else would we say they would never know who they were?" Yang quickly responded: Frances McDormand. "We know the name, but the young gays don't know the name." Yang got serious. "Here's the most important thing: Amanda Peet and Frances McDormand were costars in *Something's Gotta Give* by Nancy Meyers." The audience erupted. Rogers: "Actually, it's rule number six of culture: culture is connected." Yang laughed: "I thought you were going to say Amanda Peet and

Frances McDormand costarred in *Something's Gotta Give.*" "That's rule . . ." Rogers paused to think about it. "Thirteen." Yang agreed, "Thirteen." "Ooooooh, spooky," added Rogers, like a button on a perfect scene. Their mix of reverence and irreverence, stupidity and intellect, and an overall fluency in culture—I was in love with whoever these two humans were.

Next they had Peter Smith, a nonbinary comedian and actor, come out as Annette Bening. The impression wasn't the big character impersonation I was used to, but an understated portrayal of the actress's quirks, as in this case she was in town searching for the apples she had last time she was in New York. Finally, it was time for "I Don't Think So, Honey," a segment on their podcast, I'd learn, where Rogers and Yang take sixty seconds to rail against something in culture. Yang did "missed delivery notifications on my fucking door," telling UPS, "you're trying to domesticate the marginalized communities of America!" Rogers chose from the troll bowl (a bowl filled with topics hard to go negative on) and got *Wonder Woman*, a critical and commercial hit at the time. His response: "I don't think so, honey, *Wonder Woman*. Gal Gadot, why do we all have to match your accent because you can't do an American one?"

Others from the night: Drew Anderson on Lin-Manuel Miranda ("Honey, you don't need to star in everything you wriiiiiite"); Michelle Buteau doing "I don't think so, honey, if you don't fuck with the song 'Despacito'" ("You probably don't like 'Despacito' because you don't understand the language, and if you don't understand Spanish, you probably want to build a wall and make America great again"); Ziwe getting "Obama's two daughters" from the troll bowl

("I don't think so, honey, troll bowl. I AM A BLACK WOMAN, I WILL DO WHAT I WANT"); Morgan Miller's "I don't think so, honey, girl who won't let me go down on her on her period"; and Pat Regan's star-making "I don't think so, honey, these young girls," referring to young gay men ("I don't think so, honey, I was the first twenty-three-year-old and I will be the last twenty-three-year-old, bitch").

I saw more queer comedians that night than I had in my thirty-two years prior. When I went to the Comedy Cellar in my late teens, I never saw any out comics. When I graduated college and moved to Brooklyn, I saw Gabe Liedman, who cohosted *Big Terrific* with Jenny Slate and Max Silvestri and tried to give opportunities to queer comics, which would mean once every five shows maybe. This is to say, there were queer comedians before—Moms Mabley to Scott Thompson to Taylor Negron to Margaret Cho to Wanda Sykes to Tig Notaro to James Adomian to Cameron Esposito to Billy Eichner—but what I truly never saw or heard of or experienced before was primarily queer comedians performing for a queer audience in a mainstream comedy space.

Maybe an obnoxious, heckling audience was okay for Burr and comedians like him, but for some potential comedians it's harder to laugh off the risk of aggressive, drunk audience members. Like comedians who would be reasonably worried that a heckler who got kicked out for being drunk was waiting outside the venue for them. In his piece "The Bold and Bawdy New Queens of Comedy," E. Alex Jung spoke with Guy Branum, a gay comic of the previous generation who performs in both alternative and club spaces and has become a bit of a mentor to this class. Branum was able to articulate how big a shift this was: "We're still used to [comedy] being a space where we're going to be attacked and feel weird. If you showed up to a random showcase, you could assume that you would be told how disgusting f****ts were on a regular basis."[9] He continued, "And one of the really interesting things is that the change in the tenor of stand-up in major American cities is so much the reflection of there being actual gay people getting up [onstage]." And it self-perpetuated: Queer comedians meant more comfortable queer audience members, which meant more comfortable queer comedians.

As *Las Culturistas* the podcast grew, Rogers and Yang were able to reach potential queer comedy fans across the country, exposing their audience to a slate of guests not featured on other comedy podcasts. And when they went on tour, they'd do "I Don't Think So, Honey" live with local comedians, bringing together queer comedians and bringing out queer audiences, like Johnny Appleseeds for gay comedy. It recalls the original meaning of "safe space," which was first used of mid-sixties gay and lesbian bars.[10] These rooms were not completely free from risk but allowed for those within to be free of societal expectations and demands. It wasn't until these last few years that comedy spaces grew safe. It's more that the significant increase in both queer comedians and audience members, as well as people of color, has transformed the norms of these spaces to offer a similar practical resistance to political and social repression.

Moving beyond the physical space, it is the internet that supercharged the reach of comedy and transformed the nature of how comedians and audiences connected to each other. Growing up digitally native, young comedians are more comfortable blending their personal life and professional image. Where a comedian might've talked about their relationship with another comic at alternative comedy shows in the nineties, today, through everyone guesting on each other's podcasts, where they talk about dinners they've shared and weeks on Fire Island together, the fan gets a more accurate portrayal of comedians' friendships and, inevitably, personal lives. Stand-up comedy always lent itself to parasocial relationships, because of its conversational nature and friendly mirth, but now the average person really does have a strong sense of what their friends are doing—and, again, by friends, I mean strangers. And with this bond, these young comedians are [*grits old teeth*] influencers. Sometimes that means doing [*shudders*] sponsored content on Instagram, but this generation of comics have also used their cultural cachet for sociopolitical ends. Where past generations were adamant about distinguishing between comedians and activists (Dick Gregory's leaving comedy to pursue activism being the most famous example), millennial and Gen Z comedians are exploring what it looks like to be both. There is an inherent politics to being marginalized, and as the marginalized have acquired more social power in comedy spaces, many comedians (not just those who are marginalized) have shifted to embrace comedy's role in making or supporting social progress.

During the Trump administration, there were frequent comedy fundraisers for the most vulnerable groups monthly, if not weekly, at venues like the Bell House in Brooklyn. This included Julio Torres's benefit for the ACLU, Maeve Higgins's multiple benefits for Syrian refugees, and a Bernie Sanders fundraiser featuring comedians like River Ramirez, Jaboukie Young-White, Larry Owens, Sydnee Washington, Sarah Sherman, John Early, and Jo Firestone. Outside of comedy venues, comedians like Jamie Loftus and Mitra Jouhari have used their platforms to draw attention to, raise money for, and empower their fans to help support L.A.'s unhoused population. Hayes Davenport, a comedy podcaster and TV writer, left his job as a showrunner to work on the successful city council campaign of the progressive housing activist Nithya Raman, bringing in many members of the L.A. comedy community, like Joel Kim Booster, Sarah Sherman, John Early, Kate Berlant, Adam Conover, and Demi Adejuyigbe, to help. Comedians have always done charity work, usually in the form of hosting benefits, but those gigs are reserved for the upper echelon and often considered a bummer. But during the Trump administration (and since), there was an urgency to help, as the comedy community now included a greater number of people from the communities most at risk.

It's something I experienced firsthand. Before the 2018 midterm elections, I DMed *Top Chef*'s Padma Lakshmi, without any prior interaction, and asked if she wanted to put on a charity comedy show with me. This was not a totally random thing to do. Lakshmi had recently responded to the news that Louis C.K. had returned to live stand-up by tweeting a list of younger comedians she thinks people should pay attention to instead, like the aforementioned Yang, Rogers, Booster, and Torres.[11] And she said yes! We did three iterations during the Trump years—all hosted by Matt and Bowen, with lineups that included the people we've been talking about, raising over seventy thousand dollars for voting and abortion rights. The shows were heaven, with audiences and performers energized by each other.

Oh, remember when I said I've seen Chris Rock bomb three times, eight chapters ago? Here's number three! It was the first ever *Padma Puts on a Comedy Show* and I was in the greenroom, running the show. I told Larry Owens he was up next and heard someone open the door. It was Chris Rock. He asked if Padma was there, and I explained where she was sitting in the audience. Before I could take him there, he noticed that Michelle Wolf was performing and proceeded to sit gently on the side stage steps and just listen. "Her new stuff is great," he said, I guess to me, his friend he talks about comedy with. I asked if he wanted to go on and he said no thank you. But then ten minutes of good laughs passed, and he decided to join Wolf onstage. I peeked at the audience to watch their reaction. There was a reaction. A big "pop," to use industry parlance. It was Chris freaking Rock! Soon enough that would change, as Rock displayed a sort of irreverence that didn't jibe with the audience's earnest enthusiasm. Maybe "bomb" is unfair, but he never connected with the energy of the room. He made fun of the premise of the show—"Oh, Padma's doing comedy now." Though he probably didn't mean it exactly this way, there was a gatekeeping quality to the sentiment that was out of step with the evening and the time in comedy. This was not an audience enthused to hear someone in their fifties suggest who was or was not supposed to be doing comedy, especially if they were doing so out of a genuine desire to help. Rock eventually brought Larry Owens on, who proceeded to kill doing a song as Oprah singing to Stedman.

I don't want to suggest that this scene of alternative comedians, which has been defined by its queer vanguard, is free of irony, considering chapter 6 described the exact opposite. What there has been an increase in is what Beck Krefting called in her 2014 book, *All Joking Aside*, "charged comedy," meaning comedians who "intentionally produce humor challenging social inequality and cultural exclusion."[12] In the book she writes, "All humor locates itself in social and political contexts, but not all humor does so self-consciously or with specific intentions to promote unity and equality or to create a safe and accepting space for people from all walks of life."[13] Krefting (again, writing in 2014) notes that charged comedians struggle to "commercialize their comic personae" and that "charged humor can have a polarizing effect on audiences, diminishing its widespread appeal."[14] This becomes frustrating to these comedians when you consider that by being a member of a marginalized group performing stand-up, your comedy is inevitably charged, at least in the eyes of the "mainstream" audience. So if you aren't an able-bodied straight white male, you are at a professional disadvantage, unless you intentionally sell out your identity to make others comfortable. But having spoken to Krefting more recently, she agrees that this dynamic—partly thanks to the demand for socially engaged art during the Trump administration and the dissolution of the possibility of "widespread appeal"—has changed.

Ayo Edebiri, a comedian from this scene who would go on to costar on *The Bear*, started doing comedy when Trump was already president, and that affected her understanding of what being a comedian means. On the millennial–Gen Z cusp and growing up getting her news from *The Daily Show*, she never knew a reality where the comedian didn't have a responsibility to tell the truth and speak up against the politically powerful.[15] Relatedly, with comedians of this generation, there is a willingness to embrace the potential of comedian as journalist, whether it is Ziwe citing the pioneering investigative journalist Ida B. Wells as her hero or Loftus's work making rigorously researched narrative nonfiction podcasts about subjects like sexism in MENSA, Nabokov's *Lolita*, and American spiritualism. But beyond that, these comedians are able to be fun and funny and silly with purpose. "The comics who I like and enjoy are people who are of marginalized identities," Edebiri would tell me upon Trump leaving office in 2021. "We're finding ways to make comedy that we want to see. You can't say it exists outside of Trump and his presidency, because that's the context we're in . . . But the comedy that we roll out made ourselves laugh, made ourselves feel good during this time." It brings back Danielle Fuentes Morgan's idea from chapter 5 of laughing to keep from dying and people using comedy specifically as armor for their spirit in times when they're under attack.

My favorite example of modern charged comedy comes from Julio Torres's 2019 special, *My Favorite Shapes*. In it, Torres, who is a queer immigrant originally from El Salvador, sits in front of a conveyor belt that looks like a Memphis-designed spaceship and comments on all the objects, or "shapes," that pass by. After commenting that one of his favorite kinds of shapes is "clear with a little animal trapped inside of it," he goes off on a little tangent, in his slow, methodical deadpan: "As I was preparing this show and I was deciding which shapes were going to go in which order and I was weighing out the pros and cons of all of them, thinking which one of them were stars, which ones were more [*putting his hand up to his mouth, as if telling a secret*] supporting. And as I was just deciding on all of that, I thought, *Oh, I'm sorry, is this one of the many GOOD jobs that I'm STEALING from hardworking Americans?*" Incredibly specific to Torres's comedic point of view, the subtext of the special is about expanding the definition of American culture to include perspectives like his.

Torres made a name for himself writing for *SNL*, producing sketches like a fake commercial for Fisher Price's newest toy—a well for sensitive little boys "to wish upon, confide in, reflect by"—and "The Actress," an understated, moody portrait of "the woman who gets cheated on in the gay porn." Torres was the first of a series of comedians who would come out of this new alternative comedy community and go on to redefine America's premier comedic institution. None has done this more prominently than Yang, who was hired in 2018 as a writer and then a cast member in the next season. Yang very quickly shined, playing characters who just happened to be gay, queer-coded anthropomorphized objects, or ostensibly straight characters viewed through a queer lens. Some of his highlights include the *Titanic* iceberg mentioned in chapter 6, the bitchy Chinese trade representative or "trade daddy" Chen Biao, the SZA and Brené Brown–quoting Christmas mythical demon Krampus who is going through an existential crisis, and a spotted lanternfly with the personality of a loud, Southern reality show villain. As the great cast members always have done, Yang's work has rewritten *SNL*'s DNA. And as *SNL* goes, so goes the comedy nation. As of this writing, so many of this generation of charged comedians have found high-profile opportunities touring, on prestige television, and in film.

I am always happy when comedians I know and like get work, but it also makes me nervous. The problem is that fame is antithetical to community. Hollywood only understands top-down. Even in my short time covering comedy, I've seen multiple scenes come and go, like sandcastles. People leave New York or Chicago or Portland or wherever for L.A. with promises to return after pilot season, and then they don't, as they are instead subsumed into the larger entertainment industry. Weekly shows turn monthly, then turn yearly, and then end. Comedians turn into superheroes.

Community building and a culture of artists inspiring one another are traded for networking, big comics riding off the cred of young comics who are building off the reputation of the established names. Managers, agencies, networks, studios find your community cute. But it's hard to maintain collectivism in an individualistic business, not to mention an individualistic art form like stand-up. I don't blame anyone for making decisions about their own careers and families and lives. It's just a bummer to see a comedy scene return to being a collection of individuals who kind of know one another.

An example I often think about is Jo Firestone, a comedian as special as alternative comedy has ever produced. I went to a few of Jo Firestone's shows before I ever saw her perform. In one, she set up a comedy club for dolls, in which comedians or just people off the street could tell jokes in front of thirty dolls, with prerecorded laughs. There was the time she turned the venue Littlefield into a space where people could try to break stuff like papier-mâché sculptures, giant stuffed animals, piñatas, and balloons with pool noodles. And then there was Punderdome 3000, a monthly pun contest hosted by Firestone's father, where she didn't utter a single pun and mostly was there to react and cringe. When she does perform stand-up, it often involves crowd participation. "What I like to do with a lot of the shows is kind of leave it up to the audience," Firestone said in 2015.[16] "If the audience hates it, then it'll be a horrible show, and if the audience loves it, then it'll be a great, memorable show. But there's not a lot of control I put into it." Like the generations of alternative comedians that came before her, she is dedicated to letting the audience determine where the comedy is.

Quickly, the industry noticed her appeal. I had many conversations with TV development executives around that time, and they were all trying to figure out what they could do with her. She had "heat." For a few weeks, everyone in the scene was talking about how she *just* missed out on a major role in a *Star Wars* movie. Eventually she took a job as a writer on *The Tonight Show Starring Jimmy Fallon*. The gig included frequent on-camera work, with her playing Betsy DeVos for a while and serving as a "product correspondent," which entailed poorly recommending toys. Again, I am always happy when comedians I like and know get work, but I did miss seeing her around as much, trying to pull off the dumbest ideas she could think of.

A couple years after Firestone was New York's newest "it" comedian, Rogers and Yang were. I could feel a similar heat pointing in their direction. And the story of Yang getting *SNL* is also one of Rogers not. It is show business, not show friends. It was an uncertain moment for Rogers, having missed out on his dream opportunity and unsure what was going to happen to the partnership he spent nearly a decade building. Despite not being particularly close friends with him, Firestone ended up being one of the first people to reach out. She asked him to get coffee and they did. Rogers would later tell me, "I shudder to think about the things I said and how morose I was, but she was really, really, really important for me to have there."[17] Rogers and Yang continued doing the podcast and both career's flourished separately as well as together. It is still early, but it does feel like this current community of alternative comedians is built for the long haul. Few of them perform at the UCB anymore, but most at least studied there and learned the vitality of supporting one another.

In 2018, the *InfoWars* contributor Paul Joseph Watson tweeted, "The right is starting to get better at comedy and it's making lefties nervous," instantly creating a meme the bemused left has used to mock the absurdity of the idea of conservative comedy.[18] It is a modern version of the "why there isn't a conservative Jon Stewart" argument that floated around in the first decade of the twenty-first century, usually backed by tenuously argued "proof" that conservatives are incapable of being funny. Comedy *must* critique power structures, they'd argue; if it doesn't, it isn't comedy. Ironically, the dismissal of conservative comedy's existence has grown more frequent as its actual existence has grown more prevalent. Often I will come across dismissals of *Gutfeld!*, Fox News's nightly comedy-focused late-night show hosted by network staple Greg Gutfeld, which ignore the fact that the show is a ratings smash. But, being on TV, Gutfeld is only the most accessible example of what is happening. Starting from the post-9/11 shift, discussed in chapter 4, there has been a bubbling up of a conservative comedy underground, and it can no longer be denied. Meet the "bad little boy right," my term for comedians who have embraced the bad little boy perspective discussed in chapter 8 and leveraged it to find tremendous success among conservative comedy fans.

The first thing that must be acknowledged is that most of the popular bad little boy right comedians are not *actually* traditional conservatives. Of the biggest names that get put into this category—Joe Rogan, Tim Dillon, the *Legion of Skanks* (cohosted by Big Jay Oakerson, Luis J. Gomez, and Dave Smith), Andrew Schulz, Shane Gillis—none directly supported Donald Trump. They didn't advocate voting for him, though they did periodically support what he was doing as a disruptor. During the 2016 and

2020 elections, Bernie Sanders was the only presidential candidate I heard them routinely talk fondly of. Maybe you'd consider them libertarians, and Dave Smith of the *Legion of Skanks* is an active member of the Libertarian Party, but the "personal freedom" stuff often feels more like an expression of stubborn, loner personalities than an overarching philosophy. Sure, they're fine with the cool stuff like drugs and sex work legalization and people generally doing whatever they want, but also Rogan has publicly supported universal health care and universal basic income (though he has also publicly denounced universal basic income). Now that they are rich, none *love* taxes, but they don't really talk about them so much. Being opposed to vaccine mandates is probably the largest policy overlap with the American right wing. (It led Rogan, for example, to support Ron DeSantis's presidential hopes, though he hasn't exactly endorsed him, as of this writing.) On many policies, they seem to be completely in line with a moderate, populist Democrat perspective. Shane Gillis, the comedian who got unhired from *SNL* after clips of him making racist and homophobic jokes on his podcast were pointed out, spends the majority of his quite good 2021 hour-long special making fun of his Fox News–loving dad. But again, these comedians don't consider themselves conservative. In 2022, Luis J. Gomez—who besides cohosting the *Legion of Skanks* is the cofounder of GaS Digital, the podcast network that includes his shows and used to be the home of Dillon and Gillis's show—quote-tweeted a tweet railing against "ring wing lunatics" in stand-up, by asking them to "Name 5 right wing comedians. There are 1000s of comedians. Name 5. I can name 3."[19]

Being bad little boys, what actually matters to these comedians is "free speech." The best way I could describe their politics is that they support gay marriage and believe in LGBTQIA+ rights (Dillon himself is gay), but also would want to call me a "f****t" for asterisking out those letters. These shows' fan bases thrive on message boards where shock is currency, with each person needing to top the next, essentially radicalizing themselves, like an anonymous version of the Comedy Cellar comics' table. These shows, to different degrees, mirror what their fans like, as comedians do with their audiences. In addition, this version of free speech leads to their being anti–cancel culture, which then leads to their being anti-woke. Lastly, the key is that this freedom-of-speech-at-all-costs perspective has led to all of them giving platforms to radical right-wing podcast guests like Alex Jones, Candace Owens, and Milo Yiannopoulos, choices that have defined most of these shows in outsiders' eyes.

In 2003, Andrew Sullivan, an influential conservative (though not Republican) writer and thinker, referred to people like this as "*South Park* Republicans" and said they were the future of the party.[20] For years, this take was mocked or shot down, by people on both sides of the aisle. Two decades later, he's still wrong about the Republican party, but he did correctly predict what would soon become a trend in comedy. The *South Park* cocreator Trey Parker has said about his show: "We avoid extremes, but we hate liberals more than conservatives and we hate them."[21] It's a perspective that was echoed by Luis J. Gomez before the 2020 election, when he tweeted, "I hope Trump wins just because of how much it will bother like 4 people I hate."[22] When a fan replied, "Go vote for him Luis, help make it happen,"[23] Gomez replied, "Voting is for dorks."[24]

Maybe the easiest way to place the bad little boy right's podcasts is in contrast to their hypothetical mirror image—

the dirtbag left, the name given to non–politically correct left-leaning podcasts that sprang up and gained popularity in the wake of Bernie Sanders's failed campaign for the Democratic nomination for president in 2016. Like the bad little boy right, the dirtbag left was a response to where comedy was at the moment. For decades, comedy has been antiestablishment, but, as a result of successes such as *The Daily Show* and *SNL*, by the mid-2010s, comedy was taken more seriously by the establishment, with some political comedians arguably becoming part of the establishment themselves. In their place, a new generation of antiestablishment comedians emerged, pushing back on the now-establishment political comedy, both from the left and right.

I am just going to focus on *Chapo Trap House*, because the politics of other shows associated with the dirtbag left are all over the map to the point of not being particularly illustrative. Both *Chapo* and the hosts of bad little boy right podcasts start from the same place, as was explained to me by the professor Nick Marx, one of the coauthors, with Matt Sienkiewicz, of 2022's *That's Not Funny: How the Right Makes Comedy Work for Them*, the definitive book about the conservative comedy pipeline. At the overlap of the Venn diagram is, Marx explained to me, a feeling that, "our institutions are broken because the people running them are venal shitheads." It's why both are interested in and indulgent of conspiracy theories and appeal to a specific brand of disillusioned white guy. The difference is in how they respond to this assessment.

The libertarian podcasters, as Marx referred to them to me over email, are "cultists of the self (like Trump and DeSantis) who lampoon institutional brokenness as an economically motivated expression of their narcissism, which might be why most of them are solo club comics." They are not politically correct, because no one can tell them what to do. Whereas the hosts of *Chapo*, according to Marx, "use comedy to obliterate existing institutions, then as a foundation for solidarity to build new ones." It's a point captured by Amber A'Lee Frost, who coined the term "dirtbag left" and eventually became a *Chapo* cohost, in a 2016 *Current Affairs* essay entitled "The Necessity of Political Vulgarity," where she wrote, "Civility is destructive because it perpetuates falsehoods, while vulgarity can keep us honest."[25] As Sienkiewicz explained to me over email, irony theory has long differentiated between joking that is "aimed at an ultimate project of rebuilding" and joking dedicated to the "simple act of destruction."

This dichotomy was on display in the weeks after the Supreme Court overturned *Roe v. Wade*. Though their takes differed, these "conservative" podcasts made it about themselves, with discussion topics like whether they ever paid for a woman's abortion. Rogan defended abortion fiercely in an argument on his podcast with the CEO of *The Babylon Bee* (the right wing's answer to *The Onion*), Seth Dillon. But his argument focused on how he would react if his own daughter was impregnated through rape.[26] Gillis's response on his podcast, *Matt and Shane's Secret Podcast*, was maybe most emblematic: "[*in a sort of dumb voice*] It feels weird when the Republicans win [*laughs*]. I don't think I like it as much as I thought I would. [*out of character, as himself*] Nah . . . it's just gay . . . I don't like it."[27] (I can't overstate how much of the popularity of these shows seems to be out of a desire to call things "gay.") Conversely, *Chapo* made fun of the ineptitude of the Democrats' complete lack of substantial response to the initial leak of the decision, but proceeded to thoroughly summarize the political history of the abortion issue.[28] Soon after, *Chapo* held an abortion-rights fundraiser at one of its live shows. Though there are many on the left who quibble with the *Chapo* team's approach to political discourse, unlike bad little boy shows, it does make its politics clear, so as not to be misconstrued.

The bad little boy podcasts provide, as Sienkiewicz explained to me, "an irony forged in a sort of solipsism [that often] succeeds in using comedy to tear down all the meaning structures around you but doesn't seem to leave much left." The defining feature of their comedic philosophy is irreverence. It is dumb to believe in something and dumber to care, so if you do, we are going to make fun of you. It's a perspective of trolling contrarianism. In 2017, the comedian Hari Kondabolu, whose material Krefting uses as an example of charged comedy, released a documentary called *The Problem with Apu*, about the problem with *The Simpsons*' Indian convenience-store owner—namely that he resulted in a lot of hurt and bullying to young South Asian fans and that he was voiced by the white actor Hank Azaria. In 2022, Akaash Singh, the cohost of the *Flagrant* podcast with Andrew Schulz, released a special on YouTube called *Bring Back Apu*, arguing that Kondabolu was wrong. Singh's work models an approach of many of these comedians. It's scare-quotes comedy. And its practitioners are laughing all the way to the bank.

Flagrant's Patreon, as of this writing, has 20,785 patrons, bringing in $98,846 a month, according to the third-party Patreon-tracking site, Graphtreon.[29] Gillis's *Matt and Shane's Secret Podcast* has 41,622 patrons, the most on the platform across all shows. *The Tim Dillon Show* has 40,110 patrons and is making $208,867 a month. Again, that is each month. This is not counting the main podcast feed or YouTube channel where they make money from ads. And YouTube is the key. As of this writing, *Legion of Skanks* has 105,000 subscribers. Tim Dillon has 512,000. *Flagrant* has 1.12 million (not counting the 2.61 million Schulz has on his personal page). The *Joe Rogan Experience* YouTube channel has 14.1 million subscribers. This is where these comedians are getting a large portion of their fan base, but crucially, it is also how not-conservative comedy becomes conservative.

It's an easy-to-track formula. First, you have fans editing together clips, making videos like "Bill Burr Constant Shitting on Women" (2.8 million views),[30] or adding commentary to clips that place these comics in a more trollish, reactionary Ben Shapiro–esque conservative frame, like "Joe Rogan HAMMERS Adam Conover in 'TRANSGENDERS in Sports' Debate" (320,000 views).[31] But more than that, if you watch enough of any one of these channels, they'll refer you to clips of the other people in their orbit. Not too long in this conservative-adjacent comedy space and you are being referred to prominent right-wing and white nationalist influencers like Shapiro, Jordan Peterson, Steven Crowder, Michael Malice, Gavin McInnes, and Nick Fuentes. It happened to me when researching this chapter (don't say I've never done anything for you). In *That's Not Funny*, Sienkiewicz and Marx write, "The way in which people discover new comedy today—algorithmic suggestions on YouTube, retweets on Twitter, cross-promotion on podcasts—provides a set of pathways to connect more banal right-wing humor to the truly evil stuff, up to and including actual neo-Nazi comedy spaces."[32] "Comedy," they argue, "serves as a lubricant that helps audiences slide among the disparate aspects of right-wing ideology, with a certain gravity pulling them down into the lower, dirtier depths of the [ecosystem]."[33]

When Marx and Sienkiewicz talk about this impressionable audience, they are quick to note they largely mean mostly young, mostly white men, a group that no longer receives the sort of total cultural, societal, and political attention it once did. It is a group that the *Chapo* cohost Matt Christman knows listens to his show. "The twenty-first century is basically defined by nonessential human beings, who do not fit into the market as consumers or producers or as laborers," he said in 2016.[34] "That manifests itself differently in different classes and geographic areas. For white, middle-class, male, useless people—who have just enough family context to not be crushed by poverty—they become failsons." How these people react varies. "[Some] become aware of the consequences of capitalism," Christman's analysis continued, and "some of them turn into Nazis." These are people looking for community. Because of comedy's ability to foster allegiance, a prospective fan might listen to shows on the transgressive left and right and align themselves based not on politics but on sense of humor. No, the politics comes with time, as an extension of their loyalty to the comedy.

I'm sure it's hard to turn away your fans. Again, the issue is the audience members who don't exactly get the joke and who laugh for the wrong reason. Whereas a large portion of mainstream club comedians, not unlike Burr's fan interaction story from chapter 8, choose to be in denial, what is perversely admirable about the *Legion of Skanks* is that they accept their fans, racists and all. In October 2020, the *Legion of Skanks* subreddit, which had around twenty-five thousand members at the time, was taken down permanently, with a notice stating, "This community was banned for violating Reddit's rule against promoting hate." Gomez discussed the situation on one of his other podcasts, *Real Ass Podcast*.[35] He started by saying that the Skanks had nothing to do with the subreddit: "It was our fans; they're savages." In Gomez's telling, the subreddit was given a warning and responded by posting a meme of George Floyd and "everyone just brigading with, you know, n-words and f-words and any word you're not supposed to say." Still, Gomez, who read the subreddit frequently and posted there occasionally, believed "there was no actual hate going on in that subreddit," just folks posting memes of fucked-up shit. Later in that podcast, Gomez went on to say about the GaS Digital live chat, "There's a couple fucking actual racists. There's a couple legitimate dudes, you're like, 'Oh, that guy is probably legitimately racist.'" Laughing a little to himself, he says, "But we don't kick them out. Unless they are harassing people." If it's not clear, he means harassing other members of the community. People on the outside of GaS are a different story, because people on the outside are actually harassed for criticizing members of *this* community. "Today's fandom is more like a stateless nation, formed around a shared viewing heritage but perpetuated through the imaginations and interrelations of those who enjoy and defend it," writes Keiles.[36] These hosts might not tell their fans directly to go after someone, but they'll pick targets to joke about and never tell their fans *not* to go after them.

One of the most striking examples of this came in February 2021. Seth Simons, an activist comedy journalist, who had focused a lot of his writing on "the leading lights in the scene's transgressive edge—the place where popular, mainstream comedy bleeds into the kind of right-wing politics that animated the Capitol riot," wrote a story for *The New*

Republic called "The Comedy Industry Has a Big Alt-Right Problem."[37] The piece connects Anthony Cumia, the Trump-supporting former cohost of the popular, un-PC radio show *Opie & Anthony*, to his company Compound Media, the podcast network that at one point included shows from the Proud Boys founder Gavin McInnes and the *Legion of Skanks*, to onaforums.net, a related forum to talk about comedy and post hate speech. It was through onaforums.net that Simons and his family were doxed, and it was through onaforums.net that he got a tip from a "mole" that one user who had posted on threads like "N****r hate thread #1" (asterisks mine) and "The Kike Hate Thread" was actually Cris Italia, the co-owner of the New York comedy club the Stand. Eight months after Simons's story ran, a man wrote a post on his personal website proving that he had posed as this mole, making up everything about Italia and catfishing Simons, as a way of delegitimizing him and his journalism. He was not asked to do this by Italia (who has since used his vindication as proof of the perils with cancel culture).[38] And he was not asked to do this by the hosts of any of these podcasts. Keiles writes, "When their common cause comes under threat—through chart competition, cancellation or critique—fans can organize to increase streams, denigrate critics and rally executives to right perceived wrongs."[39] This is not unique to comedy, but within comedy, bad little boy podcast fans indulge in extreme versions of this behavior.

It is a version of a safe space, too, and these comedians know it. Gomez told one interviewer, "I wanted to create a reverse safe space to create freely, a platform where [comics] can take chances without backlash."[40] The phrase "reverse safe space" jumps out, as it implies an undoing of who safe spaces were originally created to protect. It's a vow to make spaces safe again. In another interview, Gomez calls his podcasts and podcast network "my storm shelter."[41] "One day somebody's coming for us," he explains. "One day somebody's coming to say, 'you can't say that.' Whether it's the FCC, whether it's Comcast, Verizon or the SJW's . . . it doesn't matter if they are the good guys or the bad guys. The truth of the matter is . . . *it's all of them* . . . they're all going to come." Again, many of these comedians may not be politically conservative, but in how this quote moves from political correctness to paranoia over the potential of losing their way of life, it is easy to see where their ideology overlaps with the modern conservative ideology.

What this movement in comedy is *not* is a counterpoint to this book, though it might be a bastardization. As alluded to in chapter 5, comedy's greatest strength in political action is forming and fortifying in-groups, and the "conservative" movement in comedy is maybe the strongest example of that, as it is a political cohort built largely around a belief in what humor should be. This chapter is not about how community is inherently a good thing, just that people have been looking for community and that comedy is an effective organizer. Call me a libtard cuck, but I don't think it's super great to make organizing easier for racists. (And even positive communities have histories of exclusion.) Not to be all instrumentalist, but I'm left to instead judge these communities by usefulness. So, how is this comedy being used?

It would be reasonable to see this work as an example of the superiority theory of comedy, but I see it as a group of people whose style of comedic play is a game of verbal roughhousing, as discussed in chapter 8, in which the in-group always winds up on top. Bullies need favorite comics too. But it is through play and jokes that the perversion starts happening. As I've said, jokes and memes influence people's expectations of, and interactions with, other comedy. It is here that conservative-adjacent comedy becomes a tool of the right. Andrew Anglin, the founder of the neo-Nazi website *The Daily Stormer*, is up-front about the fact that he uses humor as a Trojan horse for his bigotry. Anglin understands that most people are uncomfortable with "vitriolic, raging, non-ironic hatred," so his goal is for "the unindoctrinated [not to] be able to tell if we are joking or not." He continues, "There should be a conscious agenda to dehumanize the enemy, to the point where people are ready to laugh at their deaths. So, it isn't clear that we are doing this—as that would be a turnoff to most normal people—we rely on lulz."[42] The by-product of this strategy is that by having bigoted memes live in the same space as comedians, in the contextless internet, even if a comedian *is* just joking, they could easily be interpreted as supporters of the cause. I am not saying the bad little boy comedians are the same as the proponents of bigoted jokes on the internet; I am saying they are ignorantly or willfully—be it for profit or out of laziness, nihilism, or a desire for attention—allowing a portion of their audience to believe they are the same, that their work is bigoted even if the comedians themselves say it isn't. Their audience is no longer merely worshippers of a top-down art form, but creators and stewards of a shared, bottom-up community.

"How essential is a comedy club when you're talking about the infection rate?"[43] That's what Andrew Cuomo said when he was still the governor of New York, in the fall of 2020. The country was six months and two hundred thousand deaths into the Covid-19 experience. He continued, "Not to offend people in the comedy club—Lord knows we need to laugh—but those are the calibrations we're making."

In November of that year, Dani Zoldan, the co-owner of Stand Up NY, thought of a potential work-around. He announced a show called *Temple of Laughter* at the St. Paul & St. Andrew United Methodist Church on the Upper West Side, trying to exploit the religious exceptions in the city policies. "The pastor was behind it," he said afterward.[44] "If we can get them into the church, just to provide an evening of laughter, like, why not? I think we're doing good."

The issue is that Covid-19 is socially transmitted, meaning that a gathering, even one intended to strengthen a community, also has the potential of spreading a deadly virus to the most vulnerable members of it. Ultimately, the event was sparsely attended and poorly received online. Zoldan never did a second one. The audience decides when it wants to be an audience. As they say, a church isn't a place. It's a people.

In early 2020, Firestone, for the first time in a long time, didn't have prospects in front of her. She thought she might never work again, a fear the industry tries to instill in people so they say "yes" faster. To keep busy, she had the idea of trying to teach a comedy class for seniors. The plan was for it to last thirteen weeks. Three weeks into her class, Covid-19 forced everyone to self-isolate. The class continued, as scheduled, every Monday, but now on Zoom. As of this writing, it's still going.

Nearly two years into the experience, Firestone told me, "It does feel like it is a comedy scene."[45] "If you met all these people individually, you wouldn't necessarily think that all of them are friends," she explained. "It is very sweet to see them bonding and doing things for each other, like buying each other socks that are an inside joke or dressing up like each other." She told me a story about telling the class that when she studied at UCB, she used to get grades. "Grades!" they exclaimed in astonishment and fear. After one student started dyeing her hair blue, because she couldn't leave home to get it professionally colored, Firestone told the class, "Okay, you all get extra credit if next week you come in with blue hair, like Tequila." "When I came back the next Monday morning," she told me, "I opened the Zoom; one guy had dyed his beard blue and then another guy had [gone] out and bought a blue wig. It was so beautiful."

It reminds me of a story bell hooks told about a live conversation she had with Dr. Cornel West, in that same interview referenced in chapter 5: "The last talk he and I gave together, many people were upset because we were silly together. But I consider it a high holy calling that we can be humorous together. How many times do we see an African American man and an African American woman talking together, critiquing one another and yet having delicious, humorous delight? It's a miracle."[46] One of comedy's values, as described in chapter 5, is that it relaxes defenses and unites people with disparate perspectives without asking them to compromise.

Firestone originally wanted to do comedy because watching it as a depressed, potentially suicidal kid felt like a "reprieve," like "medicine." "I kind of thought, *Oh, if I can do comedy, then maybe I won't feel as sad and other people won't feel as sad . . .* Then I learned about the industry," she explained, "and it definitely made me more suspicious of myself. I lost sight of a lot of why I was doing it." The pandemic allowed her to get off the treadmill the industry had put her on. All she had were "these people that really were excited to do comedy and really loved comedy and really loved laughing at each other," and it was more than enough. "The people in the class made me realize you can just do comedy and it'll be fun," she explained. "Accolades are cool and it's cool to get paid, but it's not necessarily the thing that's going to make you feel okay going to bed at night."

When things opened up again, so did Firestone. It was good to get out of the house. It was good to see people. "It's made me appreciate more the community of people that do it and appreciate it," she told me. She realized that instead of just standing there and trying to make the audience laugh, "it feels better to laugh and make someone else laugh mutually." It made sense to her to turn these experiences into her first special, which went against the industry's basic understanding of what a comedy special is—one person, talking at strangers. Airing on Peacock, the result, *Good Timing*, is a documentary about members of the class trying to do stand-up for the first time, in front of a real, live audience. Heartwarming and hilarious, it makes a person feel like the Grinch at the end of the story, with their heart growing three sizes. In *Laughter*, Henri Bergson writes, "Laughter appears to stand in need of an echo."[47] What he was saying, which has been borne out in research, is that laughter is social. People are thirty times more likely to laugh with other people than alone.[48] Church isn't a place. It's a people.

11

CONNECTION

In 2022, pandemic-brained to hell and busy researching the words you have consumed thus far, I attempted to read my first novel in years. It was Sheila Heti's *Pure Colour*, a book about many things but mainly the push and pull of an artist's existence. I had already been a fan of Heti's, but I was curious after one line from the critic Jennifer Wilson's review jumped out at me: "[Art] can establish a connective thread between yourself and millions of strangers across space and time, yet the process of making it requires extensive time alone and disconnection from the three or four people in your life you care about the most."[1] After reading the book, which was a bit too abstract to give me a solution to this conundrum, I emailed Heti to ask her straight out how she felt this idea related to comedians, including her brother, the international touring comedian David Heti. She responded that she felt they had it even worse than other artists, because, while a writer might be able to take a break to get dinner with their friends, "a comic has to spend their nights in the clubs and to spend a lot of time on the road." Being a comic is a perversion of the artist's existence—they cannot be alone to create, but they are charged with carrying their disconnection along with them through life. Comedy is an art form developed by societal outsiders that grew into one for psychological outsiders. You want to know how you write five minutes of perfect observations about Halloween, like Jerry Seinfeld? While other kids are trick-or-treating, you are there next to them, thinking about the quality of the rubber bands on their masks.

When you think about it, of course comedians would be at their most valued specifically right now, in these disconnected times. Marc Maron nailed it when he told me in early 2020, "This period of history, the thing that's really gonna stand out is how isolated everyone was."[2] Because, as if out of a bad play, the day after I spoke to him, the country shut down because of a global pandemic that both demanded people self-isolate and underlined how society had already started doing so. In the late nineties, back when my fellow millennial Mark Zuckerberg and I were freshly bar mitzvahed, scholars were already writing about the so-called Internet Paradox: "a social technology that reduces social involvement and psychological well-being."[3] Oopsies. And it kept on getting worse, so that, likely, whenever you are reading this, unless something radical has happened, like cell phones start smelling really bad for some reason, you are living in a time when people have never been more connected and yet never less so. There had been some pushback during the first decade or so of Facebook about whether it had a tangible negative impact on its users, but in early 2020, a massive ten-thousand-person survey came out that revealed that 61 percent of all people surveyed felt lonely. Compared to 52 percent of light social media users, 73 percent of very heavy social media users were considered lonely.[4]

"While loneliness has the potential to kill," diagnosed Vivek Murthy, the United States surgeon general from 2014 to 2017 and again for a pandemic-era President Biden, "connection has even more potential to heal."[5] It's something I've experienced firsthand through comedy a few times.

"Laughter is the closest distance between two people." Isn't that a nice little quote? It's from Victor Borge, the Danish American pianist-comedian who became huge in the 1940s for his riffing on classical music. It gets at the feeling of closeness in the call-and-response of stand-up at its best. Some comedians like to describe stand-up as a conversation where only the person onstage is talking, but both the audience and comic are communicating. There is an intimacy to the nonverbal understanding.

Mike Birbiglia has a joke that really captures the feeling of closeness Borge was describing, in which he creates with the audience a feeling of sharing an inside joke. It comes toward the end of *Thank God for Jokes*, when he tells the story of him and his wife bringing their cat on a summer trip. He starts with this framing: "My favorite thing about marriage is that you can share jokes with your wife or husband that are funny to you and that person and no one else, other than maybe your cat. Because when you have a cat, your barometer for humor—out the window." Birbiglia continues, saying their trip was to Massachusetts, but he called it "Catsachusetts." I saw the off-Broadway version of the show twice, and both times this was received, as it is on Netflix, with crickets, which Birbiglia takes in stride by acknowledging it isn't funny but, in their house, it was "the joke of the year!"

I'm not going to recount the entire story that follows, but just know that the house they are staying in is infested with mice, which themselves are infested with a parasite that makes them unafraid of cats and people. Shenanigans ensue, as Birbiglia and his wife debate whether to let their cat take care [*wink*] of the mice. Five minutes and one mouse being carefully placed outside later, Birbiglia and co. are on their way back home and he tells the audience, "from that day forward, we have called that state . . . Mouseachusetts." Both times I saw the show live this was received, as it is on Netflix, with applause. Birbiglia continues, commenting on this response: "I want to point out something special that happened there at the end, which is, a few minutes ago, I prefaced the story with a Massachusetts-based pun. 'Catsachusetts.' Which we all agreed as a group: not funny. Moments ago, I concluded the story with another Massachusetts-based pun. It was nearly identical. It was 'Mouseachusetts.' But that time, we applauded. Which means . . . in a way . . . it's like we're married." Callbacks, at their worst, can be a cheap gimmick that just gets the comedian a free laugh of recognition from the audience, but when done purposefully it brings the audience in. As Birbiglia says in the special: "I think jokes, at their best, have the ability to make us all feel closer to one another."

As a devout believer in not yucking anyone's yum, I do not want to imply that comedy is a more connective art form than any other. Maybe you believe TV is more connective because it is in your home. Maybe you think it's food because it is essential for survival. And, yes, I've heard of music. I've had enough people talk to me about Phish to know that if you're on the right mixture of substances, all the noodling does *something*. Just as I was raised to believe

Judaism isn't a proselytizing religion, all I can do is tell you what comedy did for me as an audience member.

One Saturday morning, in the summer of 2019, my parents called my cell phone. I didn't answer. It was too early for them to just call, and I sensed that once I talked to them, I would never get to live a life without knowing whatever information they were going to tell me. So I savored a second of selfish ignorance.

Before I go forward, I want to share one comedy-related story about my older brother Simon. During his sophomore year of college, I stayed over at his dorm at the University of Arizona. I had done a similar thing with my other brother, Michael, at the University at Albany the year before, and it involved pregaming, fake IDs, and other large state university clichés. I expected the same, as we were living in *Van Wilder*'s America. Instead, Simon suggested we watch *The Simpsons* DVD commentaries. I didn't remember that part of *Van Wilder*, but that was Simon. He loved learning everything that could be learned about the culture he loved. So, we watched *The Simpsons* DVD commentaries late into the night. It was really fun. Thank you for letting me share this.

Simon, my parents would tell me that morning, had died of a drug overdose.

I found myself, once again, flipping and flipping through space. People would offer me condolences and I couldn't process the words. They'd say, "I'm sorry," and I'd just hear the noises—*eye um sar eeeeee*. I canceled an interview with Jeff Foxworthy, not in the mood to learn whether I was or was not a redneck. It took a few weeks, but the next interview I did was with Leslye Headland, the showrunner, at the time, of Netflix's *Russian Doll*. While asking her why only one of the main character's twenty-six deaths was what would be considered a death of despair, I realized I probably should've canceled that one as well.

I couldn't shake it. The grief didn't just take over my present and equate the future with dread, but it reframed my past. I have always been prone to disconnection. Losing a mother makes the most sense narratively, but it's likely that only reinforced an innate tendency. Compulsively obsessive, I could spend hours in my head without realizing I'd tuned out the world outside my skull. You want to know how you write a book about comedians' ability to write five minutes of perfect observations about Halloween? While other kids are trick-or-treating, you are there, thinking about what makes Seinfeld's joke work. Losing my brother underlined this part of myself. All I could see was disconnection everywhere. If you're less invested in people, there is less potential for hurt. But it's a bit of a baby-and-bathwater situation, because in the process of my grief, I threw away all that makes me a person, all that makes life worth living. I was not just mourning, as Freud defines the healthy conscious processing of loss, but experiencing melancholia, the unhealthy, internalized refusal to move forward. My partner was supportive and endlessly patient, but I was ashamed she had to deal with me like this. I needed to do something.

Comedy, I thought, had worked before. I asked two friends who were also having bad summers to go see Reggie Watts with me at the Bell House. I've been seeing Watts live for years. There is no one like him. The first time I saw him perform, he did the entire set in a British accent. I didn't realize he wasn't British until I watched two clips of him online after the show. Two clips, because I had to be sure he wasn't putting on a fake American accent in the first. Using a loop pedal and Moog synthesizer, he creates a performance that is less musical parody than comedic musical abstraction. His act is an entirely improvised flow state. When he was on my podcast, I asked him to improvise a song on the spot.[6] The result was a cross between the Cocteau Twins, Gorillaz, and the score of a spooky 1940s newsreel cartoon about a lonely skeleton longingly staring out their window. Afterward I asked where that came from. He didn't know. He wasn't even sure what had just happened.

Similarly, I don't remember anything specific from his Bell House show, as to properly watch Watts means to try to lock into his flow. The result is like seeing other comedians, only more so, as the audience is in constant, subtle conversation about the direction of the show. Watts builds a song piece by piece, with each musical element reacting to the last, but also reacting to how the audience is reacting. A beat comes to him, and if we dance, it becomes a dance song; if we sway, maybe it is an R&B homage. Brian Regan has my favorite way of describing what the job of a comedian is. "Let's say you have five hundred people in the audience. Who has the ability to connect to five hundred individuals?"[7] he explained. "Instead, you try to make that group one thing. And then I just try to make that one thing laugh." One thing, that's what we were.

The last famous thinker I am going to bastardize in this book is Derek Parfit, a prominent late-twentieth-century British moral philosopher best known for his book *Reasons and Persons*. Parfit thought the idea of personal identity was overrated.[8] One of his thought experiments casts you as one of three triplets who have been in a terrible accident, which leaves you with a healthy brain but a fatally wounded body, and your siblings with the reverse. Doctors implant half of your brain into each sibling, which works, but both now believe they are you. Who is dead? Who is alive? Are both you or neither? His point:

> When I believed that my existence was such a further fact, I seemed imprisoned in myself. My life seemed like a glass tunnel, through which I was moving faster every year and at the end of which there was darkness. When I changed my view, the walls of my glass tunnel disappeared. I now live in the open air. There is still a difference between my life and the lives of other people. But the difference is less. Other people are closer.[9]

It's an idea that overlaps nicely with some Buddhist concepts of self or what happens if you ever talk to someone who just took mushrooms and wanted you to know that we are the trees and the trees are their cat and their cat is their great-grandfather Frank.

In that audience that night, at times, I'm not sure I distinguished myself from the rest of the crowd and them from me. Little parts of my grief were spread among the 350 of us, making it lighter to carry. It was a start.

"We get something better. We get the moment. You know, we get the right fucking now." Remember that quote from chapter 4? During the lockdown phase of the pandemic, comedians didn't get those things. A lot of stand-ups had a hard time. I know a lot of people, period, had a hard time. This isn't a sadness competition. The pandemic was just particularly difficult for comedians, because of how singularly their art is made. It's a point I was keenly aware of when I was writing a book about comedians during the pandemic, while many of the people I was writing about couldn't do comedy. The Brooklyn comedian Nore Davis told me five months in that he "missed his saxophone."[10] Meaning he didn't just miss performing, he felt he was missing the instrument through which he was able to create. Many went looking for other outlets, like podcasts or dusting off old pilot scripts or, God forbid, Zoom shows. With time away from the lifestyle, a lot of them considered quitting. Few did. Why not? Some didn't have any other options, professionally, creatively, financially, but mostly it was what they did. It's what they needed to do. "Most people live their entire lives with their clothes on and even if they wanted to, couldn't take them off," Heti writes in 2010's *How Should a Person Be?*[11] "Then there are those who cannot put them on. They are the ones who live their lives not just as people but as examples of people. They are destined to expose every part of themselves, so the rest of us can know what it means to be a human." It's the quote I kept thinking about on May 10, 2021, when I went to see John Mulaney live at New York's City Winery, for what would be for both of us our first indoor comedy show since the shutdown.

I had last seen Mulaney over Zoom, nine months prior, but not for a performance.[12] We were discussing *The Sack Lunch Bunch*, his version of the children's variety shows of his youth and a silly sort of meditation on the loneliness of childhood fear. He told me then that he had expected to go into the project teaching his cast of fifteen eight-to-thirteen-year-olds about the business and how they shouldn't trust anyone, but he quickly realized he had nothing to tell them. He knew it was a cliché, but there was so much he could learn from them. "Those little kids had more self-soothing ability," he told me with a sense of longing. Ultimately, what the project made him realize about his own childhood was that he had a "rich inner life," but "no one seemed to care or ask me about it or pay attention." He had a desire for connection, but no one to connect with. It is a common origin for the stand-up comedian.

Sitting, socially distanced, at City Winery, in a cavernous room that looked like a warehouse space that was only halfway into being turned into a bar mitzvah venue, I learned that Mulaney had gone to rehab two weeks after our conversation, for an addiction to cocaine and alcohol. After relapsing the week he hosted *SNL* that November, he eventually checked into a sixty-day rehab facility in December. The news of his divorce from his wife of seven years came out the morning of the show I was at. Days later the news came out that confirmed the rumor of his relationship with Olivia Munn. We didn't know it at the time, but Munn was pregnant. All we knew for sure that Monday night was that this was Mulaney's first show back and he was 141 days sober. When he told us, we all clapped. He wore a long-sleeved, striped polo shirt and jeans, a notable departure from the suit fans have grown accustomed to seeing him in. He was heavier. He looked healthier. Throughout the hour-long set that followed, his appearance served as a reminder that he, like all of us, came out of the pandemic different than he went in.

The show wasn't a show. Candid, loose, sometimes hard to watch, sometimes so funny it made the audience convulse in laughter, it was a writing session. He was doing all-new material, not attempting to work in any of the jokes he had been building in outdoor shows before rehab. It was raw, both in its frankness and in the complete lack of polish typically associated with Mulaney's work. It was fascinating to see him try to figure out how to apply his stylistic signatures to more intensely personal subject matter. He is a master of faux exasperation, and a lot of his classic jokes hinge on taking not very serious things very seriously, but it is a challenging approach when the subject matter is, in fact, quite serious. How social anxiety had contributed to his drug use was not something he could easily be flippant about. Pettiness, which has always been in his act in small doses, came to the forefront. He spent a large portion of the set complaining about his intervention, organized by his college friends and his celebrity friends. *How dare they trick him into thinking he was getting dinner? Why, in a room of the twelve funniest people he knows, was no one being funny?*

A lot of this material was funny, but Mulaney has never had trouble being funny. The longest road ahead for Mulaney was not how to talk about his recovery onstage, but who to talk about it as. It is impossible to reconcile this material with Mulaney's "aw shucks" Jimmy Stewart persona. On that night, he surprised audiences by revealing that part of him still desperately wanted to continue to use. This is not an uncommon thought for someone battling addiction, but there was a lot of cognitive dissonance needed to reconcile this information with who the audience thought he was. I was reminded of the joke from his debut special, 2012's *New in Town*: "I don't drink. I used to drink, then I drank too much and I had to stop. That surprises a lot of audiences, because I don't look like someone who used to do anything." He uncomfortably laughed to himself a lot after jokes didn't get the exact reaction he expected, as if to say, *This isn't what it usually feels like for me to do stand-up.*

You know how when a caterpillar is turning into a

butterfly, their entire body decomposes before recomposing, so if you were to cut the chrysalis open in the middle, it would be just gross goo? That night was like that goo. With most of the material, Mulaney didn't come off particularly well; he knew that and leaned into it. The most exhilarating moments were when he would make fun of the tone of overwhelming support he got when the news of his addiction first came out. He would reveal something disrespectful he did to his friends and quickly remind the audience, "It's a *disease*."

Stand-up is truest to itself as an art form when a comedian has a new joke, approaches the crowd with an open mind and collaborative spirit, and is received by a present and committed audience. Vulnerability demands trusting in others. And creation makes an artist incredibly vulnerable, demanding a breaking down of their conscious self and their ego to tap into something hidden deep inside, too sensitive for the everyday. To do that in public!? It's why so many comics approach the gig defensively or combatively, as if to protect themselves. To approach the craft sincerely and openly is to be vulnerable, no matter how silly or stupid your act. When I saw Chris Rock bomb, trying to figure out how to discuss his divorce, I wasn't captivated that someone was talking about divorce, but that he was letting us help him figure out how he wanted to talk about it. And that was the same with Mulaney. I had seen Mulaney perform dozens of times. I had interviewed him a few times and run into him occasionally. I had never gotten such a sense of who he is as a person—the charming and the frustrating—than I did that first night back.

Over a year later, I saw Mulaney again, now at Madison Square Garden. Instead of 150 socially distanced spectators, it was twenty thousand people right up against each other. Mulaney was dressed in an impeccably tailored tuxedo, and his material had a similar level of polish. Obviously, he was great. He was the comedian John Mulaney. That night, at MSG, I saw a beautiful butterfly, but part of me missed the goo. E. B. and Katharine White were wrong. Frogs are a dime a dozen at any local pond, wetland, or stream. But you learn more from the innards, about the frog and yourself as a living creature.

Some audience members didn't know exactly what to make of a lot of Mulaney's performance that first night back. One person, toward the end, said they wanted to hear more about what college was like, as if to say, "Remember how much fun you used to be, John?" (He went into an extended riff about the D.C. sniper.) This was not the worst thing someone shouted out. Some felt the need to "woo!" when Mulaney listed prescription drugs he abused. When Mulaney said his relationship with audiences was the longest-lasting, most intimate one of his life, many began to clap. He cringed and asked them to stop—he hadn't meant it was a good thing. Probably even more than Mulaney, I grew frustrated as the show wore on.

I had felt connected to Mulaney and his process, but at the same time felt the audience wasn't giving him what he needed from us and, in turn, what we needed to give each other. This was supposed to be like that Reggie Watts show, a collective moment of healing, but it felt more like 150 separate experiences next to each other. To paraphrase the songwriter Ted Leo, we really weren't together at all, but parallel.

It took seeing another live show to make me realize what was missing. Developed and mounted on Broadway months before Covid-19 came to the States, *American Utopia*, David Byrne's humanely choreographed explosion of music and joy and political calls to action, is a show about connection. In it, after singing a song about brains to start the show, he explains, "Babies' brains have hundreds of millions more neural connections than we do as adults, and as we grow up, we lose these connections." The rest of his show is, abstractly, in search of those connections, trying to figure out where that leaves us as people. At the end, he wonders, "Maybe those millions of connections in our brains that got pruned and eliminated when we were babies somehow get kind of reestablished, only now instead of being in our heads, they're between us and other people. Who we are is thankfully not just here, but it extends beyond ourselves through the connections between all of us."

Watching this show live, with a fairly subdued audience, months into Broadway's reopening, was okay, but this moment in the performance made me realize that if what Byrne was saying was true, even just conceptually, then the time away weakened those connections. We need to reestablish again the reestablished wiring that bonds us together. It is not something you inherently have, but something you must work to build. It's like how a lot of people think you go to therapy to find a cure for your mental anguish, when continuing to go is the salve. That wasn't just Mulaney's first show back, it was the audience's. And it was mine.

This is how I rebuilt my connections. Soon after seeing Mulaney, I reached out to Union Hall, my favorite comedy venue on earth. Tucked in the basement under a bocce court, it has incredibly low ceilings and, even better yet, bad cell phone reception. I proposed we start a weekly comedy show with *Vulture*. The result was *Pretty Major*, every Tuesday, hosted by three comedians, Marcia Belsky, Jay Jurden, and Zach Zimmerman.

I thought it would be good for *Vulture*'s brand and the comedy community, but I hoped it would be good for me, too, who, besides living through the pandemic, was working on this book that demanded frequent mental isolation. All I was sure of was that I was getting worse. Beyond mid-pandemic melancholy, I found myself foggy, dissociative, paranoïd, and lost to the passing of time, with two years ago feeling closer than two weeks ago.

Every week, I went, first standing in the back, then sitting in the middle. Slowly people started showing up. Eventually, we stopped having to wear masks. Then we put the masks back on. And then took them off again. And so on and so on. Finally, after a couple months, we remembered how to laugh as a unit. It was, to quote hooks, a miracle.

Those first months, Jurden was working on a joke about the difficulty of doing comedy *nowadays*. No, "not because of cancel culture but because of content culture." "I'm supposed to be funnier onstage than EVERYTHING in your phone?" he asks, with a Mulaney-esque faux exasperation. "I'm supposed to be funnier than old people falling down? Funnier than babies falling down? Funnier than old people dropping babies while falling down? I'm supposed to be funnier than PUGS!?" He stays for a minute on pugs:

> I'm supposed to be funnier than a four-legged pre-existing condition?
>
> I'm supposed to be funnier than something that we bred to look like a European monarch?

> Pugs are funnier than old people and babies because they look like both of those groups.

Each week he worked on new pug tags and, without fail, we communicated our favorites.

The point Jurden was making was that a pug couldn't do what he was doing. If a pug were onstage, the audience would laugh for a second, sure, but then start worrying about whose dog it was. What Jurden was doing was an art form. An art form that can make people laugh—unless withholding laughs is necessary for the piece. An art form that is in the moment and of the moment. An art form that can be truer than the truth. An art form that can develop trust, expand understanding, give audiences the language to discuss what is most difficult to discuss, create a place to play with challenging ideas, and bring people together as one thing. It can be taken seriously. It must.

In the summer of 2021, I was waiting for a hamburger at a backyard barbecue when I met a friend of a friend, who, upon finding out I was working on this book, asked earnestly, "Why does comedy exist?" Seriously, that was his question. A question about why we as a culture, society, species have comedy. Quickly, I responded, "Because life is so hard . . ." I paused, unsure of what to say next, before adding, "Imagine if it didn't." Soon, the burgers were ready and the conversation moved on, but I couldn't. For months, I kept thinking about it. *Why on earth does comedy exist?*

In March 2022, at a point the Covid death total had reached six million worldwide (plus another projected eighteen million "excess deaths"), I was presented an answer when Maria Bamford appeared on *The Late Late Show with James Corden*, elevating what is often the safest form of stand-up, the five-minute late-night set, to the level of fine art. See, Bamford's mom, Marilyn, died in late 2020 from lung cancer. Considering that Maria's impression of Marilyn is a beloved fixture of her act—offering Maria an overly sweet albeit passive-aggressive counterbalance to her, at times, dark material—and considering that Maria has always been fearless about what she talks about onstage, of course her mother's death was a major part of the set she was working on during the pandemic. I had seen a few Zoom shows she'd performed (including one in which the premise was that after her set, the camera would stay on as she slept, only for her to end the show in the morning), and, feeling like I knew her mom through her act, I found the material very moving. But to do it on *The Late Late Show with James Corden*, a show she's never been on before, to an audience who likely doesn't know who she is and definitely doesn't know who her mom is, is such a high level of difficulty.

The entire set is incredible. But I just want to focus on the first thirty seconds and what she does to make the rest of the set work—a set in which she talks exclusively about her mother dying from lung cancer. A set, again, that is on *The Late Late Show with James Corden*. "You guys, some people love life," she starts, already getting laughs at the counterintuitive absurdity. Smiling, she continues, "I've always been on the fence about the whole thing." She speeds through so people laugh but don't think too deeply as she continues: "I could . . . go . . . at . . . any time." Medium laugh. Still building, still fairly deadpan. "What I would really like is a sharp blow to the head," she says, before her voice switches to cartoonishly, midwesternly cheerful: ". . . that I do not see coming!" She laughs maniacally as she gets a big laugh from the tourists. What she does here is find a way to introduce death as not that big a deal. *Death? That old thing. Who cares? Actually, it sounds kinda nice.* She talks about it as if it is a spontaneous vacation from life. This softens the topic, so, as she continues, the audience doesn't feel the need to tighten. A lesser comedian might've also milked this moment for an applause break, but Bamford knows she needs the momentum.

"My mom loved life," starts the next joke. *Loved*. Remember, this audience probably doesn't know Maria and almost definitely doesn't know her mom has died. This is how she tells them: subtly, gently. It's a phrase you probably hear in 90 percent of eulogies, and this set is a eulogy. She respects the audience's intelligence enough not to blurt out "MY MOM DIED!" because she knows that would just earn her rote sympathy. "My mom loved life" brings the audience in, creating a genuine feeling of closeness with Maria. All TV bullshit fades away. For the next four minutes, it is just one person telling you what they loved about their mom, in the funniest way possible. It is a stand-up version of the Jewish honorific for the dead: "May their memory be a blessing."

And you get it. Every single person in the audience and every single person at home was in the middle of a once-in-a-hundred-years traumatic event. One that was still going on. It's hard to take the time to grieve, when people don't stop dying. And, watching Maria talking about her mom who died unrelated to Covid, I realized, in a way, this is always the case. It is hard to find the time to grieve. It was barely a half a year after Simon died that Covid hit the States. But watching Maria, I laughed until I cried and cried until I laughed. I'm reminded again of the Viktor Frankl quote from chapter 4: "Humor, more than anything else in the human make-up, can afford an aloofness and an ability to rise above any situation, even if only for a few seconds." Maria gave me a tight five minutes.

Almost exactly three years from when I first interviewed Maron, we spoke again. Two months after our first conversation, his girlfriend and collaborator, the director Lynn Shelton, died unexpectedly of undiagnosed leukemia. I brought up his quote about isolation, and he acknowledged this made grieving difficult at the time. But he also said there was a "humanity bonding [aspect] to [speaking] publicly about things that are either inner monologues or taboo."[13] "It relieves something," he told me, "and that relief may be challenging, but I think that it's probably good." For Maron that meant in the days, then weeks, then months, then years that followed Shelton's passing, he would give his podcast audience an incredibly vulnerable glimpse into his grieving process, twice a week sharing whatever he felt at the moment he recorded that episode of *WTF*'s intro. A little over two and half years after her passing, he released a special, *From Bleak to Dark*, in which he spends twenty minutes reflecting on Shelton's death and his mourning. First and foremost, Maron put a premium on making the audience laugh, because, as he told me, it gives him hope. "It's really the only thing that stands between us and fascism: the humanity of decency that is available when groups of people get together." Beyond that, he believes his job as a comedian is to create things that make people see the world differently. He told me, "[Comedians can] present things that are difficult, through humor, in a way that completely recontextualizes them in someone's mind." I brought up the Frankl quote and he mentioned that he read a different book about concentration camps that resulted in this joke from his special:

> Humor that comes from real darkness is really the best, because it disarms it. It's elevating to the spirit. It's why I got into comedy. Because I'd watch comics and they would take things that were complicated or horrifying and simplify them and sort of make you see them in a different way and have a laugh. I think it is a beautiful thing and *necessary*. Like I believe there were probably some *hilarious* people at Auschwitz.

Talking with Maron, I was reminded of a study I was reading right before the pandemic. *Why on earth does comedy exist?* Well, apparently, it's not just Earth. The research suggested that whenever there is a mission to Mars, there would need to be a comedian onboard the spaceship. Now, the researchers meant just a funny person, not like it needs to be Ray Romano or something, but the reasoning was informative. "These are people that have the ability to pull everyone together, bridge gaps when tensions appear and really boost morale," the anthropologist Jeffrey Johnson said at the time.[14] "When you're living with others in a confined space for a long period of time, . . . [it's] vital you have somebody who can help everyone get along, so they can do their jobs." That is the same reason we have comedians here on Earth. They help us get through our increasingly absurd, sometimes painful, constantly frustrating lives. It's the need for legitimate foolishness. Can comedy make everything all better? Of course not. But it makes it easier.

Notes

1. COMEDY

1. Jesse David Fox, "How the Internet and a New Generation of Superfans Helped Create the Second Comedy Boom," *Vulture*, Mar. 30, 2015, www.vulture.com/2015/03/welcome-to-the-second-comedy-boom.html.
2. Bill Carter, "In the Tastes of Young Men, Humor Is Most Prized, a Survey Finds," *New York Times*, Feb. 20, 2012, www.nytimes.com/2012/02/20/business/media/comedy-central-survey-says-young-men-see-humor-as-essential.html.
3. Jennifer Keishin Armstrong, *Seinfeldia: How a Show About Nothing Changed Everything* (New York: Simon and Schuster, 2017), 18–19.
4. Judd Apatow, *Sick in the Head: Conversations About Life and Comedy* (New York: Random House, 2015), 196.
5. Jim Abbott, "Not 1 of 76.3 Million Who Saw 'Seinfeld'? Never Fear," *Orlando Sentinel*, May 16, 1998, www.orlandosentinel.com/news/os-xpm-1998-05-16-9805160257-story.html.
6. Rick Porter, "'Game of Thrones' Series Finale Sets All-Time HBO Ratings Record," *Hollywood Reporter*, May 20, 2019, www.hollywoodreporter.com/tv/tv-news/game-thrones-series-finale-sets-all-time-hbo-ratings-record-1212269/.
7. "Cable and Internet Loom Large in Fragmented Political News Universe," Pew Research Center, Jan. 11, 2004, /www.pewresearch.org/politics/2004/01/11/cable-and-internet-loom-large-in-fragmented-political-news-universe/.
8. Jody C. Baumgartner, Jonathan S. Morris, and Natasha L. Walth, "The Fey Effect: Young Adults, Political Humor, and Perceptions of Sarah Palin in the 2008 Presidential Election Campaign," *Public Opinion Quarterly* 76, no. 1 (spring 2012): 95–104.
9. Corey Robin, "The Day Zach Galifianakis Saved Obamacare," *Jacobin*, Aug. 5, 2018, jacobin.com/2018/08/affordable-care-act-website-between-two-ferns.
10. E. B. White and Katharine S. White, "Preface," in E. B. White and Katharine S. White, eds., *A Subtreasury of American Humor* (New York: Coward-McCann, 1941), xvii.
11. csch, "Norm Macdonald - Sixth & I Historic Synagogue," Apr. 5, 2017, YouTube video, www.youtube.com/watch?v=r5YQ6FHdZFI.
12. "Philosophy of Humor," *Stanford Encyclopedia of Philosophy*, Aug. 20, 2020, plato.stanford.edu/entries/humor/.
13. Ibid.
14. Ibid.
15. Robert R. Provine, *Laughter: A Scientific Investigation* (New York: Penguin, 2001), 124–26.
16. Ibid., 92.

17. Matthew Gervais and David Sloan Wilson, "The Evolution and Functions of Laughter and Humor: A Synthetic Approach," *Quarterly Review of Biology* 80, no. 4 (2005), pubmed.ncbi.nlm.nih.gov/16519138/.
18. Matthew M. Hurley, Daniel C. Dennett, and Reginald B. Adams, Jr., *Inside Jokes: Using Humor to Reverse-Engineer the Mind* (Cambridge, MA: MIT Press, 2013), 260.
19. Ibid.
20. Gervais and Wilson, "The Evolution and Functions of Laughter and Humor."
21. Henri Bergson, *Laughter: An Essay on the Meaning of the Comic* (New York: Macmillan, 1911), 69.
22. White and White, "Preface," xviii.

2. AUDIENCE

1. Mel Watkins, *On the Real Side: A History of African American Comedy* (Chicago: Chicago Review Press, 1999), 82–95.
2. Wayne Federman, *The History of Stand-Up: From Mark Twain to Dave Chappelle* (United States: Amazon Digital Services, 2021), 3.
3. Kliph Nesteroff, *The Comedians* (New York: Grove Press, 2015), 65.
4. Yael Kohen, *We Killed: The Rise of Women in American Comedy* (New York: Farrar, Straus and Giroux, 2012), 11.
5. Ibid.
6. Marc Maron, "Episode 1342—Dana Gould," *WTF with Marc Maron* (podcast), June 23, 2022, www.wtfpod.com/podcast/episode-1342-dana-gould.
7. "George Carlin Said of Andrew Dice Clay, 'His Acts Are Hardly Comedy Shows. There's Very Little Wit. They're Like Fascist Rallies,'" archived by oldshowbiz, Tumblr, Feb. 11, 2022, oldshowbiz.tumblr.com/post/675882481098113024/1990-george-carlin-said-of-andrew-dice-clay-his.
8. Sinduja Rangarajan, "The Godfather of L.A.'s Black Comedy Scene, Michael Williams, Is Plotting His Comeback," *L.A. Weekly*, Sept. 23, 2014, www.laweekly.com/the-godfather-of-l-a-s-black-comedy-scene-michael-williams-is-plotting-his-comeback/.
9. *Phat Tuesdays*, episode 1, "Hood to Hollywood," directed by Reginald Hudlin, aired Feb. 4, 2022, on Amazon Prime Video, www.imdb.com/title/tt16911950/?ref_=ttep_ep1.
10. David Mills, "Robin Harris," *Washington Post*, Mar. 26, 1990, www.washingtonpost.com/archive/lifestyle/1990/03/26/robin-harris/59df43aa-69cf-4ed4-9ee4-cca4d3c948d8/.
11. Lynn Hirschberg, "How Black Comedy Got the Last Laugh," *New York Times*, Sept. 3, 2000, www.nytimes.com/2000/09/03/magazine/how-black-comedy-got-the-last-laugh.htmlorh.
12. Mills, "Robin Harris."
13. Jesse David Fox, "Tony Woods's Travels," *Good One: A Podcast About Jokes* (podcast), Feb. 16, 2019, podcasts.apple.com/us/podcast/tony-woodss-travels/id1203393721?i=1000509405752.
14. Kohen, *We Killed*, 210.
15. Ibid., 215.
16. Beth Lapides, "Beth Lapides Reveals How UnCabaret Managed to Reach Its 25th Birthday," *L.A. Weekly*, Oct. 19, 2018.
17. Alec Baldwin, "Chris Rock," *Here's the Thing with Alec Baldwin* (podcast), Dec. 5, 2011, www.wnycstudios.org/podcasts/heresthething/episodes/173678-chris-rock.
18. Lacey Rose, "'This Is the Best Part I've Ever Had': Chris Rock Talks 'Fargo,' Aging and Why He's Spending 7 Hours a Week in Therapy," *Hollywood Reporter*, Sept. 16, 2020, www.hollywoodreporter.com/movies/movie-features/this-is-the-best-part-ive-ever-had-how-chris-rocks-extensive-therapy-helped-prepare-him-for-fargo-4060631/.

19. Judd Apatow, "Chris Rock," *Vanity Fair*, Jan. 2013, archive.vanityfair.com/article/2013/1/chris-rock.
20. *Cultureshock*, season 1, episode 5, "Chris Rock's 'Bring the Pain,'" directed by W. Kamau Bell, aired Oct. 15, 2018, on A&E, www.imdb.com/title/tt8716060/.
21. David Kamp, "The Color of Truth," *Vanity Fair*, Aug. 1998, archive.vanityfair.com/article/1998/8/the-color-of-truth.
22. Rose, "'This Is the Best Part I've Ever Had.'"
23. *Cultureshock*, "Chris Rock's 'Bring the Pain.'"
24. Ibid.
25. Ibid.
26. Ibid.
27. Ibid.
28. Ibid.
29. Ibid.
30. Ibid.
31. Kamp, "The Color of Truth."
32. Ibid.
33. *Cultureshock*, "Chris Rock's 'Bring the Pain.'"
34. Kamp, "The Color of Truth."
35. Rebecca Leung, "Rock: Bring On Oscar 'Safety Net,'" CBS News, Feb. 17, 2005, www.cbsnews.com/news/rock-bring-on-oscar-safety-net/.
36. Federman, *The History of Stand-Up*, 55.
37. Jesse David Fox, "The History of Stand-up with Wayne Federman," *Good One: A Podcast About Jokes* (podcast), May 27, 2021, podcasts.apple.com/us/podcast/the-history-of-stand-up-with-wayne-federman/.
38. Ramsey Ess, "An Appreciation of the Button-Down Mind of Bob Newhart," *Vulture*, Mar. 15 2018, www.vulture.com/2018/03/an-appreciation-of-the-button-down-mind-of-bob-newhart.html.

3. FUNNY

1. Lawrence Levine, *Highbrow/Lowbrow* (Cambridge, MA: Harvard University Press, 2009), 14–81.
2. Ibid., 198–99.
3. George Meredith, *An Essay on Comedy and the Uses of the Comic Spirit* (New York: C. Scribner's Sons, 1918), 141.
4. A. H. Weiler, "'Some Like It Hot': 2-Hour Comedy," *New York Times*, Mar. 30, 1959, archive.nytimes.com/www.nytimes.com/books/98/12/27/specials/wilder-hot.html.
5. "Film Review: 'Some Like It Hot,'" *Variety*, Feb. 24, 1959, variety.com/1959/film/reviews/some-like-it-hot-2-1200419454/.
6. Bosley Crowther, "'Dr. Strangelove,' a Shattering Sick Joke," *New York Times*, Jan. 30, 1964, archive.nytimes.com/www.nytimes.com/books/01/06/17/specials/southern-strangelove.html.
7. "The Four Marx Brothers," *New York Times*, Nov. 23, 1933, www.nytimes.com/1933/11/23/archives/the-four-marx-brothers.html.
8. Vincent Canby, "'Blazing Saddles,' a Western in Burlesque," *New York Times*, Feb. 8, 1974, www.nytimes.com/1974/02/08/archives/screen-blazing-saddles-a-western-in-burlesque.html.
9. "The General," *Variety*, Dec. 31, 1926, variety.com/1926/film/reviews/the-general-1200409824/.
10. Jay Weissberg, "The Great Buster: A Celebration," *Variety*, Sept. 1, 2018, variety.com/2018/film/festivals/the-great-buster-a-celebration-review-buster-keaton-1202924203/.
11. "B.A.P.S.," *Rotten Tomatoes*, www.rottentomatoes.com/m/baps.
12. "Step Brothers," *Rotten Tomatoes*, www.rottentomatoes.com/m/1193743-step_brothers.

13. "MacGruber," *Rotten Tomatoes*, www.rottentomatoes.com/m/macgruber.
14. Jesse David Fox, "Fran Lebowitz," *Good One: A Podcast About Jokes* (podcast), June 10, 2021, podcasts.apple.com/us/podcast/fran-lebowitz/id1203393721?i=1000524906078.
15. Brian D. Johnson, "Two Adam Sandlers Are Worse Than One," *Maclean's*, Nov. 10, 2011, www.macleans.ca/culture/movies/two-adam-sandlers-are-worse-than-one/.
16. Marc Savlov, "Jack and Jill," *Austin Chronicle*, Nov. 18, 2011, www.austinchronicle.com/events/film/2011-11-11/jack-and-jill/.
17. Michael Compton, "Sandler Falls Down with 'Jack and Jill,'" *Bowling Green Daily News*, Nov. 17, 2011, www.bgdailynews.com/community/sandler-falls-down-with-jack-and-jill/article_100d16d6-7f9e-5d69-8905-4118a5285013.html.
18. David Edelstein, Alison Willmore, Bilge Ebiri, and Angelica Jade Bastién, "Every Movie of the 2010s, Ranked," *Vulture*, Dec. 11, 2019, www.vulture.com/article/every-movie-of-the-2010s-ranked-sort-of.html.
19. Andrew Barker, "Jack and Jill," *Variety*, Nov. 10, 2011, variety.com/2011/film/reviews/jack-and-jill-1117946552/.
20. Emma Jones, "'I Didn't Get into Movies to Please the Critics': Adam Sandler Interview," *Independent*, Aug. 2, 2013, www.independent.co.uk/arts-entertainment/films/features/i-didn-t-get-into-movies-to-please-the-critics-adam-sandler-interview-a1277211.html.
21. Terry Gross, "In 'Funny People,' Lessons in Living and Dying," NPR, July 22, 2009, www.npr.org/2009/07/22/106860683/in-funny-people-lessons-in-living-and-dying.
22. Ernest Becker, *The Denial of Death* (New York: Free Press, 1973), 51.
23. Jesse David Fox, "The Lonely Island's Jose & Mark," *Good One: A Podcast About Jokes* (podcast), June 6, 2019, podcasts.apple.com/us/podcast/the-lonely-islands-jose-mark/id1203393721?i=1000440745345.
24. Chris Willman, "Dr. Luke: The Billboard Cover Story," *Billboard*, Sept. 3, 2010, www.billboard.com/music/music-news/dr-luke-the-billboard-cover-story-956518/.
25. Alex Needham, "John Seabrook on The Song Machine: 'There's a Dark Side to Pop,'" *Guardian*, Nov. 4, 2015, www.theguardian.com/music/2015/nov/04/john-seabrook-song-machine-review-pop-music.
26. Chris Kraus, *I Love Dick* (New York: Semiotext(e), 1997), 263.
27. Jesse David Fox, "Detroiters' 'Sam the Man' (with Sam Richardson)," *Good One: A Podcast About Jokes* (podcast), July 29, 2021, podcasts.apple.com/us/podcast/tony-woodss-travels/id1203393721?i=1000509405752.
28. A. O. Scott, "When Single Parents Collide on a Safari," *New York Times*, May 22, 2014, www.nytimes.com/2014/05/23/movies/adam-sandler-and-drew-barrymore-in-blended.html.
29. Ibid.
30. Madeline Leung Coleman, "Are Movie Critics Lying to You?," *Critics* (newsletter), Aug. 5, 2022.
31. Jacob Sweet, "The Context: Simpsons Writer John Swartzwelder on Comedy," *Harvard Magazine*, May 11, 2021, www.harvardmagazine.com/2021/05/the-context-simpsons-writer-john-swartzwelder-on-comedy.
32. Nancy Shulins, "America Laughs with Harvard Accent, But It Doesn't Know It," *Los Angeles Times*, Sept. 20, 1992, www.latimes.com/archives/la-xpm-1992-09-20-mn-1882-story.html.
33. Ken Tucker, "The Simpsons," *Entertainment Weekly*, Nov. 2, 1990, ew.com/article/1990/11/02/simpsons-3/.
34. Larry Rohter, "Television; Overachiever—and Learning to Deal With It, Man," *New York Times*, Oct. 7, 1990.
35. John J. O'Connor, "Review/Television; The Misadventures of the Simpsons,"

New York Times, Sept. 24, 1992, www.nytimes.com/1992/09/24/news/review-television-the-misadventures-of-the-simpsons.html.

36. Josef Adalian, "Nearly 20 Million People Have Already Watched the Game of Thrones Finale," *Vulture*, May 20, 2019, www.vulture.com/2019/05/game-of-thrones-finale-tv-ratings.html.
37. Matt Pressberg, "Why Animated Movies Are Dominating the Box Office in 2016," *Wrap*, Aug. 15, 2016, www.thewrap.com/why-animated-movies-are-dominating-the-box-office-in-2016/.
38. Lorenza Munoz, "Simpsons' Big Draw Globally," *Los Angeles Times*, July 31, 2007, www.latimes.com/archives/la-xpm-2007-jul-31-fi-nuhomerabroad31-story.html.
39. Jesse David Fox, "Brian Regan's Reading," *Good One: A Podcast About Jokes* (podcast), Feb. 25, 2021, podcasts.apple.com/us/podcast/brian-regans-reading/.

4. TIMING

1. Philip Scepanski, *Tragedy Plus Time: National Trauma and Television Comedy* (Austin: University of Texas Press, 2021), 94.
2. Jesse David Fox, "Gilbert Gottfried's *The Aristocrats*," *Good One: A Podcast About Jokes* (podcast), Sept. 9, 2019, podcasts.apple.com/us/podcast/gilbert-gottfrieds-the-aristocrats/id1203393721?i=1000449085785.
3. Jesse David Fox, "'One Giant Nerve That You Were Afraid to Touch,'" *Vulture*, Sept. 9, 2021, www.vulture.com/article/comedians-on-performing-after-9-11.html.
4. A. Peter McGraw, Lawrence E. Williams, and Caleb Warren, "The Rise and Fall of Humor: Psychological Distance Modulates Humorous Responses to Tragedy," *Social Psychological and Personality Science* 5, no. 5 (July 2014): 566–72, journals.sagepub.com/doi/10.1177/1948550613515006.
5. Fox, "'One Giant Nerve That You Were Afraid to Touch.'"
6. Scepanski, *Tragedy Plus Time*, 3.
7. Paul Liberman, "In New York, Stand-Ups Are Wrestling with Comedy's Fine Line," *Los Angeles Times*, Sept. 19, 2001, www.latimes.com/archives/la-xpm-2001-sep-19-ca-47200-story.html.
8. McGraw, Williams, and Warren, "The Rise and Fall of Humor," 566.
9. Scepanski, *Tragedy Plus Time*, 16.
10. Fox, "'One Giant Nerve That You Were Afraid to Touch.'"
11. Ibid.
12. Fox, "Gilbert Gottfried's *The Aristocrats*."
13. Frank DiGiacomo, "Why Have a Night Like This in Times Like These?," *Observer*, Aug. 8, 2005, observer.com/2005/08/why-have-a-night-like-this-in-times-like-these/.
14. Frank Rich, "The Greatest Dirty Joke Ever Told," *New York Times*, March 13, 2005, www.nytimes.com/2005/03/13/arts/the-greatest-dirty-joke-ever-told.html.
15. Fox, "Gilbert Gottfried's *The Aristocrats*."
16. Viktor Frankl, *Man's Search for Meaning* (1946; repr., Boston: Beacon Press, 2006), 54.
17. Andrew James Miller and Tom Shales, *Live From New York: An Uncensored History of* Saturday Night Live (Boston: Little, Brown, 2002), 38.
18. EJ Dickson and Andy Greene, "'In Bad Times, People Turn to the Show': Inside the 9/11 Episode of 'SNL,'" *Rolling Stone*, Sept. 8, 2021, www.rollingstone.com/tv-movies/tv-movie-features/saturday-night-live-9-11-oral-history-1221336/.
19. Ibid.
20. Mike Schur, "Mike Schur on How 9/11 Influenced the Writing on *SNL*, *The Office*, and *Parks and Rec*," *Vulture*, Sept. 11, 2016, www.vulture.com/2015/09/mike-schur-on-writing-comedy-after-911.html.

21. Terry Gross, "'SNL' Cast Member Will Ferrell," *Fresh Air* (podcast), Oct. 4, 2001, freshairarchive.org/segments/snl-cast-member-will-ferrell.
22. Dickson and Greene, "'In Bad Times, People Turn to the Show.'"
23. Ibid.
24. Amy Wallace, "Kate McKinnon Is Comedy's Not-So-Secret Weapon," *GQ*, May 21, 2018, www.gq.com/story/kate-mckinnon-profile-2018.
25. Laura Beck, "Saturday Night Live's 'Hallelujah' Opening Was a Bunch of B.S.," *Cosmopolitan*, Nov. 13, 2016, www.cosmopolitan.com/entertainment/tv/a8285155/saturday-night-live-hallelujah/.
26. Jordan Sargent, "SNL's Worst Idea Was Almost Not That Bad," *Spin*, May 21, 2018, www.spin.com/2018/05/snl-kate-mckinnon-hallelujah-gq-interview/.
27. Jesse David Fox, "Kate McKinnon's Close Encounters," *Good One: A Podcast About Jokes* (podcast), Aug. 11, 2022, podcasts.apple.com/us/podcast/kate-mckinnons-close-encounters/.
28. Jason Zinoman (@Zinoman), "Bruce came out late and his exact first words were, 'The only thing I'm gonna say is Vaughn Meader is screwed . . . And that was the only thing he said about it. he did not mention it again for the rest of the show . . . The line got a huge laugh of relief from the audience.' 3/," Twitter, Feb. 6, 2020, twitter.com/zinoman/status/1225626164892504064.
29. The 92nd Street Y, New York, "Alison Leiby with Ilana Glazer: Oh God, A Show About Abortion," June 23, 2022, YouTube video, www.youtube.com/watch?v=d4p49CCp67g.
30. Fox, "Kate McKinnon's Close Encounters."
31. Scepanski, *Tragedy Plus Time*, 3.

5. POLITICS

1. Dannagal Goldthwaite Young, *Irony and Outrage: The Polarized Landscape of Rage, Fear, and Laughter in the United States* (New York: Oxford University Press, 2020), 33.
2. Ibid.
3. Ibid., 35–37.
4. Ibid., 37.
5. William P. Hampes, "The Relationship Between Humor and Trust," *Humor: The International Journal of Humor Research* 12, no. 3 (July 1999): 253–59, www.degruyter.com/document/doi/10.1515/humr.1999.12.3.253/html.
6. Young, *Irony and Outrage*, 90–91.
7. Chris Smith, *The Daily Show (The Book): An Oral History as Told by Jon Stewart, the Correspondents, Staff and Guests* (New York: Grand Central Publishing, 2016), 156.
8. Nell Scovell, "Inside the Greatest Writers Room You've Never Heard Of," *Vulture*, Dec. 11, 2012, www.vulture.com/2012/12/inside-the-greatest-writers-room-youve-never-heard-of.html.
9. Smith, *The Daily Show (The Book)*, 215.
10. Ibid., 259.
11. Ibid., 332.
12. "Public Knowledge of Current Affairs Little Changed by News and Information Revolutions," Pew Research Center, Apr. 15, 2007, www.pewresearch.org/politics/2007/04/15/public-knowledge-of-current-affairs-little-changed-by-news-and-information-revolutions/.
13. Jesse David Fox, "Roy Wood Jr.'s Black Brits," *Good One: A Podcast About Jokes* (podcast), Nov. 11, 2021, podcasts.apple.com/us/podcast/roy-wood-jrs-black-brits/.
14. Jason Bateman, Sean Hayes, and Will Arnett, "Jon Stewart," *SmartLess* (podcast), Sept. 27, 2021, podcasts.apple.com/us/podcast/jon-stewart/id1521578868?i=1000536712335.
15. Larry Wilmore, "Malcolm Gladwell on Pioneers, Tokens, and 'The Satire Para-

dox' (Ep. 9)," *Larry Wilmore: Black on the Air* (podcast), July 10 2017, podcasts.apple.com/nz/podcast/malcolm-gladwell-on-pioneers-tokens-satire-paradox/id1234429850?i=1000390111295.

16. Catherine Kim, "The Battle over Extending the September 11th Victim Compensation Fund, Explained," *Vox*, July 29, 2019, www.vox.com/2019/6/20/18691670/jon-stewart-9-11-september-11th-victim-compensation-fund-explained.
17. *PBS NewsHour*, hosted by Gwen Ifill, aired Aug. 6, 2015, on PBS, www.imdb.com/title/tt4883696/?ref_=ttep_ep156.
18. Smith, *The Daily Show (The Book)*, 47.
19. *60 Minutes*, season 38, episode 32, "Lethal and Leaking/Priory of Sion/The Colbert Report," hosted by Steve Kroft, aired Apr. 30, 2006, on CBS, www.imdb.com/title/tt0830216/.
20. Ibid., 360.
21. Jody Baumgartner and Jonathan S. Morris, "The *Daily Show* Effect: Candidate Evaluations, Efficacy, and American Youth," *American Politics Research* 34, no. 3 (May 2006): 341–67, journals.sagepub.com/toc/aprb/34/3.
22. Smith, *The Daily Show (The Book)*, 374.
23. Debbie Elliott, "The 'Daily Effect': Cynical, Yet Informed," NPR, July 9, 2006, www.npr.org/2006/07/09/5544604/the-daily-effect-cynical-yet-informed.
24. Jody Baumgartner and Brad Lockerbie, "Maybe It Is More Than a Joke: Satire, Mobilization, and Political Participation," *Social Science Quarterly* 99, no. 3 (Sept. 2018): 1060–74.
25. Whitney Cummings (@WhitneyCummings), "Don't look to why so many people trust joe Rogan, look to why so few people trust the mainstream media," Twitter, Feb. 5, 2022, twitter.com/whitneycummings/status/1490136051163308037.
26. Adam Gopnik, "Trump and Obama: A Night to Remember," *New Yorker*, Sept. 12, 2015, www.newyorker.com/news/daily-comment/trump-and-obama-a-night-to-remember.
27. Mark Shanahan, "Was His Joke the Reason Trump Ran for President? Some Say So, and It Torments Him," *Boston Globe*, Oct. 30, 2020, www.bostonglobe.com/2020/10/30/arts/was-his-joke-reason-trump-ran-president-some-say-so-it-torments-him/.
28. Roxanne Roberts, "I Sat Next to Donald Trump at the Infamous 2011 White House Correspondents' Dinner," *Washington Post*, Apr. 28, 2016, www.washingtonpost.com/lifestyle/style/i-sat-next-to-donald-trump-at-the-infamous-2011-white-house-correspondents-dinner/2016/04/27/5cf46b74-0bea-11e6-8ab8-9ad050f76d7d_story.html.
29. Sara Schaefer, "Why Trump Jokes Aren't Funny," *Herald* (Glasgow, UK), July 29, 2017, www.heraldscotland.com/opinion/15442379.trump-jokes-arent-funny-american-stand-up-sara-schaefer-making-comedy-age-45th-us-president/.
30. Noah Garfinkel (@NoahGarfinkel), "Donald Trump is the least complicated President in history. There are like four things about him in total," Twitter, Sept. 22, 2017, twitter.com/noahgarfinkel/status/911327790821019648.
31. Malcolm Gladwell, "The Satire Paradox," *Revisionist History* (podcast), Aug. 18, 2016, podcasts.apple.com/ee/podcast/the-satire-paradox/.
32. Alan Siegel, "Tragedy Plus Time," *Ringer*, Dec. 15, 2020, www.theringer.com/tv/2020/12/15/22174371/trump-era-comedy-in-review-snl-impressions.
33. Josef Adalian, "Colbert Just Did Something the *Late Show* Hasn't Done in 25 Years," *Vulture*, May 22, 2019, www.vulture.com/2019/05/stephen-colbert-late-show-ratings-fallon-kimmel.html.
34. Emily Nussbaum, "No More Late Nights," *New Yorker*, Feb. 13, 2015, www.newyorker.com/magazine/2015/02/23/late-nights.
35. Kara Swisher, "Jon Stewart on Why the Right Would 'Rather Do a Deal with Putin Than Pelosi,'" *Sway* (podcast), Mar. 3, 2022, www.nytimes.com/2022/03/03/opinion/sway-kara-swisher-jon-stewart.html.

36. George Yancy and bell hooks, "bell hooks: Buddhism, the Beats and Loving Blackness," *New York Times*, Dec. 10, 2015, archive.nytimes.com/opinionator .blogs.nytimes.com/author/bell-hooks/.
37. Fox, "Roy Wood Jr.'s Black Brits."
38. Danielle Fuentes Morgan, *Laughing to Keep from Dying: African American Satire in the Twenty-First Century* (Champaign: University of Illinois Press, 2020), 5.
39. Srdja Popovic and Mladen Joksic, "Why Dictators Don't Like Jokes," *Foreign Policy*, Apr. 5, 2013, foreignpolicy.com/2013/04/05/why-dictators-dont-like -jokes/.
40. *Late Night with Seth Meyers*, season 5, episode 2, "Trevor Noah/Maggie Gyllenhaal," hosted by Seth Meyers, aired Sept. 6, 2017, on NBC, www.imdb .com/title/tt7322752/?ref_=nm_flmg_eps_tt_1.
41. Djamila Ould Khettab, "Algerian Media Faces 'Hostile Environment,'" Al Jazeera, July 15, 2016, www.aljazeera.com/news/2016/7/15/algerian-media-faces -hostile-environment.
42. Jesse David Fox, "Vir Das's Religion vs. Comedy," *Good One: A Podcast About Jokes* (podcast), May 6, 2021, podcasts.apple.com/bj/podcast/vir-dass-religion -vs-comedy/.
43. Soutik Biswas, "The Indian Comic in Jail for Jokes He Didn't Crack," BBC, Jan. 28, 2021, www.bbc.com/news/world-asia-india-55797053.
44. "Russia Expels Belarusian Comedian for Life for 'Insulting' Joke," *Moscow Times*, Aug. 30, 2021, www.themoscowtimes.com/2021/08/30/russia-expels -belarusian-comedian-for-life-for-insulting-joke-a74929.
45. Shreemi Verma, "Iranian Comic Zeinab Mousavi Imprisoned For 2 Years as Sarah Silverman Supports Calls for Her Release," *Dead Ant*, Dec. 19, 2022, deadant.co/iranian-comic-zeinab-mousavi-imprisoned-for-2-years-as-sarah -silverman-supports-calls-for-her-release/.
46. Fatma Khaled, "North Korea Bans Laughing for 11 Days to Mark Kim Family Anniversary: Report," *Newsweek*, Dec. 18, 2021, www.newsweek.com/north -korea-bans-laughing-11-days-mark-kim-family-anniversary-report-1660888.
47. Bernard-Henri Lévy, "Ukraine's Hero President Z.," *Tablet*, Feb. 28, 2022, www.tabletmag.com/sections/news/articles/ukraines-hero-president-z.
48. Anastasiia Mokhina, Aleksey, Viktoriia Khutorna, Petro Chekal, Leonid, Nasta, Daria Holovatenko, Danyil Zadorozhnyi, Mariia Shuvalova, Inna Zadorozhna, Victor Dobrovolskyi, Anastasia Kovalchuk, Julia Berdiyarova, Victoria Vlasenko, Anastasiia Viekua, Katya Vasiukova, Vika Zavhorodnia, Lisa Bukreyeva, Alexander, Roman Vydro, Markiian Matsiiovskyi, Yasia Myroshnychenko, Masha Varnas, Liana Muradian, Vova Prylutskyi, Yehor Shatailo, Polina Polikarpova, Lesyk Yakymchuk, Svyatoslav Fursin, and Sana Shahmuradova, "Sixteen Days in Ukraine," *Intelligencer*, Mar. 13, 2022, nymag.com /intelligencer/article/ukraine-war-diary.html.

6. TRUTH

1. Jesse David Fox, "Bert Kreischer's The Machine," *Good One: A Podcast About Jokes* (podcast), Nov. 10, 2020, podcasts.apple.com/ie/podcast/bert -kreischers-the-machine/id1203393721?i=1000497952856.
2. Bert Kreischer and Tom Segura, "Ep. 63," *2 Bears, 1 Cave with Tom Segura and Bert Kreischer* (podcast), Jan. 11, 2021, podcasts.apple.com/us/podcast/ep-63-2 -bears-1-cave-w-tom-segura-bert-kreischer/id1468013270?i=1000504976690.
3. Michael J. Arlen, "A Crack in the Greasepaint," *New Yorker*, Nov. 17, 1975, www.newyorker.com/magazine/1975/11/24/a-crack-in-the-greasepaint.
4. John Lahr, "The Goat Boy Rises," *New Yorker*, Nov. 1, 1993, www.newyorker .com/magazine/1993/11/01/the-goat-boy-rises.
5. Adam Wilson, "Louis C.K. and the Rise of the 'Laptop Loners,'" *Los Angeles Review of Books*, Sept. 25, 2012, lareviewofbooks.org/article/louis-c-k-and-the -rise-of-the-laptop-loners/.

6. David Haglund, "Half-Truths, Non-Truths, and Louis C.K.," *New Yorker*, Jan. 28, 2015, www.newyorker.com/culture/cultural-comment/louis-ck-comedy-philosophy.
7. David Marchese, "In Conversation: Louis C.K.," *Vulture*, June 13, 2016, www.vulture.com/2016/06/louis-ck-horace-and-pete-c-v-r.html.
8. "Louis C.K. Responds to Accusations: 'These Stories Are True,'" *New York Times*, Nov. 10, 2017, www.nytimes.com/2017/11/10/arts/television/louis-ck-statement.html.
9. Isaac Chotiney, "Listen to Louis C.K.: An Interview with the Comedian Jena Friedman," *New Yorker*, Jan. 4, 2019, www.newyorker.com/news/q-and-a/listening-to-louis-ck-an-interview-with-the-comedian-jena-friedman.
10. Marc Maron, "Episode 111—Louis C.K. part 1," *WTF with Marc Maron* (podcast), Oct. 4, 2010, www.wtfpod.com/podcast/episodes/episode_111_-_louis_ck_part_1.
11. Ibid.
12. Ryan Parker, "Bring On the Haters: Dane Cook Is Plotting a Comedy Comeback," *Hollywood Reporter*, Feb. 13, 2019, www.hollywoodreporter.com/lifestyle/lifestyle-news/bring-haters-dane-cook-plots-a-comedy-comeback-1185532/.
13. Matt Wilstein, "Dane Cook Never Wanted to Be a 'Frat Comic,'" *The Last Laugh* (podcast), Oct. 5, 2021, play.acast.com/s/last-laugh-daily-beast/danecookneverwantedtobea-fratcomic-.
14. Gary Gulman (@GaryGulman), "136) I believe being VULNERABLE is vital to creating MEMORABLE comedy. For the 1st few years just getting on stage is vulnerable. As a pro it means sharing a part of yourself that makes you uncomfortable and just as important, COMMITTING to the joke. #GulManTip #WriteNow," Twitter, May 14, 2019, twitter.com/garygulman/status/1128338960495849475.
15. Sean Malin, "Margaret Cho on the Groundbreaking DIY Impact of *I'm the One That I Want*," *Vulture*, Oct. 8, 2021, www.vulture.com/article/margaret-cho-im-the-one-that-i-want-interview.html.
16. Charles Duhigg, "'I Cannot Wait to Talk About How My Stepfather Died on FaceTime,'" *Slate*, Aug. 15, 2020, slate.com/human-interest/2020/08/tig-notaro-on-coping-with-cancer-and-the-pandemic.html.
17. Margaret Cho, *I Have Chosen to Stay and Fight* (New York: Riverhead Books, 2006), 16.
18. Jesse David Fox, "Beth Lapides's UnCabaret," *Good One: A Podcast About Jokes* (podcast), Jan. 27, 2022, https://podcasts.apple.com/fr/podcast/beth-lapidess-uncabaret/id1203393721?i=1000549157219.
19. Alexander Stern, "Authenticity Is a Sham," *Aeon*, Apr. 27, 2021, aeon.co/essays/a-history-of-authenticity-from-jesus-to-self-help-and-beyond.
20. Jesse David Fox, "Tig Notaro's Sixth Grade Music Class," *Good One: A Podcast About Jokes* (podcast), July 22, 2021, podcasts.apple.com/us/podcast/tig-notaros-sixth-grade-music-class/id1203393721?i=1000529681056.
21. Jesse David Fox, "John Early's Wedding Toast," *Good One: A Podcast About Jokes* (podcast), May 5, 2017, podcasts.apple.com/ca/podcast/john-earlys-wedding-toast/id1203393721?i=1000384962677.
22. Pete Holmes, "John Early," *You Made It Weird with Pete Holmes* (podcast), June 14, 2017, podcasts.apple.com/us/podcast/you-made-it-weird-with-pete-holmes/id475878118.
23. Bo Burnham (@BoBurnham), "It's the former. I've slipped into stealing Kate's vibes without trying. Most influential/imitated comedian of a generation. She figured and mastered the performance angle we were all looking for," Twitter, Dec. 8, 2018, twitter.com/boburnham/status/1071326187467624453?s=20&t=PwHDxK-yeAHzx3RXeYmdtA.
24. Bo Burnham (@BoBurnham), "And she was doing the hyper self-aware deconstructive performative liberal stuff 5 years before that stuff was part of the

popular culture. We are all playing match up to Kate. I'm being psychotic but she deserves the credit. Millennial Lenny Bruce or whatever I'm done goodbye," Twitter, Dec. 8, 2018, twitter.com/boburnham/status/1071326230069207040?s=20&t=PwHDxK-yeAHzx3RXeYmdtA.

25. Harry Gassel, "Kate Berlant Is Blurring the Lines Between Art and Entertainment," *Fader*, Jan. 16, 2015, www.thefader.com/2015/01/16/kate-berlant-interview.
26. Nathan Fielder, "Kate Berlant, in Conversation with Nathan Fielder," *Interview*, Dec. 12, 2022, www.interviewmagazine.com/culture/kate-berlant-in-conversation-with-nathan-fielder.
27. Judith Butler, *Gender Trouble: Feminism and the Subversion of Identity* (Abingdon, UK: Routledge, 1990), 139.
28. E. Alex Jung, "The Bold and Bawdy New Queens of Comedy," *Vulture*, May 31, 2018, www.vulture.com/2018/05/the-rise-of-queer-comedy.html.
29. Catie Lazarus, "The Moth's Catherine Burns on Grief and Burning Man, and Jo Firestone on Writing Jokes on Stage," *Employee of the Month* (podcast), Jan. 19, 2019, www.audacy.com/podcasts/employee-of-the-month-54569/the-moths-catherine-burns-on-grief-and-burning-man-and-jo-firestone-on-writing-jokes-on-stage-361069473.
30. Matt Rogers and Bowen Yang, "Damned and Lowly Favored (w/ Aaron Jackson & Josh Sharp)," *Las Culturistas* (podcast), Mar. 9, 2022, podcasts.apple.com/it/podcast/damned-and-lowly-favored-w-aaron-jackson-josh-sharp/.
31. Guy Branum (@guybranum), "A possible definition of camp is pretending to do a thing while actually doing it. Under these terms, is @MattRogersTho hosting Haute Dog the greatest hosting television has ever seen? Very possibly. He is great on @gaymeshowlive he is great on Haute Dog. Watch it. Love it.," Twitter, Sept. 25, 2020, twitter.com/guybranum/status/1309355571733172226/photo/1.
32. Naomi Ekperigin and Andy Beckerman, "George Civeris and Sam Taggart," *Couples Therapy* (podcast), Nov. 23, 2021, podcasts.apple.com/us/podcast/george-civeris-and-sam-taggart/id1410296631?i=1000542797982.
33. Jason Zinoman, "Bo Burnham, Discovered on the Internet, Now Challenges It," *New York Times*, June 3, 2016, www.nytimes.com/2016/06/04/arts/television/bo-burnham-discovered-on-the-internet-now-challenges-it.html.
34. Pete Holmes, "Bo Burnham #3," *You Made It Weird with Pete Holmes* (podcast), Sept. 14, 2016, podcasts.apple.com/us/podcast/bo-burnham-3/id475878118?i=1000375287243.
35. Jesse David Fox, "Bo Burnham's Can't Handle This," *Good One: A Podcast About Jokes* (podcast), July 2, 2018, podcasts.apple.com/ca/podcast/bo-burnhams-cant-handle-this/id1203393721?i=1000415049394.
36. Amy Wallace, "The Comedian's Comedian's Comedian," *GQ*, Aug. 11, 2020, www.gq.com/story/comedy-issue-garry-shandling.
37. Werner Herzog, "Minnesota Declaration: Truth and Fact in Documentary Cinema (Germany, 1999)," in Scott MacKenzie, ed., *Film Manifestos and Global Cinema Cultures: A Critical Anthology* (Berkeley: University of California Press, 2014), 471.
38. Jesse David Fox, "Kristen Schaal and Her Singing, Dancing Bird," *Good One: A Podcast About Jokes* (podcast), Feb. 27, 2017, podtail.com/en/podcast/good-one-a-podcast-about-jokes/kristen-schaal-and-her-singing-dancing-bird/.

7. LAUGHTER

1. Arthur C. Danto, "The End of Art: A Philosophical Defense," *History and Theory* 37, no. 4 (Dec. 1998): 127–43, www.jstor.org/stable/2505400.
2. Arthur C. Danto, "Introduction: Modern, Postmodern, and Contemporary," *After the End of Art: Contemporary Art and the Pale of History* (Princeton, NJ: Princeton University Press, 2021), 16.

3. Jesse David Fox, "Hannah Gadsby's Prepositions," *Good One: A Podcast About Jokes* (podcast), June 2, 2020, podcasts.apple.com/us/podcast/hannah-gadsbys-prepositions/id1203393721?i=1000476514495.
4. Marc Maron, "Episode 1358—Jerrod Carmichael," *WTF with Marc Maron* (podcast), Aug. 18, 2022, www.wtfpod.com/podcast/episode-1358-jerrod-carmichael.
5. Jesse David Fox, "How Funny Does Comedy Need to Be?," *Vulture*, Sept. 4, 2018, www.vulture.com/2018/09/post-comedy-how-funny-does-comedy-need-to-be.html.
6. Sam Sander, "*Atlanta* Wasn't for Everyone," *Vulture*, Nov. 10, 2022, www.vulture.com/article/stephen-glover-atlanta-interview.html.
7. Fox, "Hannah Gadsby's Prepositions."
8. Jenny Valentish, "'I Broke the Contract': How Hannah Gadsby's Trauma Transformed Comedy," *Guardian*, July 16, 2018, www.theguardian.com/stage/2018/jul/16/hannah-gadsby-trauma-comedy-nanette-standup-netflix.
9. "What the Hell Happened at Jerrod Carmichael's HBO Taping?," *Interrobang*, Dec. 11, 2016, theinterrobang.com/hell-happened-jerrod-carmichaels-hbo-taping/.
10. This tweet seems to have been deleted. The quote is from a transcribed version in the author's notes.
11. Jeffrey Gurian, "Jerrod Carmichael Tapes HBO Special, A Haunted Screening, Annual Benefit Brings Stars to Gotham Plus News from Jordan Rock," *Interrobang*, Dec. 12, 2016, theinterrobang.com/jerrod-carmichael-tapes-hbo-special-annual-benefit-brings-stars-gotham-plus-news-jordan-rock/.
12. Khris Davenport, "Jerrod Carmichael Doesn't Want to 'Say What Everyone Else Is Saying' About Trump in New HBO Special '8,'" *Complex*, Mar. 10, 2017, www.complex.com/pop-culture/2017/03/jerrod-carmichael-talks-hbo-special-8.
13. BUILD Series, "Jerrod Carmichael Discusses His HBO Special, '8,'" Mar. 7, 2017, YouTube video, www.youtube.com/watch?v=9WlmQjYh1Ok.
14. Jason Zinoman, "This May Be the Most Polarizing Comedy Special of the Year," *New York Times*, Aug. 24, 2018, www.nytimes.com/2018/08/24/arts/television/drew-michael-comedy-special-hbo.html.
15. Jesse David Fox, "For Drew Michael, Laughter Isn't the Ultimate Barometer," *Vulture*, Feb. 24, 2022, www.vulture.com/article/drew-michael-good-one-podcast.html.
16. Jesse David Fox, "Drew Michael's Social Media," *Good One: A Podcast About Jokes* (podcast), Feb. 24, 2022, podcasts.apple.com/us/podcast/drew-michaels-social-media/.
17. Maron, "Episode 1358—Jerrod Carmichael."
18. Ibid.
19. Chris D'Elia (@chrisdelia), "Lmaooooooooooooo wut," Twitter, Sept. 4, 2018, twitter.com/chrisdelia/status/1037045885966802944.
20. Joe Rogan (@joerogan), "LOL WUT," Twitter, Sept. 6, 2018, twitter.com/joerogan/status/1037620861358891008?s=20&t=E5E8QMu_i6Deqnf450011A.
21. Big Jay Oakerson and Dan Soder, "Bert Kreischer & Mike Vecchione in Studio, Everlast Stops In & the Guys Write Their Own 'Pete Davidson' Song," *The Bonfire with Big Jay Oakerson & Dan Soder* (podcast), Sept. 2018, podcasts.apple.com/us/podcast/bert-kreischer-mike-vecchione-in-studio-everlast-stops/id1396697981?i=1000419006292.
22. Andrew Ballantyne, "The Nest and the Pillar of Fire," in Andrew Ballantyne, ed., *What Is Architecture?* (Abingdon, UK: Routledge, 2002), 14.
23. Sarah Aswell, "'Un-PC' Comedy Lover: George Carlin and Eddie Murphy Aren't on Your Team," *Forbes*, Sept. 28, 2019, ww.forbes.com/sites/sarahaswell/2019/09/28/un-pc-comedy-lovers-george-carlin-and-eddie-murphy-arent-on-your-team/?sh=27e3058b1ed4.

24. *Charlie Rose*, "Robin Williams," hosted by Charlie Rose, aired Dec. 4, 2009, on PBS, charlierose.com/videos/24236.

8. THE LINE

1. Andrew Hankinson, *Don't Applaud. Either Laugh or Don't. (At the Comedy Cellar.)* (London: Scribe Publications, 2020), 15.
2. Ibid., 225.
3. Jesse David Fox, "Colin Quinn Will Never Stop Bombing," *Vulture*, Nov. 17, 2020, www.vulture.com/article/colin-quinn-covid-comedy-special-good-one-podcast.html.
4. Beck Krefting, "Savage New Media: Discursive Campaigns For/Against Political Correctness," in *The Joke Is on Us: Political Comedy in (Late) Neoliberal Times*, ed. Julia A. Webber (New York: Lexington Books, 2019), 239.
5. "Making Fun of People Is Inclusive, but Only If It's Funny," *Big Think*, June 26, 2015, bigthink.com/videos/lisa-lampanelli-and-politically-correct-comedy/.
6. Keegan-Michael Key and Jordan Peele, "Make Fun of Everything," *Time*, Mar. 13, 2014, time.com/22993/key-and-peele-make-fun-of-everything/.
7. Lauren Berlant and Sianne Ngai, "Comedy Has Issues," *Critical Inquiry* 43, no. 2 (winter 2017), doi.org/10.1086/689666.
8. Ibid.
9. David Marchese, "John Waters Is Ready to Defend the Worst People in the World," *New York Times Magazine*, Mar. 18, 2022, www.nytimes.com/interactive/2022/03/21/magazine/john-waters-interview.html.
10. Joe Rogan, "#1859—Louis CK & Joe List," *The Joe Rogan Experience* (podcast), Aug. 18, 2022, open.spotify.com/episode/7Hd6mqOnom9XfzvFQxoxBK.
11. *The Chris Rock Show*, season 2, episode 10, "Episode #2.10," directed by Linda Mendoza, aired Nov. 28, 1997, on HBO, www.imdb.com/title/tt0540822/.
12. The Official Steve Harvey, "Political Correctness Is Killing Comedy," Aug. 21, 2019, YouTube video, www.youtube.com/watch?v=gdVEXdr7GP8.
13. Nick A. Zaino III, "After '30 Rock,' Tracy Morgan Embraces Stand-up Comedy," *Boston Globe*, Jan. 12, 2013, www.bostonglobe.com/arts/theater-art/2013/01/12/after-rock-tracy-morgan-embraces-freedom-stand-comedy/9arhcdxFypQ8vaFZQW89RO/story.html.
14. Lisa Lampanelli, "How Political Correctness Is Killing Comedy," *Hollywood Reporter*, May 2, 2013, www.hollywoodreporter.com/news/general-news/lisa-lampanelli-how-political-correctness-450210/.
15. Marisa Schultz, "Tim Allen Joins Docudrama Taking Down PC Culture," *New York Post*, Jan. 29, 2018, nypost.com/2018/01/29/tim-allen-joins-docudrama-taking-down-pc-culture/.
16. Kliph Nesteroff, "'Cancel Culture' Has Always Been a Problem for Comedy," *Los Angeles Times*, Oct. 15, 2021, www.latimes.com/opinion/story/2021-10-15/cancel-culture-comedy-history-chappelle.
17. M. Alison Kibler, *Censoring Racial Ridicule: Irish, Jewish, and African American Struggles over Race and Representation, 1890–1930* (Chapel Hill: University of North Carolina Press, 2015), 30.
18. Ibid., 6–7.
19. Associated Press, "George Carlin Arrested for Using Profanity," *Lubbock Avalanche Journal*, June 23, 1972, 37, www.newspapers.com/clip/113974969/george-carlin-arrested/.
20. Lauren Frayer, "Comedian Vir Das Called Out Sexual Violence in India. Now He Faces Lawsuits," NPR, Nov. 18, 2021, www.npr.org/2021/11/18/1056888306/comedian-vir-das-called-out-sexual-violence-in-india-now-he-faces-lawsuits.
21. Marc Maron, "Episode 1278—'Canceled Comedy' w/ Kliph Nesteroff and David Bianculli," *WTF with Marc Maron* (podcast), Nov. 11, 2021, www.wtfpod

.com/podcast/episode-1278-canceled-comedy-w-kliph-nesteroff-and-david-bianculli.

22. David Remnick, "They're Going to Take Your Jokes," *New Yorker Radio Hour*, Feb. 11, 2022, www.wnycstudios.org/podcasts/tnyradiohour/segments/theyre-going-take-your-jokes.
23. Moira Weigel, "Political Correctness: How the Right Invented a Phantom Enemy," *Guardian*, Nov. 30, 2016, www.theguardian.com/us-news/2016/nov/30/political-correctness-how-the-right-invented-phantom-enemy-donald-trump.
24. Jesse David Fox, "Anthony Jeselnik's Three Flights," *Good One: A Podcast About Jokes* (podcast), July 1, 2019, podcasts.apple.com/us/podcast/anthony-jeselniks-three-flights/id1203393721?i=1000443304182.
25. Berlant and Ngai, "Comedy Has Issues."
26. Fox, "Anthony Jeselnik's Three Flights."
27. Jesse David Fox, "Marc Maron's Tumeric," *Good One: A Podcast About Jokes* (podcast), Mar. 24, 2020, podcasts.apple.com/us/podcast/marc-marons-tumeric/.
28. E. Alex Jung, "Who's Afraid of Ziwe Fumudoh?," *Vulture*, July 20, 2020, www.vulture.com/article/ziwe-fumudoh-instagram-live.html.
29. Jesse David Fox, "Aida Rodriguez's Wokeness," *Good One: A Podcast About Jokes* (podcast), Dec. 23, 2021, podcasts.apple.com/us/podcast/aida-rodriguezs-wokeness/id1203393721?i=1000545909294.
30. Kibler, *Censoring Racial Ridicule*, 5.
31. Lena Dunham, "The Lenny Interview: Estee Adoram," *Lenny Letter*, Mar. 30, 2018, www.lennyletter.com/story/the-lenny-interview-estee-adoram.
32. Hankinson, *Don't Applaud. Either Laugh or Don't. (At the Comedy Cellar.)*, 53.
33. Jim Carnes, "Dave Chappelle Lets Rude Crowd Have It, Sticks Up for Cosby's Comment," *Sacramento Bee*, June 17, 2004, freerepublic.com/focus/news/1156342/posts.
34. Jason Zinoman, *Searching for Dave Chappelle* (Kindle Single, 2013), 12.
35. *The Oprah Winfrey Show*, season 20, episode 73, hosted by Oprah Winfrey, aired Feb. 3, 2006, on CBS, www.imdb.com/title/tt0761021/.
36. Rachel Kaadzi Ghansah, "If He Hollers Let Him Go," *Believer*, Oct. 1 2013, www.thebeliever.net/if-he-hollers-let-him-go/.
37. Jesse David Fox, "It Took 10 Years, but Dave Chappelle Finally Weeded Out All of His Terrible Fans," *Vulture*, June 24, 2014, www.vulture.com/2014/06/dave-chappelle-live-review-this-is-why-he-quit.html.
38. Jesse David Fox, "Dave Chappelle's Netflix Specials Will Remind You Why He's One of the All-Time Best Stand-ups," *Vulture*, Mar. 21, 2017, www.vulture.com/2017/03/dave-chappelle-netflix-specials-review.html.
39. *Larry King Live*, CNN, 1990, YouTube video, www.youtube.com/watch?v=F8yV8xUorQ8.
40. Jesse David Fox, "Tom Segura's Racial Fight," *Good One: A Podcast About Jokes* (podcast), Sept. 1, 2022, podcasts.apple.com/us/podcast/tom-seguras-racial-fight/.
41. Charlie Markbreiter, "Can't Take a Joke," *New Inquiry*, Mar. 22, 2019, thenewinquiry.com/cant-take-a-joke/.
42. Sara Ahmed, "Feminist Killjoys (And Other Willful Subjects)," *Scholar and Feminist Online* 8, no. 3 (summer 2010), sfonline.barnard.edu/polyphonic/print_ahmed.htm.
43. Jason Zinoman, "His Punch Lines Cross Moral Lines. Anthony Jeselnik Gets Away With It," *New York Times*, Apr. 30, 2019, www.nytimes.com/2019/04/30/arts/television/anthony-jeselnik-netflix.html.
44. Yasiin Bey, Dave Chappelle, and Talib Kweli, "The Symphony," *The Midnight Miracle* (podcast), Oct. 1, 2021, podcasts.apple.com/us/podcast/the-symphony/.
45. Jackson McHenry, "Hannah Gadsby Decided to Quit Comedy, and Then Her

Career Blew Up," *Vulture*, June 19, 2018, www.vulture.com/2018/06/hannah-gadsby-on-her-netflix-stand-up-special-nanette.html.

46. *My Next Guest Needs No Introduction with David Letterman*, season 3, episode 3, "Dave Chappelle," created by David Letterman and directed by Helen M. Cho, aired Oct. 21, 2020, on Netflix, www.imdb.com/title/tt13317578/.
47. Danielle Fuentes Morgan, "Dave Chappelle the Comedy Relic," *Vulture*, Oct. 21, 2021, www.vulture.com/article/dave-chappelle-the-comedy-relic.html.
48. This account has been taken down and its tweets deleted. The quote is from a transcribed version in the author's notes.
49. Sylvia Rubin, "Page One—After 15 Years, Actor Apologizes for Gay Slurs," *San Francisco Chronicle*, May 11, 1996, www.sfgate.com/news/article/PAGE-ONE-After-15-Years-Actor-Apologizes-For-2982557.php.
50. *CBS Sunday Morning*, "Sunday Profile: Eddie Murphy," aired Dec. 29, 2019, on CBS, www.youtube.com/watch?v=EKeZ7NpNb3A.
51. Douglas Dowie, "Everybody's Not Laughing at Eddie Murphy," United Press International, Jan. 14, 1984, www.upi.com/Archives/1984/01/14/Everybodys-not-laughing-at-Eddie-Murphy/2002442904400/.

9. CONTEXT

1. Fox, "Brian Regan's Reading."
2. Lauren Berlant, "Humorlessness (Three Monologues and a Hairpiece)," *Critical Inquiry* 43, no. 2 (winter 2017), www.journals.uchicago.edu/doi/full/10.1086/689657?cookieSet=1.
3. Berlant and Ngai, "Comedy Has Issues."
4. Berlant, "Humorlessness (Three Monologues and a Hairpiece)."
5. Joe Flint and Amol Sharma, "Netflix Fights to Keep Its Most Watched Shows: 'Friends' and 'The Office,'" *Wall Street Journal*, Apr. 24, 2019, www.wsj.com/articles/netflix-battles-rivals-for-its-most-watched-shows-friends-and-the-office-11556120136.
6. Kate Williams, "Billie Eilish Wants to Show You Her Room," *Elle*, Mar. 29, 2019, www.elle.com/culture/music/a26984783/billie-eilish-when-we-all-fall-asleep/.
7. Ibid.
8. Melissa Dahl, *Cringeworthy: A Theory of Awkwardness* (New York: Portfolio, 2018), 8.
9. Limor Shifman, *Memes in Digital Culture* (Cambridge, MA: MIT Press, 2013), 15.
10. Ibid., 111.
11. Rachel Syme, "'I Think You Should Leave' Is a Love Language," *New Yorker*, July 26, 2021, www.newyorker.com/culture/on-television/i-think-you-should-leave-is-a-love-language.
12. Jamelle Bouie (@jbouie), "i'm going to be using this meme a lot today," Twitter, Jan. 6, 2021, twitter.com/jbouie/status/1346935868733460489?s=20&t=1-QADBU5MOK2bfGVNY6DQA.
13. Ilhan Omar (@IlhanMN), "[image]," Twitter, Dec. 3, 2020, twitter.com/IlhanMN/status/1334702809296613376?s=20&t=2XVycOnJPbbm2eI8jN-0bA.
14. Kath Barbadoro, "Stupid Times Call for Stupid Jokes," *Vulture*, Jan. 14, 2021, www.vulture.com/article/i-think-you-should-leave-memes-politics-twitter.html.
15. Megh Wright, "How the #FuckFuckJerry Movement Was Born," *Vulture*, Feb. 6, 2019, www.vulture.com/2019/02/fuck-jerry-instagram-comedians-unfollow-campaign-elliot-tebele.html.
16. Jesse David Fox, "A Conversation with the Fat Jew: 'That's Not Who I Am or What I'm About,'" *Vulture*, Aug. 21, 2015, www.vulture.com/2015/08/exclusive-interview-the-fat-jew.html.

17. Ibid.
18. Wright, "How the #FuckFuckJerry Movement Was Born."
19. Linda Hutcheon, *Irony's Edge: The Theory and Politics of Irony* (Abingdon, UK: Routledge, 1994), 6.
20. Raymond W. Gibbs Jr., "A New Look at Literal Meaning in Understanding What Is Said and Implicated," *Journal of Pragmatics* 34, no. 4 (Apr. 2002): 456–86, doi.org/10.1016/S0378-2166(01)00046-7.
21. Ted Cruz (@tedcruz), "How civilizations crumble," Twitter, Mar. 5, 2020, twitter.com/tedcruz/status/1235432247995613185?s=20&t=JWTQ1-UboC53kxoLf7yy1g.
22. Randall Colburn, "Trump's Second-Dumbest Son Falls for Months-Old 'Moves Like Bloomberg' Prank," *AV Club*, Mar. 4, 2020, www.avclub.com/trumps-second-dumbest-son-falls-for-months-old-moves-l-1842096093. Sebastian Gorka and Eric Trump's tweets have both since been deleted, but can be found archived in this article.
23. Ibid.
24. Hutcheon, *Irony's Edge: The Theory and Politics of Irony*, 18.
25. Matt Moen, "Why #FreeJaboukie Is Trending," *Paper Magazine*, Mar. 24, 2020, www.papermag.com/jaboukie-suspended-twitter-2645574689.html?rebelltitem=12#rebelltitem12. The original tweet has been deleted but can be found quoted in this article.
26. Jaboukie Young-White (@jaboukie), "The cats in Cats (2019) will have realistic spiked penises," Twitter, July 18, 2019. Original tweet has been deleted but screenshots can be found online, e.g., at twitter.com/j_rrie/status/1242296147194101762.
27. Jaboukie Young-White (@jaboukie), "Just because we killed MLK doesn't mean we can't miss him," Twitter, Jan. 20, 2020. Original tweet has been deleted but screenshots can be found online, e.g., at twitter.com/j_rrie/status/1242296147194101762.
28. Jaboukie Young-White (@jaboukie), "BREAKING: Joe Biden is not DEAD. He just getting some dick. We've all been there cnn.com," Twitter, Mar. 23, 2020. Original tweet has been deleted but screenshots of the tweet can be found online, e.g., at ifunny.co/picture/zWHC01Fr7.
29. Hunter Harris, "Jaboukie Young-White Will Probably Get Suspended Again," *Vulture*, Apr. 6, 2020, www.vulture.com/2020/04/jaboukie-young-white-twitter-quarantine-interview.html.
30. Elon Musk (@elonmusk), "Comedy is now legal on Twitter," Twitter, Oct. 28, 2022, twitter.com/elonmusk/status/1586104694421659648.
31. Brief of *The Onion* as Amicus Curiae in Support of Petitioner, *Novak v. City of Parma*, No. 22–293 (U.S. 2008), www.supremecourt.gov/DocketPDF/22/22-293/242292/20221003125252896_35295545_1-22.10.03%20-%20Novak-Parma%20-%20Onion%20Amicus%20Brief.pdf.
32. Laura June, "9 Times Pregnant Women Stole the Show," *The Cut*, May 20, 2016, www.thecut.com/2016/05/9-times-pregnant-women-stole-the-show.html.
33. Ana Marie Cox, "Ali Wong Knows How the Internet Sees Her," *New York Times*, June 22, 2016, www.nytimes.com/2016/06/26/magazine/ali-wong-knows-how-the-internet-sees-her.html.
34. Harry Dry, "The Marketing Genius of Andrew Schulz," *Marketing Examples*, Sept. 8, 2020, marketingexamples.com/content/andrew-schulz.
35. Matt Ruby, "My Instagram Reel Just Went Viral (1.3M Views). Here's Why That Sucks," *Funny How: Letters to a Young Comedian*, Substack, July 27, 2022, mattruby.substack.com/p/my-instagram-reel-just-went-viral.
36. Shirley Ju, "Chicago to Crenshaw: Comedian Lil Rel Howery Has Been Preparing for Success His Whole Life," *Hundreds*, Jan. 17, 2020, thehundreds.com/blogs/content/chicago-to-crenshaw-comedian-lil-rel-howery-has-been-preparing-for-success-his-whole-life.

37. Ibid.
38. Rashad Grove, "Why Lil Rel Turned Down a Bigger Bag from Netflix to Work with HBO," BET, Nov. 25, 2019, www.bet.com/article/8qb2pc/lil-rel-on-making-his-first-hbo-comedy-special.
39. Katie Mears, "Why Lil Rel Howery Filmed His New Special in a High School Gym," *Vulture*, Nov. 25, 2019, www.vulture.com/2019/11/lil-rel-howery-jerrod-carmichael-live-in-crenshaw-high-school-gym.html.

10. COMMUNITY

1. Bill Burr, "Monday Morning Podcast 3-26-12," *Monday Morning Podcast* (podcast), Mar. 26, 2012, soundcloud.com/themonday-morning-podcast/monday-morning-podcast-3-26-12.
2. Jesse David Fox, "How the Internet and a New Generation of Superfans Helped Create the Second Comedy Boom," *Vulture*, Mar. 30, 2015, www.vulture.com/2015/03/welcome-to-the-second-comedy-boom.html.
3. Sam Wasson, *Improv Nation: How We Made a Great American Art* (New York: Houghton Mifflin Harcourt, 2017), 12.
4. Ibid., 21.
5. Jesse David Fox, "Marc Maron's Kaddish," *Good One: A Podcast About Jokes* (podcast), Feb. 7, 2023, podcasts.apple.com/us/podcast/marc-marons-kaddish/.
6. Jamie Lauren Keiles, "Even Nobodies Have Fans Now," *New York Times Magazine*, Nov. 13, 2019, www.nytimes.com/interactive/2019/11/13/magazine/internet-fandom-podcast.html.
7. Jeffrey M. Jones, "U.S. Church Membership Falls Below Majority for First Time," Gallup, Mar. 29, 2021, news.gallup.com/poll/341963/church-membership-falls-below-majority-first-time.aspx.
8. Robert D. Putnam, "Bowling Alone: America's Declining Social Capital," *Journal of Democracy* 6, no.1 (Jan. 1995): 65–78, doi.org/10.1353/jod.1995.0002.
9. E. Alex Jung, "The Bold and Bawdy New Queens of Comedy," *Vulture*, May 31, 2018, www.vulture.com/2018/05/the-rise-of-queer-comedy.html.
10. Emily Crockett, "Safe Spaces, Explained," *Vox*, Aug. 5, 2016, www.vox.com/2016/7/5/11949258/safe-spaces-explained.
11. Padma Lakshmi (@padmalakshmi), "THIS. Why don't we give our attention to people who are actually funny: @Lesdoggg @Party_Harderson @juliothesquare @anafabregagood @bowenyang @catccohen @poregan @ihatejoelkim @MattRogersTho the list goes on!," Twitter, Aug. 28, 2018, twitter.com/PadmaLakshmi/status/1034496393950490624.
12. Beck Krefting, *All Jokes Aside: American Humor and Its Discontents* (Baltimore: Johns Hopkins University Press, 2014), 2.
13. Ibid., 2.
14. Ibid., 3.
15. Jesse David Fox, "How Comedy Survived Trump," *Good One: A Podcast About Jokes* (podcast), Jan. 19, 2021, www.vulture.com/article/good-one-podcast-comedy-under-trump.html.
16. Elise Czajkowski, "How Weird Stand-up Became a Woman's Game," *Vulture*, Apr. 2, 2015, www.vulture.com/2015/04/how-weird-stand-up-became-a-womens-game.html.
17. Jesse David Fox, "Matt Rogers's 'The Hottest Female Up in Whoville,'" *Good One: A Podcast About Jokes* (podcast), Dec. 1, 2022, www.vulture.com/article/matt-rogers-christmas-good-one-podcast.html.
18. "The Right Is Starting to Get Better at Comedy," *Know Your Meme*, Jan. 22, 2019, knowyourmeme.com/memes/the-right-is-starting-to-get-better-at-comedy.
19. Luis J. Gomez (@luisjgomez), "Name 5 right wing comedians. There are 1000s

of comedians. Name 5. I can name 3," Twitter, May 15, 2022, twitter.com/luisjgomez/status/1525874815114039297.

20. Andrew Sullivan, "South Park Republicans Are the Future, *Sunday Times*, Dec. 21, 2003, www.thetimes.co.uk/article/andrew-sullivan-south-park-republicans-are-the-future-7vgkthbhhpn.
21. *60 Minutes*, season 55, episode 1, "The Counter-Terrorism Bureau/The Murder of an American Nazi/Parker & Stone," hosted by Steve Kroft, aired Sept. 25, 2011, on CBS, www.youtube.com/watch?v=0KppaxFfPNw.
22. Luis J. Gomez (@luisjgomez), "I hope Trump wins just because of how much it will bother like 4 people I hate," Twitter, Oct. 31, 2020, twitter.com/luisjgomez/status/1322723030460674048.
23. Dr Boss (@nixonthewicked), "Go vote for him Luis, help make it happen," Twitter, Nov. 1, 2020, twitter.com/nixonthewicked/status/1322763551774134272.
24. Luis J. Gomez (@luisjgomez), "Voting is for dorks," Twitter, Nov. 1, 2020, twitter.com/luisjgomez/status/1322901637560676359.
25. Amber A'Lee Frost, "The Necessity of Political Vulgarity," *Current Affairs*, Aug. 25, 2016, www.currentaffairs.org/2016/05/the-necessity-of-political-vulgarity.
26. Joe Rogan, "1857—Seth Dillon," *The Joe Rogan Experience* (podcast), Aug. 16, 2022, open.spotify.com/episode/2SOHGmqBL2UnhwCbYSF8uu.
27. Matt McCusker and Shane Gillis, "Ep 400—Partying with Girls," *Matt and Shane's Secret Podcast* (podcast), June 29, 2022, podcasts.apple.com/us/podcast/ep-400-partying-with-girls/id1177068388?i=1000568162274.
28. Will Menaker, Matt Christman, and Felix Biederman, "640—Roe Wasn't Burnt in a Day," *Chapo Trap House* (podcast), June 28 2022, podcasts.apple.com/gb/podcast/640-roe-wasnt-burnt-in-a-day-6-28-22/id1097417804?i=1000567943038.
29. "Top Patreon Creators," *Graphtreon*, graphtreon.com/top-patreon-creators.
30. LaughPlanet, "Bill Burr Constant Shitting on Women," Dec. 3, 2020, YouTube video, www.youtube.com/watch?v=Q6UnFutP6mI.
31. The Charisma Matrix, "Joe Rogan HAMMERS Adam Conover in 'TRANSGENDERS in Sports' Debate," Apr. 28, 2019, YouTube video, www.youtube.com/watch?v=_wD6yxlW6r4.
32. Matt Sienkiewicz and Nick Marx, *That's Not Funny: How the Right Makes Comedy Work for Them* (Berkeley: University of California Press, 2022), 3.
33. Ibid., 10.
34. Jia Tolentino, "What Will Become of the Dirtbag Left?," *New Yorker*, Nov. 18, 2016, www.newyorker.com/culture/persons-of-interest/what-will-become-of-the-dirtbag-left.
35. Luis J. Gomez, "Luis J. Gomez Addresses LoS Subreddit Ban," Oct. 27, 2020, YouTube video, www.youtube.com/watch?v=o0JWaIrtnVk.
36. Keiles, "Even Nobodies Have Fans Now."
37. Seth Simons, "The Comedy Industry Has a Big Alt-Right Problem," *New Republic*, Feb. 9, 2021, newrepublic.com/article/161200/alt-right-comedy-gavin-mcinnes-problem.
38. Cris Italia, "ToxicCisWhiteMaleFat," Medium, Feb. 11, 2022, cris-italia.medium.com/toxicciswhitemalefat-2938aabfc558.
39. Keiles, "Even Nobodies Have Fans Now."
40. Seth Abramovitch, "Comedy's Civil War: How an 'SNL' Firing Exposed a Growing Rift in Stand-Up," Sept. 26, 2019, www.hollywoodreporter.com/lifestyle/lifestyle-news/shane-gillis-snl-firing-comics-mixed-reactions-exposes-growing-rift-stand-up-world-1242739/.
41. Mick Taylor, "Luis J. Gomez Is Changing the Future of Digital Comedy," *Interrobang*, Mar. 15, 2018, theinterrobang.com/luis-j-gomez-changing-future-digital-comedy/.
42. Raúl Pérez, *The Souls of White Jokes: How Racist Humor Fuels White Supremacy* (Stanford, CA: Stanford University Press, 2022), 50–84.

43. Denis Slattery, "Cuomo Not Keen on Concert as New York Infection Rate Climbs Above 1% for First Time in Month," *Daily News* (New York), Sept. 15, 2020, www.nydailynews.com/news/politics/ny-cuomo-concerts-comedy-clubs-coronavirus-reopening-20200915-yfhh6qp5dndztn4vbnlux6bkom-story.html.
44. Dan Reilly, "COVID Didn't Kill Live Comedy—It Drove It Underground," *Vulture*, Jan. 27, 2021, www.vulture.com/article/comedy-club-owners-nyc-covid-19.html.
45. Jesse David Fox, "Jo Firestone's Seniors Comedy Class," *Good One: A Podcast About Jokes* (podcast), Oct. 14, 2021, podcasts.apple.com/us/podcast/jo-firestones-seniors-comedy-class/id1203393721?i=1000538562075.
46. Yancy and hooks, "bell hooks: Buddhism, the Beats and Loving Blackness."
47. Henri Bergson, *Laughter: An Essay on the Meaning of the Comic* (New York: Macmillan, 1911), 14.
48. Robert Provine, "Laughing, Tickling, and the Evolution of Speech and Self," *Current Directions in Psychological Science* 13, no. 6 (Dec. 2004): 215–18, doi.org/10.1111/j.0963-7214.2004.00311.x,

11. CONNECTION

1. Jennifer Wilson, "Sheila Heti Does It the Artist's Way," *Vulture*, Feb. 16, 2022, www.vulture.com/article/sheila-heti-pure-colour-review.html.
2. Fox, "Marc Maron's Tumeric."
3. Robert Kraut, Michael Patterson, Vicki Lundmark, Sara Kiesler, Tridas Mukopadhyay, and William Scherlis, "Internet Paradox. A Social Technology that Reduces Social Involvement and Psychological Well-being?," *American Psychologist* 53, no. 9 (Sept. 1998), pubmed.ncbi.nlm.nih.gov/9841579/.
4. Bertha Coombs, "Loneliness Is on the Rise and Younger Workers and Social Media Users Feel it Most, Cigna Survey Finds," CNBC, Jan. 23, 2020, www.cnbc.com/2020/01/23/loneliness-is-rising-younger-workers-and-social-media-users-feel-it-most.html.
5. Matt McCarthy, "Review: Loneliness a Hidden and Serious Health Scourge, Vivek Murthy Argues in Timely Book," *USA Today*, Apr. 26, 2020, www.usatoday.com/story/entertainment/books/2020/04/26/book-review-together-loneliness-bad-health-says-vivek-murthy/5169442002/.
6. Jesse David Fox, "Reggie Watts Comes Up with a New Song," *Good One: A Podcast About Jokes* (podcast), July 16, 2018, podcasts.apple.com/us/podcast/reggie-watts-comes-up-with-a-new-song/id1203393721?i=1000415898194.
7. Fox, "Brian Regan's Reading."
8. Larissa MacFarquhar, "How to Be Good," *New Yorker*, Aug. 29, 2011, www.newyorker.com/magazine/2011/09/05/how-to-be-good.
9. Derek Parfit, *Reasons and Persons* (Oxford: Oxford University Press, 1984), 281.
10. Jesse David Fox, "Comedy Under Quarantine, Five Months In," *Good One: A Podcast About Jokes* (podcast), Aug. 4, 2020, podcasts.apple.com/ie/podcast/comedy-under-quarantine-five-months-in/id1203393721?i=1000487056312.
11. Sheila Heti, *How Should a Person Be?* (Toronto: House of Anansi Press, 2010), 54.
12. Jesse David Fox, "John Mulaney's *The Sack Lunch Bunch*," *Good One: A Podcast About Jokes* (podcast), Aug. 25, 2020, podcasts.apple.com/us/podcast/john-mulaneys-sack-lunch-bunch/id1203393721?i=1000489081331.
13. Fox, "Marc Maron's Kaddish."
14. Ian Sample, "Jokers Please: First Human Mars Mission May Need Onboard Comedians," *The Guardian*, Feb. 15, 2019, www.theguardian.com/science/2019/feb/15/jokers-please-first-human-mars-mission-may-need-onboard-comedians.

Acknowledgments

This book wouldn't be possible without Alina Hoffman. Everything I wrote before I met her was dogshit. But spending my life with her, talking to her every day, has complicated my understanding of culture in the best possible way and made me a much deeper thinker. She listened to me paraphrase most of the book's arguments over and over again for the last three years and was my most demanding reader. It was likely annoying how distracted I was this whole time, and yet she was encouraging. She believed this book could be good, and I was motivated to prove her correct. This is barely the start of why I love Alina, but everything else is personal and none of your business.

Objectively, I have the best agent in the galaxy—Adam Eaglin, of the Cheney Agency. I honestly am not sure I ever would've written a book if it weren't for Adam. I had a vague sense of something about Adam Sandler, and he was the one who suggested a book about comedy more generally. I responded, "That's a book?" He said, "Let's see!" He was a strong advocate and a patient listener. He really is so smart and nice.

Maybe this will surprise you, but there were moments throughout this process that I experienced self-doubt. In those dark moments, I'd remind myself, *My editor, Jackson Howard, believes in this project.* I don't know if there is anyone who got this book better than Jackson, myself included, and if it's any good, it is a testament to him. I also want to thank Greg Villepique and Carrie Hsieh for their invaluable copyediting and production editing work, respectively; Songhee Kim for making this book look good and cool; Thomas Colligan for making this a book I hope people *do* judge by its cover; Claire Tobin for making sure people know the book exists; and every other single person at Farrar, Straus and Giroux who made this all possible.

Speaking of invaluable, Nicole Pasulka fact-checked the hell out of this book and offered vital editorial insight and clarity late in the process, when I really needed it.

I also want to thank all the editors I've worked with over the course of my career, especially Adam Frucci, Josh Wolk, Gilbert Cruz, Gazelle Emami, Megh Wright, and Neil Janowitz, who shaped who I am as a writer and encouraged me to write about comedy in the first place. I want to give a special acknowledgments "hi" to Megh, who has been my hero and my partner in defining what comedy coverage could look like.

Lastly in the editors category: I am here writing acknowledgments because thirteen years ago Jason Diamond "discovered" me. Though I'd never had my work published anywhere but in comments sections and my personal blog, he accepted my pitch. Now we're just friends who watch Adam Sandler movies together, but he has remained my port in the storm that is media and publishing. Also through Jason I know Jami Attenberg, who granted me access to her lovely home and charming dog in New Orleans at a pivotal moment in the writing process. Jason and Megh were readers of early drafts of the book.

Other early readers include: Jo Firestone, Danielle Fuentes Morgan, Beck Krefting, Jay Jurden, Jason Frank, Anne Lim,

Christina Catherine Martinez, J. F. Harris, Nick Marx, Matt Sienkiewicz, and Kathryn VanArendonk. Anne also provided extremely helpful research work/young-person perspective. Reading Jason's college thesis was invaluable to the conception of parts of chapter 9. Christina introduced me to the work of Arthur Danto, which informed chapter 7. Kathryn graciously agreed to finish the book if I died in the middle of the process.

Very lucky was I to have Kelly Conaboy as a sounding board for many of the book's stupidest ideas. This includes the book's title, which she helped come up with. Besides being willing to listen to me worry about this book, a large reason I am able to even consider myself a writer is because Kelly, the best writer alive, considers me her friend.

Early in my life, I was lucky to be born into a friendship with Drew Blumenthal and Jonathan Lurie. Beyond supporting my various endeavors, both were undeniably foundational to my sense of humor. Two other friends who made this book possible are Dawson Ludwig, who in 2009 encouraged me to start a blog, which got me back into writing, and Drew Welborn, who that same year brought me to a *Comedy Death-Ray* live show, which reignited my love for comedy.

You know, I think it's effed that more people don't thank their therapists in situations like this. So, I want to acknowledge the work of Dr. Mazia Qaiser, who has been indispensable to my understanding of myself and the world.

Of course, I would not be here without my parents. They literally gave me life and then kept me alive, providing things like food and shelter and a TV in my bedroom growing up. They taught me how to think and analyze and be skeptical, to be funny and to value funny. They indulged me and allowed me to feel safe being a, let's say, particular person. It is through their support that I had the confidence to pursue this life, and there is a comfort in knowing they will always be my biggest fans. Thank you to my brothers, Trevor, Michael, and Simon, who are all smart and funny and annoying in their own special way. When I see things in myself and in this book that remind me of you, it makes me happy. I learned so much about being smart and funny and annoying from all of you. Lastly, thank you to all my aunts, uncles, and grandparents who contributed to me becoming whoever the person is who wrote this book.

Undoubtedly, this book would be impossible without comedians. It is never lost on me how fortunate I am that so many comedians have granted me access to how they do what they do. I am very grateful they have entrusted me with their art form.

And thank *you* for reading or listening or downloading this book directly into your brain like *The Matrix*. You've been a great audience. Good night.

Index

A NOTE ABOUT THE AUTHOR

Jesse David Fox is a senior editor at *Vulture*, where he works as the site's comedy critic and serves as the chief curator of the magazine's event series, Vulture Festival. He is also the host of the podcast *Good One: A Podcast About Jokes*, where he interviews comedians about their process. The more than 150 guests have included Judd Apatow, Maria Bamford, Samantha Bee, Aidy Bryant, Bo Burnham, Nicole Byer, Margaret Cho, Hannah Gadsby, Kevin Hart, Marc Maron, Kate McKinnon, Seth Meyers, Hasan Minhaj, John Mulaney, Kumail Nanjiani, Tig Notaro, Patton Oswalt, Martin Short, Cecily Strong, Taika Waititi, and Katt Williams. He lives in Brooklyn, New York.